DOCUMENTS OF SOCIAL HISTORY
Editor: Anthony Adams

JOHN FROST: A STUDY IN CHARTISM

JOHN FROST

John Frost: a Study in Chartism

DAVID WILLIAMS

LONDON: EVELYN, ADAMS & MACKAY

First published 1939
This edition published for Social Documents Ltd.,
by Evelyn, Adams & Mackay Ltd., 9 Fitzroy Square, London W1.
Printed in Switzerland by Reda S.A.
SBN 238. 78940. 3

JOHN FROST

A STUDY IN CHARTISM

By

DAVID WILLIAMS

CARDIFF

UNIVERSITY OF WALES PRESS BOARD

1939

To

I. M. W.

in gratitude

PREFACE

THE writing of this book was undertaken some twelve months ago at the suggestion of the Chartist Centenary Committee of Newport, Monmouthshire, who felt that their celebration of the centenary of the Chartist riot of November 1839 would not be complete without a Life of their townsman, John Frost. Moreover, no adequate treatment of the riot itself had appeared in print. Although it was the crucial episode in the history of Chartism, the standard works on that subject scarcely do more than indicate the problems involved in it, while such popular accounts as exist are inaccurate and uncritical to a degree. But to understand the riot it is necessary, above all else, to know the character and previous history of John Frost. Yet here, in particular, the existing narratives were found to be utterly untrustworthy, especially with regard to his first imprisonment. Even the notices of his life which appeared during his trial for treason were confused and contradictory regarding this incident. I have unravelled the main lines in its development at the expense of considerable labour; whether such labour was justified will be for the reader to decide. To one possible charge, however, I wish to plead not guilty in advance—that of having attempted to retell, yet once more, the general story of the Chartist movement.

I should like to acknowledge my indebtedness to the Centenary Committee for their encouragement and assistance; to the Committee of the Newport Museum and its Curator, Mr. W. A. Gunn, for permission to consult the manuscripts in their possession; to Sir Henry Mather Jackson for permission to consult the Quarter Sessions records at Usk, and particularly to Mr. J. Conway Davies, without whose assistance it would have been impossible to consult them; to Lord Tredegar for permission to consult three unpublished manuscripts in his possession; to

viii   *Preface*

Miss Myfanwy Williams for kindly placing her unpublished thesis at my disposal; to Dr. R. T. Jenkins for
reading my manuscript and offering valuable suggestions;
to Mr. D. L. Evans of the Public Record Office and to
Messrs E. H. Jones and E. J. Evans of the Cardiff Free
Library for their willing assistance at all times. But, in
particular, I am gratefully indebted for constant help to
Mr. John Warner, secretary to the Centenary Committee
and Librarian of Newport. Without his expert biblio-
graphical knowledge I should have been quite unable to
write this book in the short time at my disposal.

DAVID WILLIAMS

UNIVERSITY COLLEGE
CARDIFF
30 *June* 1939

CONTENTS

LIST OF ILLUSTRATIONS

I

BACKGROUND AND EARLY LIFE

IT was not until the second half of the eighteenth century that the English traveller discovered Wales. Hitherto he had been familiar only with the North Wales coast as part of his route to Ireland; the remainder of Wales, with its difficult roads, its forbidding mountains, and its strange language, had offered no attraction strong enough to induce him to brave its perils. But with the growth of a romantic interest in scenery and antiquities all this was changed. Its wild rocks, its foaming floods, its cascades, its cloud-topped mountains, and its dreary shores became objects to be sought out and described in prose and verse. Its people, also, with their ancient tongue, their long history and their remoteness from English ways of life now came to appear no less romantic. Numerous travellers therefore visited Wales, and when warfare on the Continent made the Grand Tour wellnigh impossible, their number was still further increased. Many were able to combine their romantic interest with an inquiry into the mineral deposits of the country, and three weeks or so provided sufficient material for a *Tour in Wales* published in quarto, and embellished with numerous plates.

Our traveller, visiting South Wales in the eighties, would cross the Severn at the New Passage. He would find himself in a richly wooded country, interspersed with fields of corn and pasture, and with gentle hills rising to considerable heights in the distance. Soon he would be able to indulge his love of antiquities by visiting the old Roman town of Caerwent. As he continued on his way he would pass Llanvaches, the cradle of Nonconformity in Wales, a fact which would scarcely be of interest to him. What would, however, attract his attention, would be that he had already reached an area which was Welsh in speech. Almost a century later, when George Borrow visited these parts, he found half the people habitually Welsh-speaking, and Archdeacon Coxe, in 1798, was glad to avail himself of a Welsh-speaking guide. The 'level', immediately along the sea-coast, had been anglicized for a considerable time, and the market-towns, built as they generally were around a castle, had never been Welsh. But although the English language was gradually penetrating up the valleys which opened on to the English border, its progress was slow, and, like an incoming tide among the sand dunes, it left the hills untouched for a time, while in the mountains in the north and west of the shire a large part of the population spoke no English at all. Continuing westwards from Caerwent the undulating road which our traveller had to follow gradually ascended until it reached the village of Christchurch, and then descended quickly to a bridge across the River Usk at Newport.

This old borough (for it was new only in comparison with ancient Caerleon, the fortress of the Roman legions, nearby) did not present a very attractive appearance. The bridge by which it was approached was a rickety wooden structure, built upon exceedingly high piles of wood. The boards with which it was floored were always left loose (although stopped from slipping by small tenons fixed at their ends), apparently because the high tides, if obstructed, might carry away the whole bridge. Once safely across, the traveller found himself by the castle, the shell of which was still almost entire, and before him lay the town, which consisted of hardly more than one long, narrow, straggling street, ascending a hill until it reached the church of St. Woollos. All accounts agree that Newport was unusually dirty and ill-paved, and that its houses wore a gloomy appearance. It comprised about 190 tenements, so that its population could hardly have been a thousand all told.[1] Nevertheless it was an incorporated borough, governed under a charter granted by King James I in 1623. It had its mayor, its twelve aldermen, and its burgesses, the appointment of the mayor being subject to the confirmation of the lord of the manor, the Duke of Beaufort. This was the sole privilege which the lord possessed, in spite of the enormous power which he wielded elsewhere in the shire, particularly in the borough of Monmouth. Everyday affairs in the little town were governed by a series of some fifty ordinances, drawn up in 1711, which themselves present a detailed picture of life at Newport, at least in the early eighteenth century. Particularly numerous are the regulations concerning trade, preventing strangers from infringing the liberties of the town and counteracting the devices used to avoid the payment of tolls. Butchers were strictly forbidden to sell any meat which had been 'blown' by them, under pain of forfeiture and the payment of a fine. Neither could they offer any bull's flesh for sale, unless the bull had been baited, without the payment of a fine of six shillings and eight pence, and even so, a candle must be placed by the meat during the time it was offered for sale, for the baiting of bulls in the bullring still provided the burgesses with their chief sport, and also was supposed to improve the flavour of the meat. The rural nature of life in the town may be seen in the regulations about the repair of the hedges between the tenements, and the fines imposed for casting dung into the street, from the bridge to the church, or suffering pigs to go about the town without yokes and pims. In religious matters the ordinances tend to be puritanical, although this may well be evidence of laxity

[1] J. M. Scott, *The Ancient and Modern History of Newport* (Newport, 1847), p. 43, gives a survey of the 192 tenements in Newport in 1764. Archdeacon Coxe, *An Historical Tour in Monmouthshire* (London, 1801), p. 46, gives the number of houses as 221, and the population 1,087.

3

on the part of the inhabitants. The constable was strictly enjoined to search inns and ale-houses for tipplers in time of divine service, and any one riding through the town to merry-making on Sundays, 'which is usual', must pay the large fine of six shillings and eight pence for each such offence. Moreover every one who had no reasonable cause for absenting himself must resort every Sunday to the Parish Church of St. Woollos, under pain of forfeiture for each default of one shilling, and if any there might be who were so unhappy as to dissent from the Church of England, but were exempted from the penalties of the laws for not coming to church, they also must resort to some place allowed by law for the practice of religious duty, and not stay at home, or go to any place not allowed, under pain to forfeit ten shillings for each default. The language of the townsmen was English, but on market-day the street would be crowded with farmers from the country-side, bargaining animatedly with the inhabitants in their own language, yet speaking among themselves the soft Welsh dialect of Gwent.

If our traveller wished to proceed still farther westwards he would have to ascend the hill by St. Woollos, for the lower turnpike road to Cardiff was built a little later. On reaching the church he might be tempted to ascend its tower, although this could not be done without some trouble, as the winding staircase was in an indifferent state of repair, but having gained the summit he would be amply recompensed for his exertions. In the distance, across the Bristol Channel, he would see the hills of Somersetshire. On this side, along the seashore, were the 'levels' of Caldecot and Wentloog, fertile low-lying lands which had frequently been subject to inundation, and were protected by a sea wall, maintained at great expense by a Court of Sewers. To the north were a number of rivers, flowing from the mountains through narrow valleys almost parallel with one another, and then converging on

4

Newport. Here the iron industry had already been begun, and it was this geographical feature which was to convert the little market-town into a flourishing seaport in the next hundred years. Even now the traveller would see the masts of several ships in the river, but these were all engaged in the coastal trade, especially with Bristol. To the west, his eye would be caught by the park and mansion of Tredegar, the home of the Morgan family who had played such a large part in the history of the district.

The house of Morgan was of great antiquity. Fanciful genealogists even traced its descent from Ham the accursed, second son of Noah, while others, who disputed this, connected the Morgans with the junior but more respectable line of Japheth. Some stopped with Brutus, the conqueror of Britain, but all were agreed (and for this there is sufficient evidence) that the family traced an almost unbroken male descent from Cadivor the Great, lord of Dyfed, who died in 1084. The other great Monmouthshire family, that of the Somersets, Dukes of Beaufort (descended only from John of Gaunt, and even so, on two occasions out of wedlock), could offer no comparison with this. In addition, innumerable branches of the Morgan family were scattered over the country-side, and some of their members had attained great distinction. The names of two persons only, and those very different in repute, may be mentioned here: Ivor the Generous, in the fourteenth century, the greatest of all patrons of Welsh literature, and in the seventeenth century, Sir Henry Morgan, the buccaneer. But the direct male line of the Morgans came to a sudden end in the eighteenth century. Thomas Morgan succeeded his nephew in 1763, but possessed the estates for only six years. His son, Thomas, died two years after his father, and was succeeded by his brother Charles, who ruled at Tredegar for eighteen years but died childless. The third brother, John, then came

5

into possession of the estates. He was now fifty-five years of age, but he hurriedly married a young woman in the hope of producing an heir. If we are to believe the *Gentleman's Magazine*, he was more than once disappointed, and even after his death four years later, his young widow experienced her usual ill fortune. Thus the estates passed in 1792 to John's elder sister, Jane, and her husband, Sir Charles Gould, judge marshal to His Majesty's forces. It was the common fate of nearly all the old Welsh families; they ended in heiresses married to Englishmen, and thus became anglicized. In November of the same year Sir Charles became a baronet in his own name, and on the following day he assumed the name and arms of Morgan. His estate was even then valued at £30,000 a year,[1] and the mineral wealth beneath its surface was almost incalculable. He died in 1806 and was in turn succeeded by his son, Sir Charles, the opponent of John Frost.

Not only did the Morgans possess enormous wealth; they exercised a political influence scarcely less important. Politics in Wales in the eighteenth century were in a feudal, if not still in a tribal stage of development. The radical historian of Monmouthshire wrote in 1796 that 'the feodal ideas and habits of an oppressed and degraded peasantry are not wholly abolished',[2] and an acute observer of Welsh life maintained that half a century later candidates for Parliament were concerned not with matters of national policy but 'with asserting and maintaining their own family consequence against rival claimants in a county or neighbourhood', while the behaviour of the people 'was less that of citizens contending for their rights than of clansmen vehemently battling for their respective chieftains'.[3] Contested elections, therefore, whenever they

[1] *Gentleman's Magazine*, 1792, p. 673.
[2] David Williams, *History of Monmouthshire* (1796), p. 348.
[3] Henry Richard, *Letters on the Social and Political Condition of the Principality* (London, 1876), p. 80.

6

took place (it is true that they were infrequent) were fought with great bitterness and at great expense. The contest for Flint in 1734 is said to have cost the two candidates nearly £70,000, and one of them eventually became insolvent. Nor were the consequences sometimes less disastrous for the recipients of this largess, as the following extract from the *Cardiff Records* will show.

'Coroner's inquest taken at Bridgend, 7 April 1768, on view of the body of Morgan Thomas, found that the deceased, "being at Bridgend aforesaid the sixth instant, at the time of the General Election there for a Member to serve in Parliament for the said County, when great ffeastings, drinking and rejoicings were made on the Occasion, he the said Morgan Thomas, being very much at all times addicted to drinking, from alehouse to alehouse went for meat and drink, and having had a good deal offered he refused none, till at last he became full gorged with Meat and Drink, which not being able to bear, about four o'clock in the afternoon sickened at the Stomach, and not being able to discharge the said meat and drink, at Bridgend the day and hour aforesaid he then languished, and languishing lived about ten minutes; and by over eating and drinking in manner aforesaid suffocated and dyed".'[1]

But the election which remained in popular memory was that of 1802 for Carmarthenshire, when the poll was kept open for fifteen days, and the unsuccessful Whig candidate's expenses amounted to £15,690. 4s. 2d. This sum included payments to innkeepers for 11,070 breakfasts, 36,901 dinners, 684 suppers, 25,275 gallons of ale, 11,068 bottles of spirits, 8,879 bottles of porter, 460 bottles of sherry, 509 bottles of cider, and eighteen guineas for milk punch. The charge for ribbons was £786, and the number of separate charges for horse hire was 4,521.[2]

[1] *Cardiff Records* (Cardiff, 1900), ii. 222.
[2] *Report of the Royal Commission on Land in Wales and Monmouthshire* (H.M. Stationery Office, 1896), p. 161.

The landed gentry therefore exercised undisputed sway. In North Wales the ruling family was that of Wynnstay, especially in the period of Sir Watkin Williams-Wynn, the friend of the Pretender, and it is said that the peasantry there would always qualify a determination to do anything with an 'if it please God and Sir Watkin'. And what Wynnstay was to North Wales, Tredegar was to the south-east. In Monmouthshire itself political matters were amicably arranged. Unlike the other Welsh shires it had been granted two members at the Union of England and Wales in the sixteenth century, and as there were only two powerful families in the shire they divided its representation between them. Thus from the time when the shire first received the right of representation, a member of the family of Morgan and one of the family of Beaufort, or, on occasion, their respective nominees, had sat for the county of Monmouth. Twice only throughout the eighteenth century was there a contest, in 1722 and in 1771, and in both cases a Morgan was successful. In the boroughs the right of electing a member was vested, after a decision had been made by the House of Commons in a disputed election in 1680, in the resident burgesses of Monmouth, Newport, and Usk, and not in the burgesses at large,[1] so that they were saved from the abuse common elsewhere in Wales of swamping the electorate just before a contest by the creation of honorary burgesses for party purposes. Contests here, however, were very infrequent. The power of Morgan in Newport, where sixty-five of the one hundred and ninety tenements belonged to him, was supreme, while Beaufort completely controlled the larger borough of Monmouth. It was a Beaufort nominee, therefore, who represented Monmouth boroughs throughout the century. But the Morgan influence was equally strong in Brecon. The borough franchise was here vested in the burgesses, who

[1] *Journal of House of Commons*, ix (26 Nov. 1680), p. 663.

numbered about two hundred in 1698, but the contest of that year was one of the last for Brecon, and during the century which followed the 'common council' of burgesses had been reduced by omitting to fill vacancies when they occurred, until it had reached the tractable number of seventeen.[1] A Morgan nominee, therefore, sat for Brecon borough without dispute for over eighty years. The same was true of Brecon county, but here an unexpected opponent appeared in 1806 in Thomas Wood of Gwern-yfed, a proprietor in the East India Company, and the only nabob in the parliamentary history of Wales. Before his overwhelming wealth even a Morgan had to retire defeated, and although strenuous efforts were made to unseat him, especially in 1818 when the poll was kept open for the maximum of fifteen days, he retained his seat until 1847.

Such was Newport at the end of the eighteenth century, a small market-town, scarcely more than a village, and entirely under squire rule, and here it was in all probability that the future Chartist, John Frost, was born on 25 May 1784.[2] Very little can be ascertained about his family, and the unwary is liable to be trapped by the presence at

[1] Anon., 'The Reform Bill and its Operation in Wales', *Cambrian Quarterly Magazine*, iii (1831), pp. 273–4.

[2] *Western Mail*, 17 Mar. 1877, quoting Frost's remark in 1874 that he was 90 years of age on '25 May last'. Frost very frequently states his age, and in every case this agrees with the date given in the text, but he nowhere else states the day of his birth. Several accounts contemporary with his trial for treason give the date as 1786, and this was accepted by W. N. Johns, *The Chartist Riots in Newport* (Newport, 2nd ed., 1889), p. 8, and has been followed by all subsequent writers. This would involve an ignorance on the part of John Frost of his own age, which is incredible. His baptism was not registered at St. Woollos. There is a tradition that he was born at Llantarnam, but he was not baptized there. The St. Woollos register has the following entries: John Frost baptized 9 Nov. 1783; John Frost buried 23 Dec. 1784; John Frost baptized 3 July 1785; John Frost buried 12 Apr. 1787; John Frost baptized 1 Mar. 1795; John Frost, a boy, buried 23 Dec. 1800; John Frost, a very pious and aged man, buried 12 Oct. 1803.

this time in the little town of several persons bearing his name. Even during the trial for treason there were in Newport two John Frosts, both Chartists.[1] Further, there were Frosts in Newport who were not related to him at all.[2] He himself states that his family had been settled there for nearly a century.[3] It is certain that his grandfather was 'old John Frost, the cordwainer', and that his parents were John and Sarah Frost, of the Royal Oak Inn in Thomas Street. During his infancy or very early childhood his father died, and soon afterwards his mother married again,[4] remaining, however, the tenant of the Royal Oak, which was now the property of her son. She was destined very soon to lose her second husband, but she consoled herself with a third, William Roberts, who, again, joined her at the Royal Oak.[5] She lived to witness her son's difficulties, his condemnation to death and transportation for life, and died only five years before his return, when she had reached the age of ninety-two.[6]

After his father's death the boy was brought up by his grandparents. Even in his own old age he had vivid recollections of the 'stern old man', his grandfather, and of his kindly grandmother, behind the ample folds of whose skirts he often used to hide.[7] What education he received it is very difficult to say, though one account contemporary

[1] The other Chartist was his cousin John (born in 1803, entry in family Bible of Thomas Frost, now in Newport Library). He was a baker and beer-house keeper. His Chartism is mentioned in Newport Museum MS. 839. He was active as a Chartist in 1848 (broadside signed by him and others, Mar. 1848). He died in 1853.

[2] J. and T. Gurney, *The Trial of John Frost* (London, 1840), p. 492, evidence of William Frost.

[3] *A Letter to Thomas Prothero* (1821), p. 8. *A Letter to Sir Charles Morgan* (1821), p. 22.

[4] Possibly 7 Mar. 1792. Entry in St. Woollos register: 'Edward Jones, batchelor, and Sarah Frost, widow, married.'

[5] Usk MSS. Land Tax Assessment for 1808 and subsequent years.

[6] *Monmouthshire Merlin*, 9 May 1851, obituary notice. She was born 14 Apr. 1760 and died 2 May 1851.

[7] *Star of Gwent*, Letter of John Frost, 2 Feb. 1861.

with his trial states that he was sent to Bristol to be educated, as the schools there were better than those at Newport.[1] However this may be, he somehow acquired an extraordinary command of the English language. It was the old man's intention to bring up the boy in his own trade, and he seems to have apprenticed him to himself,[2] but the boy did not care for bootmaking. He was, in his own words, excessively fond of reading, and there was not a novel in the town which he could borrow which he did not read. Years later he was to recall how he and a young friend would manage to order a few books from Bristol, how they would wait in St. Woollos Churchyard, looking out for the packet, *Tredegar*, which plied between the two ports, and how they would rush down to the wharf to claim their books when the boat put in.[3] According to one account his indentures were broken, and at the age of sixteen he was apprenticed to a tailor at Cardiff.[4] Even the very hostile writer of this account admits that his conduct there was steady and exemplary. Possibly it was at the end of his apprenticeship that he proceeded to Bristol and became assistant to a woollen draper in Bridge Street.[5] This must have been about 1803 or 1804. It is probable that his grandfather was now dead; he may have been the 'John Frost, a very pious and aged man' who was buried at St. Woollos in October 1803. All accounts agree that the boy was released from his apprenticeship to his grandfather through the intervention of an 'uncle', and that it was this uncle, a mayor of Newport, who supplied him with letters of recommendation on his departure for Bristol. This was William Foster, a well-to-do and prominent

[1] *The Charter*, 29 Dec. 1839; *Life of John Frost* (anon.) 1840, p. 3.
[2] *Full Report of the Trial of John Frost*, by a Barrister (London, 1840), p. v.
[3] *Star of Gwent*, loc. cit.
[4] Anon., *The Rise and Fall of Chartism in Monmouthshire* (London, 1840), p. 7. (The author was Mr. Dowling, proprietor of the *Merlin*. *Merlin*, 28 Mar. 1840.)   [5] *The Charter*, loc. cit.

tradesman of Newport who became an alderman in 1803 and mayor in 1804.[1] Frost did not remain long in Bristol, for he soon moved to London, where he became a shopman to a merchant tailor. Critics of his later life found reason to condemn the 'restlessness' which made him abandon the cobbler's last and seek to improve his situation in life by moving to Bristol and to London, but even they had to admit that he was assiduous and successful in his new calling.

His period in London, short though it was, was formative in so far as his ideas were concerned. It is true that in later life he was to state that he 'had never read a book that required thought' until his thirty-second year,[2] that is, until well after his return to Newport, but by the time he wrote this, anything lighter than his favourite book, Blackstone's *Commentaries on the Laws of England*, had come to appear frivolous reading. There is every indication that he devoted his leisure hours to study, and that he frequented radical debating societies. The period was a difficult one for the radicals. The prosecutions for sedition in 1793 and 1794, together with the savage sentences of transportation which were inflicted and the repressive legislation passed to meet the occasion, had almost destroyed the radical movement. Nevertheless Major Cartwright, a survivor of the first radical generation, was still active, and the acquittal of Thomas Hardy, John Horne Tooke, and John Thelwall was still in every one's mind. Moreover, in 1799, Francis Place had already opened his tailor's shop at 16 Charing Cross, soon to become the

---

[1] *The Charter*, loc. cit., identifies him with William Foster; elsewhere his name is not given. Borough of Newport Council Meetings Record, vol. i (1739–1834), MS. in the Newport Library, gives the information about his mayoralty. The account given in the text agrees better with the facts than the commonly accepted version that Frost left for Bristol on being released from his indentures to his grandfather. He would have to be apprenticed to his new trade, and the Bristol Apprentice Books which cover this period contain no mention of his name.   [2] *Star of Gwent*, loc. cit.

meeting-place of all who were interested in radical ideas, while in 1802 Cobbett began to publish his *Political Register*. Whether Frost came into contact with these men or not, there is no documentary evidence to prove, but he may very well have done so, for the number of radicals in London was now small, and the meetings which they held in their coffee-houses were very intimate. In particular he seems to have come under the influence of John Gale Jones,[1] a Welshman whose middle name the wits among his friends were accustomed to change into 'gaol', for an adequate and obvious reason. He was an apothecary and a surgeon, although it is doubtful if he ever practised, for his time was entirely occupied in political agitation. Apparently he was a fluent speaker, and he was chosen by the London Corresponding Society to go on a mission in 1796 to explain to provincial radicals how to obviate the penalties of the repressive acts of 1795, but he was arrested at Birmingham and sentenced to imprisonment. Later on he was to be prosecuted again, on that occasion for a libel on Lord Castlereagh. Prominent among the radicals in the opening years of the century, also, was John Frost, the friend of Horne Tooke. He had twice presented addresses from the London radical societies at the bar of the French Convention. On the second occasion he had learnt in Paris that a reward of £100 was offered for his arrest, and he immediately returned, in order, as he said in an open letter to Pitt, to 'afford an opportunity to some fellow-citizen to profit by the proposed bounty of the Treasury'.[2] He was charged with having declared in the public room of a coffee-house that he was for equality and no kings. For this he was tried in May 1793. Erskine, who defended him, showed that the Crown witnesses had

[1] Barrister, loc. cit.; *The Life of John Frost* (London, 1840), p. 3.
[2] G. S. Veitch, *Genesis of Parliamentary Reform* (London, 1913), p. 270. See also *The Times*, 12 Mar. 1840.

forced him against his will into the conversation in which he had used these words, and that he was drunk at the time, but nevertheless he was sentenced to six months' imprisonment and to stand on the pillory at Charing Cross. The second part of the sentence provided the occasion for a great demonstration, for the mob destroyed the pillory and released Frost, who calmly walked back to prison. It is interesting to speculate whether the Newport Frost met his famous namesake, whether, indeed, it was the latter's reputation which made him interest himself in radical ideas. However this may be, the older man lived to see the other sentenced and transported for ideas very like his own. It is stated that Frost never ventured to speak at these meetings in the coffee-houses, and this may well be so, for like many facile writers he was a poor speaker, at least in early life. Even when he had committed a speech to memory, he said, the sight of a public audience drove it out of his head.[1] Certain it is that he returned to Newport with a good knowledge of the causes and course of the French Revolution derived from these discussions, and fully convinced of the soundness of many of the theories of the French eighteenth-century thinkers. His lack of a formal education made him self-opinionated, and led him to hold these ideas more dogmatically than he might otherwise have done. Many of them he was never to change.

It was the earnest entreaties of his mother which induced him to return to Newport. This must have been about 1806,[2] though he was not sworn and admitted a burgess until 3 November 1809.[3] He took over the house and

---

[1] *Letter to Sir Charles Morgan* (1833), p. 18.

[2] In his *Letter to Sir Charles Morgan* (1821), p. 3, he mentions that Sir Charles and Lord Arthur Somerset came to his shop to canvas his vote 'about fifteen years ago'. This must have been the election of 6 Nov. 1806 or 12 May 1807. His name on the list of freeholders 2 Oct. 1810 is given as 'John Frost shopkeeper'. He must therefore have returned to Newport before 1811, the date given in Johns, op. cit., p. 9, and all other accounts.

[3] Newport Council Meetings Record, as above.

business of a Mr. Thomas, draper and tailor in the High Street,[1] and seems to have prospered immediately. His name is included in the list of freeholders drawn up by the constable and sworn before the mayor, 2 October 1810,[2] and in the list of burgesses agreeing to the assessment of a poor rate on 12 February 1812.[3] He must therefore have taken part immediately in local affairs. They did not, however, occupy all his time. In his reminiscent old age he recollected many and many a pleasant evening spent wandering in the meadows between Newport and Caerleon, at that time entirely free from buildings (what atrocities had since been committed on them in the name of improvement, he was then to reflect),[4] and it may well have been there, and in the woods towards Bettws, that he courted his wife. She was a distant relative of his own, a niece of his 'uncle' William Foster, and the widow of a timber merchant named Geach.[5] She had two young children, William Foster Geach and Mary Foster Geach. Since her husband's death she had lived, at least for a time, with her uncle, though in her marriage entry she is described as living in the parish of Bettws, and it was in Bettws Parish Church that Mary Geach and John Frost were married on 24 October 1812.[6] Of her two children by her first husband, her daughter Mary married in 1830 a George Lawrence, tanner of Pontypool,[7] and she plays no part in this story; William Foster Geach, on the other hand, was destined in a very remarkable way to share the fortune of his stepfather.

Thus at the age of twenty-eight John Frost was married,

[1] *The Charter*, loc. cit.   [2] Usk MSS., List of Freeholders.
[3] Newport Library MSS., Overseers of Poor.
[4] Newport Library MSS. Frost letter, 27 Oct. 1870.
[5] Charles Geach and Mary Morgan married 29 Sept. 1803. Witnesses, William Foster, C. Morgan. St. Woollos Register.
[6] Entry on inside endpaper of Bible kept in Bettws Parish Church. Information supplied by Miss Edith M. Hartland.
[7] *Merlin*, 16 Oct. 1830.

15

and showed promise of becoming a successful tradesman of Newport. He was robust and active, a little above the medium height, with his face very slightly marked by the small-pox. Even his bitter opponents admitted that he was 'gifted by nature with far more than ordinary powers of mind', that he was quick in apprehension and possessed energy and a rough vigour of intellect.[1] He was interested in religion, and was, like his uncles, a nonconformist. Reverend critics after his trial were to attribute his downfall to his lack of religion, and the foulest calumnies were preached from their pulpits concerning him,[2] but there is not one word in all his writings to justify this. Soon after his return to Newport he is found lending £100 to the Mill Street Congregational Church.[3] He, himself, seems to have worshipped at Hope Chapel; here, at any rate, all his children were baptized.[4] They were eight in number: John, born 8 October 1813; Elizabeth, 18 March 1815; Sarah, 16 January 1817; Catharine, 16 October 1818; Ellen, 17 September 1820; Henry Hunt, 1 August 1822; James, 7 August 1824 (he died five months later),[5] and Anne, born 1 July 1826. All his affairs seemed to prosper, and, in 1820, old William Foster, thrice mayor of Newport, from whom he and his wife had great expectations, died. The old man had taken advantage of the growth of Newport to amass a considerable fortune as a merchant and a builder—one group of houses in the town was known as Foster's Court—and he possessed a fair property at Newport and at Roath, near Cardiff. But he had married

---

[1] *Rise and Fall*, p. 6.   [2] *The Times*, 20 Apr. 1840.
[3] Newport Library MSS. Mill Street Congregational Church Account Book, 1791–1831. Entries 1815, 4 Nov. 'Paid Mr. John Frost's interest of money £5. Borrowed to pay Frost's £100, £38.' In 1800 there are the entries Edward Frost and William Frost 'dismissed to the English'. These were his uncles.
[4] Somerset House. Non-parochial Registers, Monmouth 26, Register of Hope Chapel, Commercial Street, Newport.
[5] St. Woollos Registers, Burial 12 Jan. 1825, 'James Frost, an infant'.

a second time, and his will proved a keen disappointment to John and Mary Frost, in fact the impulsive nephew bluntly called it a fabrication.[1] The second Mrs. Foster had evidently been able to influence the old man; possibly, also, he did not altogether approve of the young radical, his former protegé, and his niece's second husband. He left all his property, both real and personal, to his wife, Margaret, for her life, or until she married again. Should she marry again, she was to be paid one hundred pounds on the day of her marriage. In the event of her death or remarriage the property was to be handed over to a trustee to be administered in three parts. The first part was to be held in trust for the maintenance, education and advancement in life of William Foster Geach, until he attained the age of twenty-one, when it became his property, provided, of course, that the second Mrs. Foster had died or remarried. The second part passed to his sister under similar conditions, and, should either die before he or she reached the age of twenty-one, his or her share was to pass to the other. Should both die before they came of age, the property was to be united to the third part, which included Foster's dwelling-house and Foster's Court and passed to their mother, Mary Frost. The old man, however, stipulated that it should be held in trust for her, for the term of her natural life, so that it should be for her own disposal only, and 'not to be at the disposal of, or subject to the control, forfeiture, debts or engagements of John Frost, her husband', or any future husband she might marry, even if she should wish it to be so applied, although on her death it should pass to her heirs absolutely. As the second Mrs. Foster might live for a long time, and was unlikely to sacrifice an ample fortune for the sake of a second husband, Mary Frost and her two children might not benefit under this will for a number of

[1] *A Letter to Thomas Prothero* (1821), p. 4.

years, while the greatest care had been taken that John
Frost should not benefit at all. Out of the family quarrel
about this will came all John Frost's early troubles, and
out of these arose his vendetta with Mrs. Foster's lawyer
which persisted for twenty years, colouring all his activities
in the local politics of Newport and contributing largely
to the train of events which eventually brought him to the
condemned cell and Van Diemen's Land.[1]

[1] Will of William Foster, dated 6 June 1819, in Llandaff Diocesan
Registry. He died 29 Feb. 1820. (The will is endorsed 'goods, chattels,
credits of the deceased under £3,000'.) In the Newport Library is a lease
(dated 1810) transferring the Wharf warehouse, quay, &c., from William
Foster and Robert Jones, merchants, at the rent at which they had leased
them from Sir Charles Morgan together with £285, and a bill of sale of
their sloop *Tredegar* for £450. In the Library also are two seven-year leases
dated 1822 of some of Margaret Foster's property, at the rents of £85 and
£23 a year respectively. They are witnessed by William Foster Geach and
Thomas Jones Phillips.

II

THE MAKING OF A CHARTIST

IT is said that the radicalism of Madame Roland was due
not so much to the ideas which she had absorbed in her
early reading of Voltaire and Rousseau as to the personal
slights which she and her mother had suffered at the
hands of the aristocracy. In the same way John Frost's
radicalism was intensified by the sense of injury which he
felt at his treatment by the all-powerful town clerk of
Newport. His struggle for the rights of the burgesses was
inextricably mixed up in his personal quarrel with this
man, and his political ideas, which eventually became
merged into those of the Chartist movement on a national
scale, were formed in the local politics of the small
borough of Newport.

This great opponent of his was Thomas Prothero, a
man only four years his senior. He was the grandson of
Edward Prothero, a currier of Usk, a fact of which John
Frost never ceased reminding him, for he invariably
referred to Prothero's mansion in Newport, the Friars, as
Lapstone Hall. Edward's son Thomas, at one time a bum-
bailiff, if we are to believe Frost, had become an attorney
in his native town, and clerk of the peace for the county
of Monmouth. He, himself, was not above suspicion of
sharp practice,[1] and Thomas Prothero of Newport seems
to have been his illegitimate son.[2] The latter arrived in

[1] Agreement between Edward Bowyer and Thomas Prothero, 16 Feb.
1818, in Cardiff Public Library.

[2] His name is not included amongst the offspring of Thomas Prothero
of Usk in Sir Joseph Bradney, *History of Monmouthshire. The Hundred of Usk*
(London, 1904), p. 38. Burke's *Landed Gentry* traces the family no further
back than himself. Frost, *A Letter to Thomas Prothero* (1821), p. 23, calls him
'a spurious begotten son of Old Prothero of Usk'. The *Newport Review*, xii
(20 Nov. 1822), p. iii, deals with his illegitimacy. He does not seem to have
been on good terms with his father, who, on one occasion, in his capacity as

19

John Frost

Newport in the early years of the century. He set up in a modest way as an attorney, was sworn and admitted a burgess on 9 October 1807, and three days later was appointed town clerk.

The time was opportune for an enterprising man. The iron industry of Monmouthshire, only in its infancy some twenty years earlier, had suddenly acquired enormous importance. The narrow, parallel valleys among the hills were found to be abundantly rich in iron ore, and in the coal and limestone necessary for smelting it. Large-scale iron works were therefore started, one after the other, in rapid succession. At the head of the so-called 'eastern valley' (Afon Lwyd) were the Blaenavon works, where a blast furnace was first introduced in 1790. So rapidly did the industry develop here that there was scarcely time to erect houses for the workers, and living conditions were primitive in the extreme. Lower down the same valley was Pontypool, already for a century and a half the home of a famous industry, the making of Japan ware, which obtained its name because the finished product resembled Japanese lacquered wood. This industry, however, decayed rapidly in the first years of the nineteenth century, and eventually the very secret of japanning died with the last workman engaged in it. But its place was being taken by the heavy iron industry, and, in 1796, the historian of Monmouthshire prophesied that the area around Pontypool would be a second Birmingham. Across the mountains from the Afon Lwyd came the first of the 'western valleys', that of the Ebbw Fach, and at the head of this were the great works of Nantyglo. These had been started at the same time as the Blaenavon works (actually they were only some five miles apart by the mountain road)

clerk of the peace, attempted a forcible entry into his house, to recover goods which were thought to be hidden there. J. Frost, *Letter to Inhabitants of Newport* (1832).

but had not prospered until 1809 when they were bought by Joseph Bailey. Rumour had it that their new owner had been a tramp in his youth, but he became one of Wales' greatest iron-masters, and he was joined in 1811 by his still more famous brother, Crawshay Bailey, who has passed into Welsh folk-song as the owner of 'Crawshay Bailey's engine'.

Under the two brothers the Nantyglo works came to rival even Dowlais, and developed a world reputation for iron rails. Joseph soon retired to Parliament and to his Breconshire estates; Crawshay remained at Nantyglo till 1871. He was stern and tyrannical, the hardest of task-masters, and we shall meet him again. Parallel to the Ebbw Fach flowed the Ebbw Fawr, and near its source were the works of Ebbw Vale, purchased in 1796 by Messrs. Harford & Co., from Jeremiah Homfray. Still farther west ran the Sirhowy River. Here were the small Sirhowy works which passed in 1795 into the possession of Richard Fothergill, but in 1800 Sir Charles (Gould) Morgan leased land in the Sirhowy valley, with full mining rights, to his son-in-law Samuel Homfray (the brother of Jeremiah) and Richard Fothergill, at an annual rent of £300 for the first five years, and £500 for the following ninety-four years. In addition the lease stipulated an outlay of £100,000 on the erection of new works, £40,000 of which must be spent by 1808. More-over all the iron and coal produced must be shipped from Morgan's wharves at Newport and in Morgan's ships, so that Sir Charles would collect all the port and shipping charges. The new works, and the town which grew up around them, were called after Sir Charles's seat, Trede-gar. Last of the Monmouthshire rivers was the Rhymney —in fact the boundary, throughout its course, between Glamorgan and Monmouth. Its valley, also, with that of the other rivers, converged on Newport until the railway (and the tunnel through Caerphilly mountain) connected it with Cardiff. Here the Rhymney ironworks were started in 1800, and were bought in 1803 by Richard Crawshay, the iron-king of Cyfarthfa, for £100,000. In the next year he gave them as a regal marriage portion to his daughter who had married his partner, Benjamin Hall.

All this industrial development found its outlet in Newport, where its effects were immediate. First came the canal, here, as elsewhere, both the evidence and the cause of industrial prosperity. In 1792 an Act of Parliament was obtained to authorize the construction of a canal from Newport along the Afon Lwyd to Pontnewynydd, near Pontypool, with a branch along the Ebbw river as far as Crumlin bridge. The latter section was opened to traffic in 1798 and the former in 1800, and immediately railroads were built to join the canal-ends with the works at Blaenavon and Ebbw Vale. This canal, however, did not serve the Sirhowy Valley, and in 1802 powers were secured to construct a railroad which would connect the Sirhowy and Tredegar works direct with Newport. It passed through Risca, and then, for a mile, actually through the grounds of Sir Charles Morgan's seat at Tredegar Park. For this inconvenience, the tolls levied soon compensated Sir Charles at the rate of £3,000 a year;[1] it was, surely, a more than golden mile. In the meantime a new Act had been obtained to extend the canal a mile and a half beyond Newport itself, and at the same time (1797) Newport obtained exemption from the duties levied on coal and culm carried in the coastal trade. This, above all else, was the foundation of Newport's prosperity, for it already possessed an excellent tidal river suitable for the trade. Its coal exports therefore increased from under 10,000 tons in 1798 to 18,000 in the next year, while ten years later they had reached the figure of 148,000

[1] *Merlin*, 30 Mar. 1833; 11 Jan. 1834.

tons. Moreover the old rickety bridge with its sliding
floors, which had for a long time been unsafe for car-
riages,[1] was taken down in 1800. It was replaced by
a new stone bridge of five arches, the work of David
Edwards, the remarkable son of a very remarkable father.
William Edwards, a self-educated farmer and nonconformist preacher, had built, about 1750, a bridge over the
Taff at a place subsequently known as Newbridge, and
now called Pontypridd. It was a single span of 140 feet,
in its day the largest arch in the world, and it still remains a thing of beauty. His son David continued his
work, and constructed a large number of bridges in South
Wales, and it was he who built the one at Newport at a
cost of £10,165. The canal, the tramroad and the bridge,
together with the turnpike roads soon constructed both
towards the east and towards the west, led to the growth
of Newport itself. Its population rose from 1,135 at the
first census of 1801 to 2,346 in 1811 and 4,000 in 1821.
Most of the new-comers were drawn from the immediate
neighbourhood, a sure proof of this being the number of
Welsh Nonconformist chapels erected in the first decades
of the century in Newport, where none had been before.
Thus the little town, grown up around the castle and
English in origin, became for a few decades predominantly
Welsh, until it was swamped once more by the greater
immigration later on in the century.

It was this rapidly growing town which Thomas
Prothero brought entirely into his own power. Of the
methods which he used to do so, it is now difficult to speak
after this long lapse of time, but even to-day his name is
apt to rouse a feeling of resentment, and where there ha_s
been so much and such persistent smoke it is permissible
to suspect that there was some fire. Besides, it was n ͏

[1] John Evans, *Letters Written during a Tour through South Wales* (London,
1804), p. 64.

only John Frost who accused him in print of sharp practice. A brother attorney issued a lengthy pamphlet detailing his unprofessional conduct in transacting legal business. He showed that this amounted to intimidating witnesses, influencing the counsel of his opponents in one action by supplying him with five briefs while the action was pending, whereas he had never supplied him with one before, splitting fees with auctioneers, and making extortionate charges for arranging loans,[1] and as this pamphlet does not seem to have been followed by a libel action, it probably contains some truth. He was certainly a pugnacious and domineering man—the future member of parliament for Monmouthshire, William Addams Williams of Llangibby Castle, addressed him in his letters as 'my dear Prize Fighter'[2]—and he found ample scope for exercising his desire for power. For he was not only town clerk of Newport; much more important was the fact that he was agent to Sir Charles Morgan and to two other landowners in the district. This gave him almost unlimited power over their tenants. It enabled him to compel them to bring all their legal work to his office, and according to Frost, he even inserted clauses in their leases unknown to them which prevented them from transferring their leases without Sir Charles's consent. In this way he made sure that any transfers to be arranged or mortgages to be effected should be done by him, and this gave him the opportunity to set up a considerable business as a banker. Further he was the treasurer of the Caerleon Charity, which owned considerable property very rich in mineral deposits, and in his capacity as slate and timber

[1] Walker at the suit of Phillips. The Facts upon which the Defendant rested his Pleas of Justification, and the Motives which led him to consent to compromise the Suit, with a Report of the Proceedings in Court, by C. H. Walker, the Defendant. London, Nov. 1832, pp. 32. (In Lord Tredegar's Library.)

[2] Newport Library MSS.

merchant he was himself able to supply the Charity with materials which it required. Again, in addition to being town clerk, he acted as deputy-recorder of Newport (for the recorder, Sir Charles, took no part in municipal affairs). This office, it is true, was largely honorary, but it strengthened his hold upon the municipality. All the important legal work which the growth of the town involved, the procuring of Acts of Parliament for the improvement of the town, and for the regulation of the harbour, for example, was thus done by him, and well was he paid for it. He was also treasurer, and, for some years, deputy sheriff for the county of Monmouth. In all these ways he was able to amass a considerable fortune. The admittedly hostile Frost maintained that he had come to Newport with only a shirt to his back, while in less than twenty years he boasted of being worth £20,000, and Frost declared that setting a beggar on horseback had had its usual results. At any rate he had a financial interest in every new undertaking, in the canal, the turnpike roads, the new gas company and the docks. But his chief speculation was in coal-mines, and he soon became the largest exporter of coal from Newport. In this connexion somewhat incredible stories are told of his activities. It is stated (on fairly reliable authority) that in 1833 he and Thomas Powell, the other important coal exporter of Newport, induced several colliery proprietors to sell them all their coal for a number of years at a price of about eight shillings a ton, in order to avoid underselling each other, and that having obtained this agreement, Prothero and Powell immediately raised the price to eleven shillings a ton, while one person who owned two small collieries and refused to join in the agreement, was forced to capitulate through the obstruction of his export facilities at Newport.[1] However this may be, it is certain that in the same

[1] Alderman H. J. Davis, 'A Short Account of the Rise and Progress of

year, 1833, of the £3,000 which Sir Charles was receiving for his golden mile, between £600 and £700 were being paid by Thomas Prothero, who had only two years previously ceased to be his agent.[1]

Others had not been slow to realize the possibilities of Newport. With the cutting of the canal, pieces of land, especially along the river bank, which had hitherto been entirely useless, now became very valuable. The Duke of Beaufort seized one of these pieces, and proceeded to build a wharf upon it. Immediately the freemen were up in arms. A 'hall' was held in 1794, attended by both Sir Charles (Gould) Morgan and his son, and an inquiry was ordered into the territorial rights of the burgesses. They were able to substantiate their claim, and in 1799 the Duke had to resign the wharf to them on condition that part of the money which he had expended should be refunded to him. Some of the property of the corporation seems to have been sold to pay off the Duke's claims[2] (although Frost maintained consistently that the Duke did not receive a penny),[3] and from this time on the wharf was known as the Corporation Wharf. Eight years later, when Thomas Prothero had become both agent to the Tredegar estates and town clerk of Newport, the younger Sir Charles leased to his brothers-in-law, Samuel Homfray and Rowley Lascelles, and to Richard Fothergill 200 acres of land on which they proceeded to build the Tredegar Warehouse and Quay. Once more the burgesses put forward a claim; they said that a third or more of the land on which these were built was their property. This time they were not successful, but for

Newport' (his reminiscences) in Conyers Kirby, *Pictorial Guide to Newport* (Newport, 1891), p. 27. Thomas Powell was the founder of the Powell Duffryn Coal Company. [1] *Merlin*, loc. cit.

[2] Newport Library MSS. Corporation Records, 1836–43, pp. 68–9, give a lengthy report on this matter.

[3] *Second Letter to Sir Charles Morgan* (1822), and elsewhere.

thirty years the matter was being continually raised until it was eventually abandoned with the collapse of the Chartist agitation.

In all the boroughs of the country, the freemen were now beginning to assert their rights against the borough mongers. In Monmouthshire the first struggle took place in the borough of Monmouth itself, and this incident is particularly notable, because it brought John Frost for the first time before the public as an active reformer. It is difficult to find out what part he took in the struggle, but more than one account states that he was an active supporter of the burgesses.[1] Here the borough monger was the Duke of Beaufort, a man of great wealth and influence. He was lord-lieutenant of three counties; his brother was governor of the Cape of Good Hope; one of his sons was a lord of the Treasury, while another was an ex-lord of the Admiralty. In addition he had twenty-nine livings in his gift. He returned several members to Parliament and was rewarded for this influence by having his sons appointed to some of the most lucrative offices in the gift of the Crown. In Monmouth he asserted the right of appointing the municipal officers and controlling other business within the borough as well as of conferring the freedom of the borough upon individuals, a privilege which would be of great importance in a contested election. The burgesses disputed his claims, and the matter was brought before the courts in 1818. The Duke tried to intimidate his opponents by threatening to take the contest, if necessary, to the House of Lords, thus involving them in ruinous expense, but the Court of King's Bench decided in their favour and refused to accede to a new trial, so that the triumph of the burgesses was complete.[2] This 'glorious struggle' greatly encouraged

[1] *Rise and Fall*, p. 8; *The Charter*, 10 Mar. 1839.
[2] *Bristol Mercury*, 20 Apr. 1822, 24 Nov. 1823.

the reformers, particularly in the neighbouring borough of Newport.

Here, however, the contest was of a different nature, for the freemen and the corporation were on opposite sides. Freedom of the borough could be obtained by birth, by marriage, by apprenticeship within the borough, by gift, and by purchase, although admission by apprenticeship had been discontinued for a long time, and regulations with regard to gift and purchase were somewhat vague. Aldermen, on the other hand, were appointed by their own body, and only when vacancies occurred, so that the corporation was a closed one. The possibility of a struggle between the aldermen and the burgesses arose mainly out of the existence of common property in Newport. Part of this property was a large common field to the north of the town, called the Marshes. It was generally kept in hay, and the grass was sold by auction each year, the aftermath being grazed by cattle turned on the ground by the burgesses. About this there was not much room for dispute, for the proceeds of the sale were divided in equal parts among the resident burgesses and the widows of their dead colleagues, according to the ordinances of 1711, although Prothero was suspected of arranging the sale so that he could buy the hay himself at half its value and then resell it at a profit. The dispute arose concerning the rent of the Corporation Wharf, which amounted to about £100 a year, and of two small plots of ground, together with small sums levied in fines and dues. The corporation claimed the right to use this money for public purposes; the freemen demanded that it should be divided among themselves. Moreover it was the corporation which had arranged for the sale of a plot of land to compensate the Duke of Beaufort (although the purchase seems never to have been completed),[1]

[1] *Merlin*, 27 July 1833.

while Frost stated that Sir Charles Morgan, himself a member of the corporation as its recorder, based his claim to part of the land covered by the warehouse and wharf on the gift of the corporation. Obviously this was becoming a matter of importance with the increased value of land, and as no accounts were published of the money received by the corporation, it was suspected that the public purposes on which it was spent were dinners for the mayor and aldermen. Consequently the matter was taken up with great vigour by Frost, who championed the rights of the larger body at the expense of the smaller. Curiously enough this led him later into a false position, for even after the Municipal Corporation Act he still consistently championed the rights of the freemen of the old borough, but these rights were then opposed not to those of a closed corporation but to those of the citizens at large. As no more freemen could be created after 1835, their number was small and diminishing, in contrast to the growing population of the town, and the democratic Frost found himself defending the rights of this small body, while those who had supported the claim of the mayor and aldermen to the control of the money for 'public purposes' then became the champions of public rights. Payments out of the Marshes money continued to be made, in fact, until the last claimant died in 1924.[1]

The person who first appeared in print on the matter was, however, not Frost, but Samuel Etheridge, a man some seven years older than Frost, who issued two letters *To the Burgesses of Newport* in 1820. He was a printer by trade, the proprietor of the 'Radical Printing Office', and he wrote under the name of Hampden.[2] Both the name

[1] J. Warner, 'The Marshes Estate', *Monmouthshire Review*, v. 122–36.

[2] Etheridge took the necessary oath with regard to the possession of a printing press in Jan. 1822. He first used his own press 26 Jan. 1822. Usk MSS. Quarter Sessions Records. He became an assistant overseer of the poor.

of his press and his pseudonym were significant of the new development which was taking place in radical ideas. Some four years before Waterloo Major Cartwright, the indefatigable reformer of a previous generation, had tried to revive interest in parliamentary reform by the foundation of the Hampden Club. The name was chosen because of the refusal of the seventeenth-century leader to pay taxes, but the club was distinctly a Whig body, for no one was eligible for membership unless he had an income of £300 a year derived from land. Major Cartwright made two missionary tours to propagate its ideas, in 1813 and in 1815, but without much success. When the war was over the club was revived on a much more popular basis. Branches were established throughout the country and membership extended to all who paid a subscription of one penny a week. This was about March 1816; by January 1817 a government agent reported that the clubs in England, Scotland, and Wales claimed a membership of almost half a million.[1] Whether there was a branch in Newport or not is not known, but Etheridge certainly propagated the ideas of the club, publishing among other things a copy of the charter of Newport, so that the burgesses might know their rights. At his shop, also, could be bought Cobbett's *Political Register* and other radical literature. It was he who published all of John Frost's early pamphlets, but he was not a financial success, and Frost eventually took over his printing press. He continued, however, to write to the local newspapers on matters of reform, always under the name of Hampden, and later became the secretary of the Newport branch of the Working Men's Association.

The cause of reform was also being taken up locally by other and more 'substantial' men. Of these the most active was John Hodder Moggridge. He was apparently

[1] H.O. 40/3.

a native of Gloucestershire, and had acquired wealth by 'spinning English broadcloth'. With this wealth he had bought an estate in the extreme west of Monmouthshire and embarked on the life of a country gentleman. His relations with his tenants were not always happy, and he, in his turn, was the recipient of public letters which show that his attitude towards them was the one which has always been considered typical of 'new men'—tradesmen turned squires—and which Bishop Hugh Latimer had condemned nearly three centuries before.[1] He was a prolific writer of pamphlets, mainly on agricultural distress, and the Monmouthshire news in the *Bristol Mercury* (the chief paper circulating in the shire at this time) was taken up almost exclusively with his activities. After their quarrel Frost insinuated that these reports were written by Moggridge himself. His political ideas were those of the Whig industrialists. Party politics, however, were not solidified in Monmouthshire, and when Sir Charles Morgan was elected for the fifth time as member for the shire in 1812, his nomination was proposed by Moggridge. Possibly the latter hoped in this way to be fully accepted into the circle of the county families. But his ideas were soon shown to be radically opposed to those of Sir Charles, and in February 1817 he induced the high sheriff to call a meeting of the gentry, clergy, freeholders, and householders of the county of Monmouth at Usk. Here certain resolutions were passed, proposed by Moggridge himself. Profound regret was expressed at the recent assault on the person of the Prince Regent, but the meeting hoped that this would not be held to prejudice the cause of reform. In this cause the meeting presented a petition to His Highness. The extreme poverty of the country was stressed, and this was attributed to excessive

[1] Peter Lauder, *A Letter to John H. Moggridge* (Cardiff, 1816); id., *A Letter to John H. Moggridge* (Gloucester, 1817).

taxation which was itself due to the corrupt representation of the people. Fewer than two hundred persons returned a decided majority in the House of Commons, while members of that House enjoyed places and emoluments exceeding £200,000 annually. The petition therefore called for shorter parliaments and a more equitable distribution of the franchise, together with the reduction of the military and civil establishments and the abolition of sinecures. A counter resolution to the effect that the reform of Parliament would not relieve distress was negatived by a large majority. Unfortunately the petition was signed by the high sheriff only, in his capacity as chairman of the meeting, and there is no means of knowing who or how many people supported it. A counter petition was immediately circulated, maintaining that those who supported the resolutions were not representative of the county, that taxation was not the cause of distress, and that the reform of Parliament was inexpedient, and this was signed by no less than 520 people, 45 of whom were magistrates, among the signatories being most of the landowners and iron-masters of Monmouthshire.[1]

The issue therefore was clearly joined between the two groups on the matter of reform, and this at the time when the burgesses of Monmouth were struggling for their rights. Consequently when a general election was held in March 1820, on the accession of George IV, John Hodder Moggridge decided to contest the boroughs against the Marquis of Worcester, son and heir to the Duke of Beaufort.[2] The excitement was enormous. There had been no contest in the boroughs within living memory, and it was forty-nine years since the last contest in the shire, when Valentine Morris of Piercefield, a West India

[1] Lauder's second letter gives a full account of these resolutions.
[2] *Bristol Mercury*, 13 Mar. 1820. W. R. Williams, *Parliamentary Representation of Wales* (Brecon, 1895) is inaccurate on this matter.

planter and 'spirited landowner', had ruined himself by opposing old John Morgan of Tredegar. When nomination day came, and all who were interested crowded to the Shire Hall at Monmouth, the honour of seconding Moggridge's nomination fell to John Frost.[1] The latter was under thirty-six years of age at the time, and his selection on this important occasion indicates that he had already become well known for his political views. Unfortunately, however, although the *Bristol Mercury* supported Moggridge, there is no report of Frost's speech. The result of the election, also, was disappointing, for the Marquis defeated his opponent by ninety votes to forty, and he remained in undisputed possession of the seat for another eleven years. In vain did John Partridge, Etheridge's foreman, when the next election came in 1826, publish a song:

> Shall the sons of Newport free
> E'er to Worcester bend the knee?

The free sons of Newport had to wait until their cause was championed by a man of still greater wealth in the person of Benjamin Hall, grandson of the iron king of Cyfarthfa.

The election of 1820 had taken place only a few days after the death of old William Foster. Frost's disappointment at the terms of the will was intense, and he contemplated taking the matter to the law courts. Powell, the coal exporter, however, dissuaded him, as the expense might well be enormous, and induced him to see Mrs. Foster's solicitor, Thomas Prothero, who might arrange things amicably, as he was pleased with Frost's support of Moggridge. Prothero's affairs had, indeed, progressed so far that he had begun to hold views on politics contrary to those of Sir Charles. His interests were those of the Whig merchants; Sir Charles's were those of the Tory landowners, and this eventually led to a separation between

---

[1] *The Charter*, 10 Mar. 1839; *Dublin Review* (Feb. 1840), p. 276.

the squire and his agent in somewhat acrimonious circumstances. Besides, Moggridge was his personal friend.[1] There had so far been no actual strife between him and Frost, although the latter had a temperamental dislike for any one who had arrogated to himself as much power as Prothero had done, while Frost was the chief leader of the burgesses in their struggle against the corporation. Frost went to see him, and according to Frost's account, Prothero was inclined to agree with him that the will was a fabrication. But nothing was done in the matter until July, when Frost realized that Prothero had accepted the will, for in that month he acted under the instructions of Margaret Foster, and wrote to John Frost's uncle, William Frost, threatening to put the law into execution against him unless he repaid money which he had borrowed from William Foster.

This was not the first time that William Frost's financial embarrassments had involved his nephew. The older man had engaged in some unfortunate building speculations. Frost declared that his uncle's misfortunes had been due in the first place to Prothero's insertion, without his knowledge, of a clause in his lease which made it impossible for him to transfer the lease without Sir Charles's consent. William Frost had therefore been unable to arrange a mortgage at all for some time, and even then only at a ruinous rate through Prothero himself. Moreover, in 1815 Prothero had served him with a writ for the repayment of this money. John Frost had immediately paid £200 into the hands of Prothero's clerk, who promised to stay proceedings, but when Frost brought the remaining £100, he was told that proceedings had not been

---

[1] Moggridge had expressed high approbation of his ability as Treasurer for the County at the Usk Quarter Sessions (*Bristol Mercury*, 26 Oct. 1818), and seconded a motion for an increase in his salary. Prothero acted for Moggridge in the Lauder affair.

stayed, and he had had to pay an additional £13 for legal expenses. In August of that year William Frost's title-deeds, which had been in Prothero's possession as security for the debt, were handed over to John Frost, and in May 1816 William Foster lent William Frost £195, the sum which Margaret Foster now sought to reclaim as part of her vendetta against John Frost.

When John Frost heard of this he wrote immediately (July 1820) a private letter to Thomas Prothero. He accused him of using his position as agent to Sir Charles to compel his tenants to come to his office, and of charging them exhorbitant rates for the work done. He demanded redress for the injuries William Frost had sustained, and threatened that he would otherwise lay the matter before Sir Charles. Should he, also, refuse to take any notice, then Frost would show Prothero what industry and perseverance could do—presumably a threat to publish the letter. He ended by giving Prothero some sound moral advice. Let him think of his young and growing family, and let him make it possible for it to be said that while he had devoted his youth to amassing wealth in a dubious manner, in his declining years he had made amends.[1]

The letter was a private one; it was, in fact, delivered by Frost's servant into the possession of Prothero. Probably, however, news of it got abroad, for Frost was not the man to hide the fact that he had told Prothero what he thought of him. It must, in any case, have infuriated that imperious man beyond endurance. Moreover, the matter of the Corporation Wharf was raised once more. In 1819 the burgesses had claimed that the rent from the wharf should be divided among themselves; the aldermen had replied that there was no evidence to justify this, and

[1] This private letter is printed in Frost's first public letter to Prothero.

decided that the rent should be 'distributed as heretofore for public purposes'.[1] In October 1820 thirty-six of the burgesses, urged on by Frost, presented a memorial on the subject to Sir Charles Morgan, as recorder of the borough, and Sir Charles consented to a meeting at the Heath Cock Inn to discuss the matter. The proceedings were stormy. Sir Charles as chairman allowed Prothero continually to interrupt the burgesses while they put their case, in fact maintained that he had every right to interrupt them, and Prothero did his utmost to bully them into submission. The only result was that feelings were embittered on both sides, and no agreement was reached. By this time Frost and Prothero had become bitter enemies on both public and private grounds, and that was why Prothero in January 1821 took action with regard to the letter written in July 1820. He brought the matter before a Grand Jury at Usk. He was, at this time, under-sheriff for the county, and it is at least extraordinary that nine of the Grand Jury were from Caerleon, seven of them being tenants of the Caerleon Charity, of which Prothero was treasurer, while the foreman was unable to read—and this in a trial for libel. The jury found a True Bill, a verdict which can only be explained by Prothero's influence. Further he had Frost arrested and instructed the constables to take him immediately, not before a Newport magistrate, but before a Reverend Mr. Thomas of Caerleon, a master under the Caerleon Charity, and therefore prepared to do his bidding. Frost had scarcely time to arrange for bail, but the reverend gentleman was about to accept two bails in £20 when Prothero's messenger appeared and instructed him that he must demand twenty-four hours' notice of the bail. Frost was therefore kept in custody by the constables in his own home for thirty hours, and when he was for a second time brought

[1] Newport Library MSS. Corporation Records.

before the magistrate, the latter now demanded two bails in £50 each, with Frost himself for £100.

In the meantime Prothero had taken action against William Frost. The old man was arrested and taken to Monmouth gaol. John Frost and his cousin Thomas Frost accompanied him, and it was the old man's intention to take advantage of the recent Insolvent Debtors Act of 1820. But he became so ill on the journey that John and Thomas Frost decided to give bail for his appearance rather than leave him in Monmouth. The clerk to the magistrate at Monmouth made an unfortunate mistake in spelling Margaret Foster's name as Forster, and Prothero promptly took advantage of this to upset the bail. The matter was eventually brought before Mr. Justice Bayley at the Court of King's Bench in the Easter Term of 1821.[1] It was represented that the cousins had become security not for William Frost's appearance but for his debts. Moreover, a clerk in the office of Prothero's London agent, one John Miles, gave evidence that the bail had in their possession deeds belonging to William Frost to cover his debts and the cost of the action, and further that they had tried to prevent Margaret Foster from continuing with the case by threatening to make William Frost bankrupt, representing to her that she would never recover her money and would only involve herself in great expense. The judge came to the conclusion that William Frost had attempted to effect a fraudulent bankruptcy—a not uncommon occurrence—and so John and Thomas Frost were held responsible for his debt of £195 together with £30 costs. To add insult to injury, Prothero

[1] P.R.O. King's Bench Calendar of Pleas, Easter Term, 1821, no. 1628. The calendar for the Hilary Term 1821, no. 746, records a case Thomas Jones Phillips, plaintiff, John Frost, defendant. I have been entirely unable to find any further record of this case. A Thomas Jones Phillips was a clerk in Prothero's office in 1810; it was he or his son (of the same name) who arrested Frost in November 1839.

boasted in public that he had 'fixed Jack Frost with his uncle's debt'. He went further. He put an execution into Frost's house for £67, interest and costs, although receipts could be produced to show that William Frost had paid the interest, and although his client was quite satisfied that she had recovered the money in full. Prothero's clerk, meanwhile, taunted Frost that he supposed he would take action to recover this money, while, as deputy-sheriff, Prothero charged him £3. 7s. for collecting it.

Prothero may well have thought that he had silenced the ringleader of the burgesses. If so, he was mistaken. He had not proceeded with the libel action against Frost. It is difficult to see how he could, in any case, have proved libel in a letter delivered into his possession, while the letter could hardly be interpreted as an attempt to extort money, as all it demanded was redress for William Frost's grievances. According to Frost, Prothero hesitated because he was unwilling to risk being cross-examined in court, and this may have emboldened Frost to take the next step. He now had printed a forty-page *Letter to Thomas Prothero*, incorporating his first letter. This he sent to Prothero on 31 August, at the same time intimating that unless the injuries which he and his family had received at Prothero's hands were redressed, copies of it would be exposed for sale on the next day, and as he received no reply, Frost proceeded to carry out his threat.[1] In this public letter his accusations were definite enough. He accused Prothero of using his position as under-sheriff to pack the jury at Usk. Trial by jury, he said, was the boast of the country, and a wretch who tampered with it was unfit to live. Compared with him a highwayman or a pickpocket was a virtuous character. He proceeded to give an account of the William Frost affair. The clerk of Prothero's London agent, he claimed, could not possibly have known that

[1] *Trial of Prothero v. Frost in Court of King's Bench* (Newport, 1822).

Frost held title-deeds belonging to his uncle. He could only have obtained this information from Prothero. But Prothero knew that he held these deeds as security for a debt contracted in 1815, for Prothero himself had handed them over to him. Consequently in getting this clerk to swear that Frost held title-deeds to cover his uncle's debt to Margaret Foster, Prothero had suborned a witness to perjury. Frost accused him further of using his power to injure Sir Charles Morgan's tenants and specified other cases of sharp practice on his part. He placed before the public a detailed account of his relations with Prothero and of the claims of the burgesses in the matter of the Corporation Wharf. He spoke moreover of the hypocrisy of men who were so regular in their attendance at church, but who were found on other occasions in the churchyard in a compromising situation, a matter as notorious as the sun at noonday, and he concluded with the same language as in his private letter. Let Prothero review his past life and devote the evening of his days to making amends.

This was Frost's first essay in authorship. His model was very obviously William Cobbett, and passages of the pamphlet are worthy of being placed beside the work of his 'master'. He showed a remarkable command of language and a power of humorous invective which might well have been used in a better cause. His success in Newport was immediate. Nothing like this had happened there before, and the majority of the four thousand inhabitants of the little town, who hated and feared Prothero, were delighted with the character sketch of him which Frost had drawn. Every copy was sold, and a second edition was called for immediately. Frost was therefore encouraged to continue in his new avocation. The mayor and aldermen had agreed to a resolution (drawn up by the town clerk himself) stating that they believed the accusations against Prothero to be false. They, therefore, were the recipients of Frost's second letter. It was far more scurrilous than the first—Frost had evidently enjoyed the reputation for diablerie which he had acquired —and the very human weaknesses of the mayor were dissected at great length. In addition, the accusations against Prothero were repeated and other specimens of his extortionate practices were given. Frost challenged him to a public debate on the matter. Further he roundly accused Sir Charles of receiving for a number of years money which rightfully belonged to the burgesses of Newport. He kept up the excitement of the latter by an announcement at the end of the pamphlet that he had already in the press a *Sermon for the Lawyers* (the first of a series which he hoped to issue), and that he would shortly publish *A Letter to Sir Charles Morgan*. The sermon proved to be innocuous; the letter to Sir Charles, on the other hand, not only challenged his right to the land on which the Tredegar warehouse was built, but questioned the ways by which large estates had been acquired at all.

Prothero had now no alternative but to prosecute. He chose to take advantage of the privileges of an attorney in having the case tried before the Court of King's Bench and not in the local courts. Eleven indictments were brought against Frost, three based on the private letter, and the remainder on the published pamphlet. Of these the most important related to the accusation of having packed the jury at Usk and suborned a witness to perjury. In this way, read the plea, an attempt had been made to bring Prothero into public scandal and disgrace, especially with Sir Charles Morgan, as a person unfit to be employed, whereas, in fact, Prothero had in all his actions been marked by 'great honesty and integrity, regard for truth, justice and humanity'.[1] In reply Frost pleaded justifica-

---

[1] P.R.O. King's Bench, Plea Rolls, Hilary Term, 1822, no. 289.

tion on all counts. He went further and specified a date on which Prothero had been found in the churchyard, to wit on All Fools' Day, 1821.

The case came before Lord Chief Justice Abbott at the Court of King's Bench on 1 March 1822, Prothero claiming damages to the extent of £5,000. Frost took up with him four witnesses: his uncle, to prove Prothero's insertion without his knowledge of a clause in his lease; his cousin, to prove that he had gone bail for his uncle's appearance only; a person to prove tampering with the Caerleon witnesses, and another who had witnessed the churchyard affair. He had briefed two very remarkable men, Thomas Denman, later Attorney-General and Lord Chief Justice, and young Frederick Pollock, who was to defend Frost in still more difficult circumstances. They advised him to plead guilty, for Pollock gave it as his opinion that the remarks were libellous, even if the accusations were true, and explained to Frost (already sufficiently dissatisfied with the ways of the law and of lawyers) that 'the greater the truth, the greater the libel'. Frost, however, refused, and persisted in his plea of justification. They, on the other hand, would not call his witnesses, and when Frost tried to insist, Denman told him sharply that he had entrusted his case to them and so must abide by their decision, which was to plead only in mitigation of damages.

A Mr. Puller opened for the plaintiff. He came at once to the weak point of his own case: why had Prothero, if he was so well known and admired in Monmouthshire, chosen to have the matter tried in Middlesex, and this he explained by Frost's accusation that Prothero could select his own jury in Monmouthshire, so that the latter had chosen to take the case elsewhere. Mr. Puller then proceeded to detail the various points in the indictment, admitting incidentally that the cousins had been fixed with their uncle's debt in consequence of a clerical error. He dwelt upon the injury done to Prothero's good name, the attempt even to poison his domestic happiness by a foul imputation, which was highly improbable, as Prothero on that very day had attended the high sheriff at the assizes, and called for damages as exemplary as ever were given in a court of justice. Mr. Denman, in reply, drew emphatic attention to a cause between neighbours being brought almost two hundred miles to be tried before strangers. It was passing strange that a gentleman, so honoured as the plaintiff was said to be by the gentry of his neighbourhood, should bring this action for trial to a place where he had never been heard of. Character, which this proceeding was intended to vindicate, was a local subject; it was not transferable from city to city like a bill of exchange. Modes of expression used on the borders of Wales could only be understood by those who lived there; virulence of language there might imply little deliberate malice, and the heat of these sons of Cadwallader was as little understood in Middlesex as their aboriginal tongue. The jury would remember the couplet:

> Sir Toby MacNegus much spirit has got,
> And Sir Philip ap Keppel is apt to be hot.

This trial should never have been transferred to another atmosphere of feeling, nor should a Middlesex jury be called upon to give £5,000 damages for excess of Welsh anger. If the argument with regard to Prothero's influence were brought forward, did he then admit this illicit influence? Were there no coroners in Monmouthshire who might select the jury, and even if the whole of the shire was under Prothero's influence, were there not the neighbouring counties of Gloucester, Somerset, and Hereford where the case might have been tried without this enormous expense? The plaintiff had not even averred his impartiality as under-sheriff, had not proved the charge of subornation false, had not shown that there was nothing mysterious in Mrs. Foster's affair. The defendant had been fixed with the payment of a debt by a mere error in one letter of the alphabet, and this injustice had goaded him to write a pamphlet which, even in its culpable warmth, carried to every heart a conviction of his sincerity. His indignation at the fact, not denied by the plaintiff, that seven of the Caerleon jury were tenants of the Charity of which Prothero was treasurer, had Denman's hearty concurrence, and that of all who wished to preserve the noblest institutions of England. What damages could be awarded? Prothero had already had ample revenge. Frost had been brought to the verge of ruin; he must pay the expenses of the case and those of his witnesses who made their first visit to London in this way and had been waiting there a fortnight in expectation of the trial. The jury would appreciate the impenetrable mystery which shrouded the case, over which Prothero could have shed the clearest light; they would never blindly give large damages in Middlesex in a case which could only have been fairly and fully investigated in Monmouthshire. The Lord Chief Justice then addressed the jury. They must not infer from the silence of the plaintiff that the imputations were true; no man should be called upon to prove his own innocence. Generally speaking, he agreed that cases should be tried in the county where they arose; a special reason for not doing so had been given in the present instance, and the jury must decide upon its merits. Damages must be given, for the defendants had admitted the offence, but he left the amount to the jury, enjoining them to give their verdict temperately, dispassionately, and justly. The jury took the pamphlet with them when they retired. They shortly returned and declared Frost not guilty on one count arising out of the private letter, but guilty on all the others.

Damages they assessed at £1,000—costs being later fixed at £316.[1]

Frost's exposure of Prothero had cost him dear. He derived what solace he could from the fact that his friends were preparing to welcome him, and although his arrival was delayed by bad weather and workmen had been threatened with dismissal if they took part in the affair, a large crowd awaited him when he stepped off the packet from Bristol on Tuesday, 5 March. He was determined to give the matter as much publicity as possible, as this was the best way to injure Prothero, so he now published a full account of the trial, with his own comments, in two pamphlets of some ninety pages. He was bitterly critical of his counsel—the couplet about Sir Toby MacNegus infuriated him into incoherence—and as Denman and Pollock had refused to call his witnesses, he proceeded to state the evidence which they had been prepared to give, including an affidavit relating to Prothero's adultery. He also produced a second *Letter to Sir Charles Morgan*, repeating his charges, which were now becoming a trifle monotonous.

Prothero in the meantime had so far lost his temper as to assault Etheridge, the printer, at Sir Charles's cattle show, and had been indicted for it. The matter was dealt with at the Usk Quarter Sessions in April, when Prothero thought it wise to withdraw his plea of not guilty, but his fine was set at one shilling, which he immediately paid to the sheriff in court.[2] His friends had also held a dinner in his honour at the Westgate Hotel, one of the speakers being J. H. Moggridge. This brought from Frost a public letter to the recent Whig candidate in which he doubted

---

[1] This account has been reconstructed from Frost's pamphlets, King's Bench Plea Rolls, a full account in *The Times*, 2 Mar. 1822, a brief account in *Bristol Gazette*, 7 Mar. 1822, and *Trial of Prothero* v. *Frost* (Prothero's account).

[2] Usk MSS. Quarter Sessions Orders, 1821–30, under date 15 Apr. 1822.

whether the latter was 'the flaming patriot' he had pretended to be. Moreover, placards were posted throughout Newport and the neighbourhood advertising a 'full and particular account of the trial between Thomas Prothero and John Frost' which was to appear shortly. This was apparently the work of Prothero and Moggridge, and, if we are to believe Frost, the printer sold only thirteen copies. It was, in any case, a very lame reply, for it did little more than reproduce the Lord Chief Justice's summing up.

All this did not exculpate Prothero in the eyes of the burgesses of Newport, and Frost was threatening to publish a satirical poem entitled *The Wanderer of Usk* which, no doubt, was already circulating in manuscript. Prothero, therefore, decided to take further action. Possibly taunted by Denman's remarks at the trial, he decided to bring another action against Frost at the summer assizes in Monmouth on the ground of two libellous statements in the *Letter to the Mayor and Aldermen* and the *Letter to Sir Charles Morgan*, both published before the London trial.[1] The case came before a special jury at Monmouth on 13 August.[2] Puller once more appeared for Prothero, but this time Frost defended himself. He received short shrift from the judge, Sir William Garrow, especially when he tried to make disparaging remarks about Denman, and consequently sat down without completing his defence. Puller intimated that if Frost expressed compunction, Prothero would not proceed, but this brought from Frost only a passionate refusal. He gloried in what he had done and would do it again, for he had only exposed tyranny. The jury without hesitation found him guilty, and he was required to give bail for his appearance before the Court of King's Bench in November to receive judgement.

[1] P.R.O. Assizes 1/28. Oxford Circuit Minute Book, 1822.
[2] *Newport Review*, 24 Aug. 1822.

He now had little time to lose. He immediately sold off his stock for £700 (scarcely half its value, so he claimed).[1] He then paid his debts, except one of £200 to his step-father, William Roberts, who had him arrested, and on 28 August Frost went to Monmouth gaol, intending to claim the benefit of the 1820 Insolvent Debtors Act. From gaol he continued to issue his pamphlets, including a bitter attack on the highway commissioners, in which he accused Prothero of causing the death of a woman turn-pike keeper at Newport, by arresting her husband for debt when she was in an advanced state of pregnancy, and another letter *To the Radicals of Monmouthshire*. But he had neglected to complete his arrangements before entering gaol, and, curiously enough, he now under-estimated his opponent's power. He wrote from prison a letter to his wife, instructing her how to enter the shop at the Excise Office as belonging to their son, and how to dispose secretly of part of their furniture, and this letter was evidently opened at Prothero's request.[2] When Frost appeared before the Commissioners of the Insolvent Debtors Court (that is, the magistrates in Quarter Sessions) at Usk on 14 October, his release was opposed by Prothero on three grounds: (i) that he had been actuated by malice in the libel which he had published; (ii) that he had given undue preference to some of his creditors; and (iii) that he had fraudulently made away with some of his property to deprive his creditors of their rights. The magistrates included both Moggridge and Lord Worcester's brother, both embittered against Frost. Possibly Prothero was unable to use the knowledge he had illegally gained of Frost's undoubted attempt at fraud. At any rate, the court somewhat surprisingly overruled the first and third objections. But they held that

---

[1] *Newport Review*, 26 Oct. 1822.

[2] This letter was printed in a broadside attack on Frost by Detector in 1837.

the second objection was substantiated, and so Bosanquet, the chairman, sentenced Frost to six months' detention, after which period he should be allowed the benefit of the Act.[1] Undoubtedly, in this matter, he got off better than he deserved, and he seems to have outwitted Prothero, for the Royal Oak Inn remained his property for another fifty years, although it may have nominally passed into his mother's possession.[2]

His detention in Monmouth gaol was not technically an imprisonment, and he always looked back on it as one of the happiest periods of his life, for it gave him ample leisure for reading and writing.[3] His friends subscribed to his support and to that of his family,[4] and his own chief concern was to obtain a good knowledge of Welsh and French, so that when he came out he would be a more formidable opponent to Prothero and Sir Charles.[5] But he still continued his public letters, now printed in the *Newport Review*, which the irrepressible Etheridge had started in order to continue the struggle. Among these letters was one *To the Radicals of Newport*.[6] In it he foretold the day of reckoning which was at hand, and urged the radicals to fix upon some house or farm which they would like to have. He already had his eye on one—Werndee (a farm belonging to Sir Charles); he would be satisfied with that. The whole letter is written in a tone of banter, but throughout the Chartist period this reference to

[1] Usk MSS., op cit., 14 Oct. 1822; *Newport Review*, loc. cit. By an order of the Insolvent Debtors Court, Westminster, 1 Nov. 1822, William Roberts, detaining creditor, was ordered to show cause why Frost should not be discharged. There was a technical error in the return made of his bankruptcy, which involved some correspondence, Usk MSS. Insolvent Debtors. Miscellaneous Papers. Notice of bankruptcy, *The Times*, 31 Mar. 1823; 'bankruptcy superseded', *The Times*, 15 Sept. 1823.
[2] It is given as Frost's property in Usk MSS. Register of Electors, 1832.
[3] *Western Vindicator*, 22 June 1839.   [4] *Newport Review*, loc. cit.
[5] *Letter to Radicals of Monmouthshire*, Sept. 1822.
[6] *Newport Review*, 20 Nov. 1822.

Werndee was brought up against him, and however much
he denied it, he was accused of favouring the division of
property.[1]

Frost did not appear before the King's Bench until
Monday, 3 February 1823, when he was brought up by the
gaoler of Monmouth. The Lord Chief Justice asked him
if his defence would take long, and on being told that it
would, he proposed that the case should stand over for
a week, and arranged that Frost should be committed
to the custody of the Marshal of the Marshalsea. Frost
complained of this preliminary confinement, and of the
expense he was compelled to bear, but he was told that he
could not be relieved, and was advised to try by a judicious
concession to the prosecutor whether he could not prevent
the necessity of inflicting further punishment on him. In
the Marshalsea he remained until Tuesday, 11 February,
when he was brought up again. He now tried to read a
long address attacking Prothero, but Lord Chief Justice
Abbott cut him short, and sentenced him to six months'
imprisonment. Frost requested that this might be served
at Monmouth, but Abbott told him that it was his duty to
see that he was removed from the county where he had
done so much mischief, at least for a time, and so he was
sent to the prison at Cold Bath Fields. He was also to find
security for his good behaviour for five years, himself in
£500 and two sureties in £100 each.[2] Thus on a dismal,
damp day in February he was placed in one of the worst
prisons in London. His companions there were a pro-
miscuous group of felons, and he found the conditions
almost intolerably repugnant. Yet he survived them, as
he was to survive even worse conditions twenty years
later.[3] When the time drew near for his release, great

[1] Broadside by Vindex, 1837; *Particulars of Trial of John Frost*, 1840.
[2] *The Times*, 4 Feb. 1823; 12 Feb. 1823; *Bristol Mercury*, 24 Feb. 1823;
Particulars of Trial, 1840; *Merthyr Guardian*, 16 Nov. 1839.
[3] *Letter to Radicals of Newport*, 1832, describes these conditions.

preparations were made at Newport, and on the day a large crowd met him some four miles out of the town. (Enthusiastic Chartists stated later that there had been 15,000 present on that occasion[1]—nearly four times the total population of Newport—but the Chartists were never much good at figures.) With banners flying, and a band playing (somewhat inappropriately) *See the Conquering Hero Come*, they escorted him into Newport, and then carried him in triumph through the streets, where they made a point of passing in front of Prothero's mansion, the Friars, the 'Lapstone Hall' of the pamphlets.[2] But the security for good behaviour had effectively silenced Frost for a time, and nothing further came from his pen for the next nine years.

In these two years, 1821 and 1822, Frost had thus produced some dozen pamphlets, and one is enabled to discover what his ideas on social and political matters were at this stage. Two considerations immediately force themselves on our attention. In the first place, his ideas were now completely formed. Ten years later he was to take part in the long struggle for reform; seven years later still he had become an important Chartist leader, but in all his writings and reported speeches at these times there is scarcely an idea which is not to be found in the early pamphlets. This makes the second consideration all the more surprising. Chartism is generally thought of as a product of the industrial areas, as a reaction against the misery produced by industrialism. The years 1815–22 were certainly years of acute distress in South Wales. The price of iron had dropped 60 per cent. in 1816, and wages were drastically reduced, with the usual result of strikes, riots, and the calling in of troops. Throughout 1817 a

---

[1] *The Charter*, 29 Dec. 1839; *Life of John Frost*, 1840, p. 4; even the hostile *Decline and Fall* gives the figure 10,000.

[2] Ibid.; *Western Mail*, 30 July 1877.

cordon of detachments was stationed around the coal-field. Even in 1822, when Frost was busily writing, strikes were taking place within twenty miles of Newport,[1] but apart from one very passing reference he pays no attention to them at all. He cannot have been unaware of their existence; it was merely that his radicalism was derived from other sources, from the doctrinaire systems of the previous century, from the struggles for reform in the pocket boroughs and from the misery caused by squire rule in the country-side.

It was through reading Cobbett's *English Grammar*, he says, that his mind was turned to radicalism. It was then that he realized that respect was paid to rich and powerful men not through voluntary admiration but through fear and compulsion. He then began to inquire into the means by which this wealth and power was acquired. Many of the great men, he found, held their estates only because of the plunder of William the Bastard; almost all the other large estates were acquired at the expense of the Church. He held strongly with Cobbett that lands had been given to the Church to support the poor, and that the obligation to do so was taken over by the Cecils, the Bedfords, and the others when they appropriated these lands at the Reformation. If they did not fulfil this obligation, their title to their property ceased to be valid. Nowhere, apart from the unfortunate reference to Wern-dee, does he advocate the division of property. 'If by equality is meant equality of property,' he says, 'the doctrine is too foolish to bestow a word on it.' But he insisted that the right of property could never be so absolute as to sanction oppressive conduct in its owners. No owner could turn a mad bull on to his property be-cause it was his own—or, for that matter, a mad lawyer, a far more dangerous animal; neither had he the right to

[1] *Bristol Mercury*, May 1822, several issues.

extort rents from his tenants which kept them in misery. The owner's wealth was derived solely from their labour; if they did not get their just deserts, Frost seriously considered whether they were obliged to pay rent at all. Again, as in the case of Cobbett, his ideal was a country in which an independent yeomanry flourished, and their happiness should be the chief concern of the landowners.

Why, then, was there so much distress in the countryside? It had two causes. One was the resumption of cash payments as a result of Peel's Act of 1819. The French landing in Pembrokeshire in 1797 had produced a run on the Bank, and cash payments had been stopped for twenty years. Prices had soared in consequence. Now that the issue of notes was restricted, commodity prices had rapidly fallen. Thus, according to Frost, a farmer obtained only a third as much for his produce, but he paid the same rent and taxes as before, and the only people who benefited were fund-holders and pensioners, among them most members of Parliament. The second cause was high taxation. 'Taxation causes poverty; poverty causes misery; misery causes crime' remained an axiom for Frost throughout his life, and it is well to remember that this was the time of which Sydney Smith spoke in the famous passage where he described how everything was taxed from the schoolboy's top to the marble which handed down his virtues to posterity when he was gathered to his fathers to be taxed no more. This taxation was due to the enormous national debt contracted in an unnecessary war waged against the French democrats, and to the existence of innumerable pensions and sinecures. In this respect the unfailing source of information for Frost and his fellow radicals was the *Black Book* of 1820 (followed by the *Extraordinary Black Book* of 1831). Here it was that they found their details of jobbery and corruption in Church and State.

51

Thus while Etheridge revealed to the public the enormous emoluments received out of public funds by the Beaufort family, and the *Cardiff Reporter*, in its brief life, rendered a similar service to the Butes, Frost confined himself to the family of Tredegar. Colonel Lascelles, Sir Charles's brother-in-law, had secured the lucrative sinecure of receiver-general of the taxes for Monmouthshire, a post involving merely the signing of his name. Lord Rodney, Sir Charles's son-in-law, was in receipt of a pension, which the *Black Book* fixed at £2,923. 1*s*. 6*d*. a year. Surely his services must be remarkable, said Frost, if they could be measured to the accuracy of eighteenpence. The *Black Book* was admittedly not entirely accurate, but one is forced to the conclusion that at no other time in the history of Monmouthshire has one class exploited the community as much as was then the case.

Frost's methods of bringing this home to the public were picturesque. He calculated that every farmer, workman, and tradesman in Monmouthshire paid one-half of his earnings in taxation; he assumed that the taxes of one group of people, say of the inhabitants of Newport, went exclusively to pay Lord Rodney's pension; he further asked his readers to imagine that the taxes had to be paid in kind and that Lord Rodney collected them himself. How much food, then, would Lord Rodney have to take off every workman's table in Newport to make up the pension paid to him not because of any service of his own to the community, but merely because of the services of an ancestor?

This state of affairs could not last much longer, and was it not better that the change should be brought about peaceably than by violence? He reminded Sir Charles that men with larger estates than Tredegar had been forced to become fiddlers, dancing-masters, and even shoe-makers as a result of the French Revolution. Already revolts were taking place again in Spain and Portugal and 'a new light was beaming on the world'. Was Frost, then, an advocate of insurrection? The question is important because he was later accused of being a physical force Chartist, and his attitude in 1839 was still the same as in 1822. He was continually exasperated at the impossibility of getting a Parliament of placemen to reform itself, and was infuriated by this impotence into heated expressions. Moreover, the Peterloo affair had shown the antipathy between the workers and the middle-class yeomen cavalry, who were the 'heroes' of that day and not the regular troops. Characteristically, Frost gave the name of Henry Hunt to his second son (born a few weeks before he entered Monmouth gaol), and the Newport radicals held a dinner while Frost was in prison to celebrate Hunt's release, when the healths of Hunt, Cobbett, and Frost were drunk.[1] Etheridge went even further, and spoke of Thistlewood, the agitator of the Cato Street Conspiracy, as a martyr.[2] Frost was well acquainted with John Locke's justification of resistance to a government, and his favourite quotation was Blackstone's remark that the law of nature was dictated by God himself, so that no human laws were of any validity if they were contrary to it. Consequently, if an obviously unjust situation was not reformed by Parliament, force must be used.

This, however, should be done only as a last resort. The solution was parliamentary reform. He was under no illusion with regard to the two parties. The disillusionment which the Chartists were supposed to have felt after 1832 was not true in the case of Frost, for, ten years earlier, he was already stating that the workers should not base their hopes on either the Whig or the Tory party— 'two plunderous factions who have robbed the people without mercy'. He showed that both parties were uniting

[1] *Newport Review*, 9 Nov. 1822. [2] Ibid.

against the workers' aspirations, ostensibly in the interests of Church and king, whereas the great majority of radicals were opposed to neither the Church nor the king. (He allowed himself a doubt as to whether Parson Thomas of Caerleon had received any special commission from the Holy Ghost for the cure of souls, but otherwise he has no single remark disparaging of religion.) A reformed Parliament, however, would not allow pensions and sinecures to remain for a day. His remedy was a simple one. Every county should return members in proportion to its population. Every man above the age of twenty-one should have the vote. Candidates' names should be posted on every church door a month before the election, so that the electors could inquire into their merits, and the voting-papers should be placed in a box in each church. As the mechanism was so simple there was no reason why elections should not take place each year. Thus, in 1822, Frost had adopted what was to become, sixteen years later, almost the full programme of the Chartists. By this means he confidently hoped that taxation would be reduced and poverty abolished so that crime would therefore disappear.

III

THE MAYOR OF NEWPORT

'I HAVE stopped Frost's mouth for ever; we shall hear no more of him', is said to have been Prothero's remark after the sentence of imprisonment passed upon Frost in 1823. Frost's triumphal entry into Newport may have caused him some doubt, but the next few years seemed to prove that his forecast had been accurate. For a time Frost was entirely silent. The reason for this is not difficult to find. He had given security for his good behaviour. Moreover, even though he had arranged his bankruptcy fairly successfully, his struggle with Prothero must have nearly ruined him, for, apart from the thousand pounds damages, he had been involved in great expense, and had had to pay his uncle's debts. He had been away from his business for nearly a year, and he had a young and growing family to support. When he returned from prison the eldest of his six children was barely thirteen, and two more children were yet to be born to him. He was therefore forced to devote his energies and abilities to setting his affairs in order, and once more he seems to have been an uncommonly successful tradesman.

One of the chief reasons for his success was the continued growth of Newport, and of the industrial villages of West Monmouthshire of which Newport was the shopping centre. Frost must have taken advantage of this to expand his drapery business. Even within Newport itself the population grew from 4,000 at the census of 1821 to over 7,000 in 1831. Newport had, in fact, outstripped the neighbouring market-town of Cardiff, and the rivalry between them had commenced. There was sufficient reason for it, for officially Newport was still reckoned to be merely a creek of Cardiff. The papers of all ships

55

loading and unloading at Newport had to be taken to the customs office at Cardiff, and the ships' masters had to appear there in person. This involved considerable delay and expense. A 'humble memorial' was therefore presented to the Treasury in 1820, and after the usual inquiry and delay, Newport obtained the status of an independent port on 1 May 1823. The trade of Newport flourished accordingly. The annual export of coal had risen from 148,000 tons in 1809 to nearly half a million tons twenty years later, while in much the same period the export of iron rose from 16,000 to 114,000 tons a year. Means of transport and communication were being improved at the same time. In July 1830 the newly established *Monmouthshire Merlin* was proud to draw attention to the fact that Mr. Thomas Prothero had introduced a locomotive engine which drew a load of over fifty tons along the tram road belonging to the Monmouthshire Canal Company from his collieries to his wharf below Newport, a distance of some thirty miles. Travelling facilities were also improving, and in 1834 the journey from the neighbouring town of Monmouth all the way to London could be done within one day. A daily service was therefore introduced. The coach, *Mazeppa*, left the Beaufort Arms at Monmouth every morning at five o'clock, and reached the Bull and Mouth in Regent Street in the evening at eight o'clock precisely. Any one prepared to travel at this break-neck speed on the outside of the coach could do so for fifteen shillings; a seat inside the coach cost double the money.

All this progress and the rapid growth of the population of Newport made it necessary that there should be some improvement in the dirty, ill-paved streets of the town. An Act of Parliament was therefore prepared for the watching, lighting, paving, cleansing, and improving of the streets and highways of Newport in 1826. The work was, almost of necessity, entrusted to Prothero and to his new partner, Thomas Phillips. This young man (he was then twenty-five) later displaced Prothero as Frost's chief opponent. He was a native of Llanelly, Breconshire, though he had spent his youth at Pontypool, and he had been articled to Thomas Prothero in 1819, afterwards becoming his partner. Frost, who was prepared to admit in 1822 that he possessed some talent, soon came to speak of him as an empty, loquacious young man, affected in his manner, and parading his knowledge on every occasion. There is no doubt about the last characteristic, for his speeches both on political and municipal matters were reported at length in the *Merlin*, and he was accustomed to make his pronouncements with the authority and completeness of a Lord Chief Justice. He was little in stature, and one gets the impression that he was somewhat over-conscious of his own rectitude. Certainly there is not the slightest suspicion about his integrity. He and Prothero now drew up an Act for the improvement of the town. Over sixty 'improvement commissioners' were named in the Act, and these included the Marquis of Worcester, his brother Lord Granville Somerset, Sir Charles Morgan, with his four sons and his brother-in-law, the mayor and corporation as well as Prothero and Phillips themselves. They were authorized to levy rates not exceeding 1s. 3d. in the pound, and minute regulations were drawn up with regard to the care and cleanliness of the streets. As the list of the commissioners was so exclusively representative of property, it is not surprising that the Act met with much opposition in Newport, and although Frost had only been out of prison some two and a half years one can suspect that he was again one of the ringleaders. The opponents of the Bill briefed Frederick Pollock to argue their case before both the House of Commons and the House of Lords. Their contention was that the meeting which had petitioned Parliament for the Bill was not a public one but

57

a selected committee, but Thomas Phillips, the chief witness for the other side, maintained on oath that this was not so, and the Bill became law in March 1826.[1] The fees and expenses of Messrs. Prothero and Phillips amounted to £1,224. 9s. The commissioners, as will be seen, did not carry out their duties efficiently, but the body remained in existence for some time and was not superseded even by the Municipal Corporations Act of 1835. In fact, the functions of the improvement commissioners and of the new town council overlapped, to the detriment of municipal administration, until the earlier body was absorbed by the other in 1850.

With the death of the 'first gentleman of Europe' in 1830, more stirring times began. His brother, William IV, was proclaimed at Newport on 10 July with the customary jollification. Bell-ringing and cannon-firing continued throughout the day. Fourteen barrels of beer were distributed among the populace, and it was thought prudent because of the crowd to close all the shops and suspend business for the day. The boys of the National Schools were regaled with plum cake, while a handsome dinner was provided by the corporation for a company of Highlanders stationed in the town. Every countenance, we are told, beamed with conviviality, and in the evening a large company of the freemen, among them John Frost, sat down to a public dinner.[2] After this, it was perhaps ungracious on the part of Frost to have appealed against the rates on the grounds of the inclusion of £3 for 'bell-ringing on Coronation Day' in the expenses of the town. Nevertheless he won his case at the Usk Quarter Sessions, where this item was disallowed, and he obtained two guineas costs in addition.[3] The demise of the Crown still, in those

[1] 7 Geo. IV, ch. 6. The Act is given in Scott, op. cit., pp. 63–7. See Frost, *Letter to Reformers* (1832), p. 22.
[2] *Monmouthshire Merlin*, 10 July 1830.
[3] Usk MSS. Sessions Record Book, 1830–4. Entry 2 July 1832. There

days, involved a general election, which took place in August. It passed off in Monmouthshire without any excitement, for there was no contest. Lord Worcester was again returned unopposed for the boroughs, while his brother, Lord Granville Somerset, and Sir Charles Morgan continued to represent the shire as they had done for such a long time. Political feeling had not yet become crystallized, and, in view of what was soon to happen, it is worth noting that Prothero supported Lord Worcester, speaking of his parliamentary activities in the highest terms (Frost insinuated that this was because he wished to get his son into the army), while the seconder of Lord Granville Somerset's nomination was William Addams Williams of Llangibby Castle.

It was not, however, the senselessness of this electioneering which roused Frost into activity, nor was it the prolonged coal strike in Monmouthshire earlier in the year. The future Chartist was still (as, indeed, he was throughout his life) most easily moved by distress in the countryside. In November 1830 there broke out in southern and western England a serious peasants' revolt. The conditions of the farm labourers had become intolerable. Their wages, according to Cobbett's *Rural Rides*, amounted to no more than 7s. to 9s. a week, while the introduction of the threshing machine deprived them of their occupation in the late autumn, when the corn harvest was over. It was the bitterness roused by the threshing machine which probably accounts for the form taken by the riots—the burning of corn ricks. The outbreak was most severe in Hampshire, and the class-feeling aroused cannot be better appreciated than in the Duke of Wellington's advice to the Hampshire magistrates:

were two other items disallowed: 'Labour and roads £26. 14s.'; 'Mrs. Mathews to enable her to get a husband £1.' With Frost in his appeal were associated his uncle Edward, and George Oliver, who later became one of Frost's most violent enemies.

John Frost

'I induced the magistrates to put themselves on horseback, each at the head of his own servants and retainers, grooms, huntsmen, game-keepers, armed with horsewhips, pistols, fowling pieces and what they could get, and to attack in concert, if necessary, or singly, these mobs, disperse them, destroy them, and take and put in confinement those who could not escape. This was done in a spirited manner, in many instances, and it is astonishing how soon the country was tranquillised, and that in the best way, by the activity and spirit of the gentlemen.'[1]

There was a mild outbreak of this jacquerie in Monmouthshire, and on Monday, 6 December 1830, a meeting was held at the King's Head, Newport, under the presidency of Sir Charles Morgan, himself, 'to adopt measures for the effectual preservation of the peace and property of the town of Newport and its neighbourhood'. Resolutions were proposed by Prothero and seconded by his brother-in-law, William Brewer (who declared bluntly that 8s. a week was a sufficient wage for a labourer) urging all property owners to set a nightly watch to guard their property and to keep an eye on strangers. Special constables were to be sworn in the following Wednesday, and the poor were to be informed that while property owners were compensated by insurance, the eventual suffering through the destruction of corn would fall on the poor themselves, and that the punishment for incendiarism was death. This infuriated Frost, and he produced at the meeting a counter-proposal which deplored violence but sympathized with the sufferings of those driven to violence, and declared that this suffering was due to high taxation, high rents, and tithes. Although the meeting was presided over by Sir Charles, who owned half of Newport, seventeen people voted for Frost's resolution, while twenty-six

[1] Wellington, *Despatches*, quoted H. W. C. Davis, *Age of Grey and Peel* (Oxford, 1929), p. 224.

abstained from voting, and the motion was only defeated by twenty votes.

Once more Frost was in striking agreement with Cobbett. The master himself had appeared in Monmouthshire on 1 June. He had ridden over from Ross, arriving at Monmouth at five o'clock in the morning, and had circulated handbills, inviting people to listen to a lecture at the King's Head Hotel in that town at four o'clock in the afternoon, the price of admission being two shillings. According to the hostile account in the *Merlin*, only thirty people attended. Cobbett's theme was the familiar one. Misery was due to the enormous debt contracted during the French war, and to the currency legislation of 1819, resuming cash payments. Yet he did not advocate the re-issue of paper money, but produced the surprising proposal that the borough mongers who had been in Parliament during the French War should be made to pay off the debt themselves. On this, and on the abuse of pensions, Cobbett dilated for almost two hours.[1] There is no reason to believe that Frost met him on this occasion. In any case, this was before the outbreak of the riots. It should be noted, moreover, that the date of the meeting at which Frost spoke was 6 December, for Cobbett's article on the same subject did not appear in the *Political Register* until five days later. This showed an astonishing agreement between Frost and Cobbett, yet it would be wrong to state that Frost was merely influenced by Cobbett. The truth is that the two men thought alike on nearly all social matters. Until public distress was relieved, said Cobbett, it was useless to use coercion. This the authorities interpreted as encouraging outrage, and they decided to prosecute him. The trial did not come on until the following April, but it was destined to be a celebrated one, for

[1] *Merlin*, 5 June 1830. It should be noted that he spoke at the King's Head, Monmouth, and not the King's Head, Newport, as is usually stated.

Cobbett conducted his own defence, and castigated the Whig ministry. 'The Tories rule us with rods,' he said, 'the Whigs scourge us with scorpions.' He called both Lord Melbourne and Lord Brougham as witnesses, but the jury disagreed, and after fifteen hours failed to reach a verdict.

After the meeting of 6 December, Frost could keep silent no longer. He decided to become a printer himself, so he acquired Etheridge's type, and published early in the new year *A Christmas Box for Sir Charles Morgan*. How different things were now, he said, from what they had been when he was a boy, in the days of old John Morgan. Then Tredegar was an open house to all its tenants; now it had to be specially guarded at night. It was no wonder that ꞇʰ ᵉ labourers were driven to desperation, for they had to subsist on 9*s*. or 10*s*. a week, and half their wages went into the pockets of pensioners. Special constables had enrolled, but they knew well that they would lose their farms or be dismissed from their employment if they did not. Would they act against their fellow sufferers? But there would soon be a great change. Within a week of the first meeting, at the King's Head, Newport, another had been called at the same place, to petition for a remission of taxes, and a few days later a third meeting had called for parliamentary reform. Even Prothero and Phillips, said Frost, were now reformers. At this meeting two Newport radicals had proposed a resolution in favour of reform, dwelling specifically on the pensions of Lord Ellenborough (£15,000) and Lord Bathurst (£13,000), but that 'empty, loquacious young man', Thomas Phillips, had argued that too much must not be expected from parliamentary reform. It would neither clothe the naked nor feed the hungry, he had said, and so he had proposed an alternative resolution. It is in this that the significance of the *Christmas Box* lies; it shows clearly the breach between the radicals and the reformers. Frost was never under any illusion as to how far the latter would go, though his perspicacity in this was no doubt due to the fact that the two chief reformers in Newport were his personal enemies. He himself demanded an extension of the franchise, triennial elections (if not more frequent), and the ballot, and he urged Sir Charles to join the reform movement, for he had everything to lose and nothing to gain by opposing it. He ended his publication with a *Letter to the Married and Single Women of Monmouthshire,* commending Hunt and Cobbett to their support, and soliciting subscriptions towards Hunt's expenses at the Preston election which he had just won. Frost's pamphlet was a bitter one. It had none of the humorous scurrility of the earlier series; neither did he now allow his feelings to drive him into extravagant expressions. The times were too serious, and his personal experience still rankled, for at the foot of the last page he printed in heavy type, 'Six Months in Cold Bath Fields'. In view of Cobbett's prosecution, it is surprising that Frost did not find himself once more in the courts.

The movement for reform had suddenly attained great importance, possibly because of the July Revolution in France. (The last election had occurred the day after Charles X's abdication, and had come too soon to be affected by it.) In Wales there were the usual anomalies in parliamentary representation. Merthyr Tydfil, which had over twice the combined population of Cardiff and Newport, was not represented at all, while Swansea, which had half as many again as their combined population, was only a contributory borough to Cardiff. Haverfordwest, on the other hand, had its own representation, even apart from the tiny Pembroke borough, while in Brecon there were only seventeen electors. Montgomery, a mere village on a hill-side, had its own member, while the neighbouring large towns, Llanidloes, Newtown, and

Welshpool, the homes of the Welsh woollen industry, were unrepresented. In the boroughs there was the usual variety in the franchise, while in the shires the number of the forty shilling freeholders had been sadly depleted by the prevailing economic distress. The meeting to which Frost referred had taken place on 21 December, and the chief speakers had been Thomas Phillips and himself.[1] Phillips, in his usual manner, had traced the history of the reform movement. He agreed emphatically with Chatham's declaration that unless Parliament reformed itself from within, it would be reformed with a vengeance from without. But he warned his hearers against expecting too much, and, moreover, he thought the ballot of doubtful value, although he was not positive on this subject. Of what use was reform, Frost had asked in reply, if it did not feed the hungry and clothe the naked? Parliament took so much in taxes that hunger and nakedness were the consequence. If Parliament were elected by the people, it would suffer them to enjoy a fair proportion of their earnings, and this would remove much of the existing distress. The ballot was obviously necessary, for the Duke of Newcastle and the Marquis of Exeter had already turned out of their property those who had voted against their wishes. The meeting agreed, with one dissenting voice, to petition for a uniform franchise, a fair and equal representation, shorter parliaments, the abolition of pensions and sinecures, and either the ballot or some equally effective regulation.

With the new year the struggle became intensified. The Marquis of Worcester had replied to the townsmen of Newport refusing to support their petition for reform. Another meeting was therefore held on 5 February. It expressed its belief that the country could only be saved from the horror of revolution by effectual reform of the representation, and declared that at the next election

[1] *Merlin*, 25 Dec. 1830.

only a candidate pledged to reform could be supported.[1]
On 1 March the Reform Bill was introduced into Parliament. Meetings in its support were held throughout the
county. At Newport, on 3 March, the chief speaker was
Thomas Phillips. He advocated reform, but not universal
suffrage, for that would apply to females, and not even
the most visionary reformer would contend for their
admission to the franchise. (It may be worth noting that
the speaker remained a bachelor throughout his life.) It
was a question not of principle but of degree. He, therefore, advocated a property qualification in the counties,
and ten pound householding in the towns. At Usk, two
weeks later, the chief speaker was Benjamin Hall. It was
his father who had married the daughter of Richard
Crawshay, iron king of Cyfarthfa, and had become the
proprietor of the Rhymney Ironworks. The elder Benjamin Hall was the first industrialist to enter the political
field in Wales, and so great was his wealth that the Bute
candidate withdrew before the contest in the election for
the shire of Glamorgan in 1814. He held the seat only a
short time, for three years later he died. The son, who was
now starting his political career, was destined for a sort of
anonymous immortality, for it was he who bestowed his
name on Big Ben. He was eventually raised to the peerage
in 1859 as Baron Llanover. Now he was a strong advocate
of reform. Were the wishes of those who represented the
whole wealth and importance of the county to be spurned
and set at naught by the two great houses of Beaufort and
Tredegar, he asked. If the members did not agree with
their constituents they must be ousted in favour of men
who would. Other meetings were held at Monmouth and
elsewhere, and an address to the king in favour of reform
was forwarded from Newport.[2]

But on the 22 March the Bill passed its second reading

[1] Ibid., 12 Feb. 1831.   [2] Ibid., 26 March 1831.

by only one vote. This made dissolution almost inevitable, and in preparation for it the townsmen of Newport met at the King's Head. Sir Charles Morgan and his son, the member for Brecon, had thought it wise to vote for the Bill, and received the thanks of the meeting. Those who had opposed it, and they included the Marquis, were declared enemies of their country, and it was resolved that a determined attempt should be made to defeat them at the coming election.[1] Eventually it was decided to contest both the shire and the boroughs. For the former, William Addams Williams was chosen; for the latter Benjamin Hall. This placed Sir Charles in a quandary. He was now seventy-two years of age, and unprepared for a strenuous contest. Moreover if there were a three-cornered fight in the shire, Williams would undoubtedly head the poll, and the contest would then be between Beaufort and Tredegar. On the 18th he wrote to his constituents soliciting their support; on the 20th he declared his intention not to stand. At the same time he dismissed his agent, the great Thomas Prothero. Their relations had become strained, and within two years they were at law with one another. Prothero's young dog had wandered off the tram road—the golden mile—through Tredegar Park, and the gamekeeper on learning whose dog it was had put the muzzle of his gun into it and shot it. Prothero sued him for damages, and was awarded the contemptuous sum of one farthing.[2] Even he must learn that it was still unwise to cross the county families. But that was in the future; the business now was electioneering, for on 22 April Parliament was dissolved. The excitement was so great in the boroughs that even the London papers commented on it. Hustings had not been erected since 1820, and Prothero was busy urging those who were entitled to their freedom to claim admittance. Rowdiness

[1] *Merlin*, 9 April 1831.   [2] Ibid., 30 March 1833.

and rioting prevailed; windows were smashed, and on 29 April it was only the intervention of Frost which prevented the crowd at Newport from assaulting the Marquis and possibly throwing him into the river. Frost, at a considerable sacrifice of his feelings, was co-operating with Prothero in support of Hall, and when nomination day came, he was one of the chief speakers at Monmouth. The private character and reputation of the Marquis (he had fought at Waterloo) had nothing to do with the question, said Frost. What he had done in his fifteen years in Parliament, was the important matter. He had for a time been a Lord of the Admiralty, of which he knew nothing, and might have brought the country to ruin had war broken out. He had opposed reform; let the electors now try Hall. The gallant Marquis replied by pointing out that Prothero and others had supported him as recently as the last election of the previous August. He publicly thanked Frost for his protection at Newport. When the poll was declared closed at the end of two days, Hall had won with 168 votes to Worcester's 149. A hundred and forty of Hall's supporters were from Newport; 120 of Worcester's from Usk and Monmouth. Hall was then chaired, and presented with bouquets of flowers. When he arrived at Newport some days later he was given a triumphal entry. A crowd of 10,000 had gathered from the neighbouring towns, bells were rung and cannon fired. He was drawn in state through the streets, and the houses were wreathed in flowers and the crimson colours of his party. At five o'clock dinner was served at the King's Head, with Thomas Prothero in the chair, and among the persons toasted was John Frost. Unfortunately no one has recorded Prothero's words or demeanour when this toast was announced. But Prothero had been too clever. Worcester petitioned against the result and many of the freemen whom Prothero had 'created' were disallowed, so that two months later Worcester once more took his seat in the House.[1]

Almost immediately there was a cry of victimization, both from among the burgesses of Monmouth and the tenants on the Beaufort estate.[2] Moreover, the curate of St. Woollos was dismissed by his vicar. Another meeting was held at the King's Head, and a resolution passed (proposed by Frost) expressing the opinion that this was due to a difference on public matters. A deputation including Frost was appointed to wait upon the Bishop of Llandaff, but he, no doubt incensed by this interference on the part of the dissenters in a matter of church discipline, replied to Frost's request for an interview by refusing to pursue the matter any further.[3] Local politics were also occupying Frost's attention. He had formed a Patriotic Society, of which he himself was secretary, and on its behalf he wrote to the corporation asking it to receive a deputation to consider the claim of the burgesses to the Corporation Wharf. The mayor and aldermen, however, denied the right of the Patriotic Society to interfere in the matter, and resolved to apply the rent of the wharf as heretofore to public purposes.[4] Frost, moreover, arranged a public meeting to oppose a bill which Prothero and Phillips were promoting for the improvement of the roads. He communicated with the new member for the shire, and learned that the ministry was about to introduce legislation to deal with highways in general, and so, he contended, the local bill was unnecessary. He accused the two lawyers of merely wishing to collect fees by pursuing the matter, and further accused Prothero of using his position as a highway commissioner to remove a tollgate which was near his own house.[5]

[1] *Merlin*, 30 April 1831, 7 May, 14 May.
[2] Ibid., 26 Nov. 1831; 10 Dec. 1831.   [3] Ibid., 1 Oct. 1831; 8 Oct. 1831.
[4] Newport Library MSS., Corporation Minutes, 26 Sept. 1831.
[5] Frost, *Letter to the Reformers*, 1832.

But all this was overshadowed by the excitement caused when the House of Lords rejected the Reform Bill (8 October). A meeting was addressed on the subject by Phillips and by Frost on 14 October, at which Frost was particularly violent. He saw nothing before them but years of commotion. The interests of the governors and the governed were so opposed (for the former desired to retain power and the latter to obtain freedom) that the only way to obtain reform was for the king and fifty life guards to turn out the old applewomen in Parliament and lock the door. Yet he advised non-violence, though it was easier for the well fed to have patience than the poor who had looked for relief to the Reform Bill. He ended with a bitter attack on the Duke of Wellington. The Duke had just expressed his contempt for the people, but from his earliest infancy he had been a pensioner—'a pauper on the public'—and had no contempt apparently for the people's money. He must be taught that the people of England would not be insulted with impunity.[1] Phillips and his associates were probably embarrassed by their doughty ally, and can hardly have been pleased when a branch of the Political Union of the Working Class, recently established in London, was formed at Newport at the beginning of November. Its manifesto declared that all men were born free and had certain natural and inalienable rights. Governments were based on these rights and should exist for the protection and security of the people. All property honestly acquired was sacred and inviolable, but hereditary distinctions should be abolished. The vote should be given to all men over the age of twenty-one, and Parliaments should be annual.[2] Early in the following year Frost published a *Letter to the Reformers* which was a further attack on his Whig associates. They were rapacious and unprincipled men, he

[1] *Merlin*, 22 Oct. 1831 and 29 Oct.   [2] Ibid., 12 Nov. 1831.

said, and it was madness to suppose that those who were rolling in wealth would do anything for the benefit of the people.

Excitement was intensified in May, when the ministry was defeated and Wellington attempted to form a government. It was on the twelfth that the placards bearing the words 'To stop the Duke, go for gold' were posted all over London, on the advice of Francis Place, an incident which undoubtedly influenced Frost, for it lent support to his theories about currency. So much was he now taken up with public affairs that he decided to abandon his business to his family, and devote himself entirely to politics. In the nine years since his release from prison he had prospered considerably, and he thought that his children could easily carry on the business for their own benefit. His eldest boy was, in fact, nearly nineteen years of age. He fondly supposed that as far as his own modest needs were concerned, he could support himself by his pen. He believed that great changes were about to take place, and he thought it the duty of every man to accelerate these changes and to avert the serious consequences which would follow if they were violently produced. For this purpose the only effective instrument was the press, and the first-fruit of his decision was the issue of a new periodical, *The Welchman*. In his introduction he outlined his programme. He would attend petty sessions and consider the ability and impartiality of the magistrates. He would deal with the question whether they should be elected by the people, and not, as was the case, merely chosen on account of their wealth. He would attend churches and examine the sermons delivered there, together with the general conduct of the parsons, for he was told there were 'drunken parsons, unclean parsons, hunting and shooting parsons' in Monmouthshire. He would discuss the question whether the Church should be disestablished.

He would examine the situation with regard to the Charity lands of Monmouthshire. He would carefully watch the conduct of their representatives in Parliament, and record their speeches. In particular he would deal with the subject of paper money, and the whole of the first issue was devoted to this.

Like most reformers at the time, Frost paid great attention to the manipulation of the currency. In 1821 he had already written against Peel's Act for the resumption of cash payments, on the ground that the sudden restriction of the currency would ruin the farmers and benefit the holders of stock created during the depreciation. In this, his inspiration was, without doubt, Cobbett's *Paper against Gold*. Some months after the *Welchman* had appeared occurred the great debate between Cobbett and Attwood at Birmingham (September 1832). Attwood strongly advocated a paper currency as an antidote to all financial distress; Cobbett again opposed it. Both claimed the victory in the debate, and it was apparently the audience alone which received a knock-out blow, for the meeting continued interminably.[1] Frost once more held the same standpoint as Cobbett. He admitted that the issue of paper money might for the moment render rents, taxes, and debts easier to pay, but this would be offset by the danger of panic which might be caused by another run on gold. There would be general insecurity due to rapid changes in prices, together with a repetition of the crop of forgeries, hangings, and transportings which had accompanied the previous issue of paper money. This was not inconsistent with his previous attitude, for what he had then opposed was the sudden restriction of the currency, and, in fact, the government had had to mitigate its evil consequences. Frost's new plan was some kind of 'equitable adjustment' between currency and prices. He had

[1] *Merlin*, 8 Sept. 1832.

suggested a plan of this kind in a letter to Lord Granville Somerset as early as 1829, but the member for Monmouthshire had not taken it up. He would now, in the second issue of the *Welchman*, produce such a plan as would 'make the labourer leap for joy', but as the second number did not appear there is no way of comparing it with Cobbett's own 'equitable adjustment'.

Frost's abandonment of his business to devote himself entirely to politics is a fair indication of his ambitious nature. Undoubtedly his great desire was to enter Parliament (a fact which goes far to explain his part in the Convention of 1839), and he put forward in the *Welchman* a tentative suggestion that he might be adopted as a candidate for the Monmouth boroughs, with Hall and another industrialist for the shire. No doubt the gentlemen in Parliament would ridicule the idea of sitting with a tradesman, but he reminded them of the French Revolution, and he warned them that their ridicule might mean the loss of their estates. The presence of tradesmen in Parliament would be a lesser evil for them than the exile across the Atlantic which might result if they continued to resist all reform. He was surprised that ironmasters should support the county families, whose interests were so different from their own, and he insisted again that the only visible sign of hard work on the part of the Monmouth legislators for the last fifty years was on the pensions list. They had always had a steady eye for that. But Frost may have been discouraged by his failure to continue the *Welchman*, and the Reform Bill may have become law sooner than he expected (4 June). At least, no more is heard for a time of his candidature. By the Reform Act Merthyr Tydfil and Swansea received separate representation, and the shires of Carmarthen, Denbigh, and Glamorgan were granted a second member each, but in the shire and boroughs of Monmouth there was, in this respect, no change. There was, however, great activity in registering those who were now entitled to vote, in preparation for the coming election. The registering barrister visited the shire in October and the boroughs in November. The Tories contested almost every claim—in Newport alone, they raised no less than 227 objections—while the case of the reformers was defended by Thomas Phillips. Eventually some 800 were declared qualified to vote in the boroughs.[1]

Already canvassing had begun. In the shire, Sir Charles once more decided not to stand, and as the reformers did not feel confident enough to contest both seats, William Addams Williams and Lord Granville Somerset were again returned in December, the one a reformer and the other a consistent opponent of reform. Early in June a public meeting at Newport had declared that it would support for the boroughs only a candidate who had been in favour of the Bill,[2] and Benjamin Hall was once more adopted. The struggle which ensued was even more bitter than in the previous year. Hitherto the landed interest had exercised undisputed power, and there had been comparatively little need for bribery and intimidation. Now their title had to be defended, and every possible device was used to influence the electors. So disgusted with the actions of his opponents did Hall declare himself to be that he pledged himself to introduce a measure for the ballot within six weeks of his election to Parliament,[3] while his own expenses proved a serious drain even on his enormous fortune. The Tredegar influence strongly supported Lord Worcester, but the combined strength of Beaufort and Tredegar proved insufficient, for Hall was returned with 393 votes as against his opponent's 355. Even more spectacular was the defeat

[1] *Merlin*, 27 Oct.; 17 Nov. 1832.
[2] Ibid., 23 June 1832.　　　[3] Ibid., 8 Dec. 1832.

of Sir Charles's son by six votes in the borough of Brecon, so that for the first time since the Restoration (apart from the two years 1720 to 1722, when the lord of Tredegar happened to be under age) there was not one Morgan at Westminster. Frost was carried away by this success so far as to forget his distrust of the Whigs. He wrote exultantly to Sir Charles Morgan (who had attributed the victory to the 'rabble' of Newport) that power had passed forever out of the hands of the aristocracy into those of the middle classes of society.[1] He expressed great confidence in the reformed Parliament. It would be willing to listen to the complaints of the people, and would redress their grievances. Lord Rodney's pension would not be paid for another year. Reforms would be introduced in the currency and in the Church, and slavery would be abolished. At a reform dinner in Pontypool (where his stepson was vice-president of the Reform Association) he reaffirmed his confidence in the new government, and praised the poor who had done their duty at the election in spite of threats and promises.[2] But the victory was more evident than real, and Frost was soon disillusioned. It is true that the Monmouth boroughs were never recovered by the Somerset family, but within two years a Morgan was returned unopposed for the borough of Brecon, and held the seat for another twelve years. In time a Morgan even recovered Breconshire, for so long the constituency of the 'nabob', Colonel Wood. Again, within nine years of the Reform Bill William Addams Williams had withdrawn in favour of Sir Charles's son, and until 1880 a Somerset and a Morgan represented Monmouthshire without a break. The transference of power from the landed to the commercial and industrial interests which is supposed to have taken place in 1832

[1] *Letter the Second to Sir Charles Morgan*, 1833.
[2] *Merlin*, 19 Jan. 1833.

was certainly not obvious in Wales. Certain fundamental changes, indeed, there had been; the system of patronage was diminished if not destroyed, and this deprived the Crown of its chief means of influencing the government, but this was revealed only with the passing of time.

For the next two years Frost was engaged in local affairs. He once more raised the question of the wharves. He approached Sir Charles's new agent, asking him to produce his title to the land on which the Tredegar Wharf was built, only to be told that Sir Charles would retain possession of the land until the burgesses could prove that he had no right to it. In the matter of the Corporation Wharf he gained an unexpected and, as it proved, an inconvenient success. The corporation suddenly reversed its decision of September 1831, and the rent was paid over to Frost, who was asked to act as treasurer on behalf of the burgesses. He then found himself unable to divide the money, for he feared that he might be held personally responsible for it, if an action were brought by some one to recover it, and he may well have feared a trick on the part of his wily antagonists, Prothero and Phillips, in this too sudden submission on their part. He himself wished to apply the money to recover the land occupied by the Tredegar Wharf. He now also brought another accusation against Sir Charles, on what seems very slender evidence, of being in possession of lands formerly belonging to a free school at Newport.[1] At the time Lord Brougham's commission was inquiring into the property of the charitable institutions of the country, and this exercised Frost greatly. At a public meeting in October 1833, under the presidency of Thomas Prothero, and in the presence of Benjamin Hall, he urged the member to inquire into the abuses in the charitable institutions in the boroughs,[2] and

---

[1] *A Letter to Sir Charles Morgan,* and *Letter the Second,* 1833.
[2] *Merlin,* 15 Oct. 1833.

in 1834 he succeeded in inducing the solicitor for the Attorney-General in charity matters to prepare a case for the Court of Chancery against three local persons, who promptly promised to discharge the arrears due from them.[1]

The Reform Parliament lasted only a year and eleven months, and a new election had to be held in January 1835, the fourth in a little over four years. The representation of Monmouthshire remained unchanged. Lord Worcester decided not to contest the boroughs, and within a few months he had succeeded his father as Duke of Beaufort. It was suggested that Sir Charles's fourth son, Octavius Morgan, should take his place, but eventually the choice fell upon Joseph Bailey, Junior, the son of the member for Worcester, and nephew of Crawshay Bailey of Nantyglo. One industrialist, therefore, opposed another, and the whole influence of Tredegar and Newport was exercised in support of Bailey. The greatest exertions were made, especially in Newport, for Bailey could count upon a large majority at Monmouth and Usk. Thomas Phillips accused Joseph Bailey, Senior, of 'the most gross and unblushing bribery', and enumerated instances at Newport. He had hesitated to advocate the ballot, but his experience now proved to him that there was no other way of protecting the poor. Bailey's supporters denied the accusation, while accusing their opponents of the same thing. Eventually, on 12 February, Hall was successful with a majority of only four votes (428 to 424). Writs were issued against various persons for bribery, and £100 reward was offered for information leading to a conviction. Bailey, on the other hand, petitioned the House of Commons, complaining that the returns had been tampered with. Fifteen days were occupied in examining this complaint, but, in the end, Hall retained his seat.[2]

[1] *Merlin*, 23 Feb. 1839. Letter to Lord John Russell.
[2] Ibid., 6 Dec. 1834; 10 Jan., 17 Jan., 28 Feb., 6 June, 13 June 1835.

The Mayor of Newport

The year 1835 was taken up almost entirely with two matters. One was the harbour. The trade of Newport increased to such an extent, especially when the export duty on coal was repealed in this year, that its harbour facilities became entirely inadequate. It was therefore decided to obtain parliamentary sanction 'for making and maintaining a dock and other works in the borough of Newport, with a railway and stone road therefrom'. The preparation of the Bill was, as usual, entrusted to Prothero and Phillips. Royal assent was obtained for it in July, and work on the dock was immediately begun. It took seven years to finish, and it involved the presence in Newport of a large body of navvies during the critical year 1839. The controversy which arose concerned the appointment of a harbour board. Some such body was obviously necessary, for hitherto control had been vested in the mayor who was entitled to levy 'mastage' on all ships (ranging from 4*d.* to 3*s.* according to the size of the vessel), and who appointed two water bailiffs to supervise the river. This arrangement had now become totally inadequate. A public meeting was held in April at which Phillips urged that the board should be representative of the 'interests' concerned, that is, the landowners, the iron-masters, the coal exporters, and the shipping and wharf companies. Frost maintained that there were only two 'interests', public and private, and strongly opposed granting the power of levying and expending public money to persons who were not responsible to the public. Phillips retorted that those who would be taxed were not the public but the owners of shipping, yet the meeting supported Frost and broke up amid considerable tumult. The matter was continued into the following year, and Frost himself went up to London to oppose the new Bill. He obtained the support of both William Addams Williams and Benjamin Hall for the principle of public control and responsibility, but their only success was the inclusion of the mayor and three councillors on a board of thirty-six members. It was one of Frost's objects (indeed he maintained that it was his primary concern) in getting himself elected mayor later on, to become a harbour commissioner in virtue of his office, and thus to be able to expose what he considered the excessive charges of Prothero and Phillips for promoting the Bill.[1]

The other, and even more important, concern of the year 1835 was the passing of the Municipal Corporations Act, which revolutionized the local government of Newport, as of other towns. As early as July 1833 Thomas Phillips, who had acted as town clerk for about ten years (the office was still nominally in the hands of his senior partner), was examined by a select committee of the House of Commons. This examination showed the need for radical reform. The freemen (not to speak of those who were not burgesses) had no share whatsoever in the management of corporation affairs, but with the growth of the town this management had come to involve the control of a considerable amount of public money. The town clerk acted as treasurer, and no accounts were published. Occasionally contributions were made to the poor, but in 1830 all the corporation money had been spent on dinners and wine in connexion with the king's coronation. Even the mastage dues, which were a perquisite of the mayor's and had formerly barely covered the fees paid to the water bailiffs, now amounted to some £300 or £400 a year. In fact, an action had been threatened in the previous year (was this possibly the work of Frost?) to test the legality of the mayor's claim to the money, and as the individual mayor concerned was not prepared to fight the case at great expense, he had accepted a compromise of about £100 to £150 a year. The property of the cor-

[1] *Merlin*, 23 April 1835; 16 April 1836; 21 May 1836; 4 June 1836.

poration, also, had greatly increased in value in the meantime. Particularly unsatisfactory was the administration of justice. The recorder, who had held his position since 1807 (he was, in fact, Sir Charles Morgan), was non-resident, and was not even learned in the law. The steward to the lord of the manor, a magistrate in virtue of his office, was also non-resident, and had never acted in that capacity. He attended only on the second Thursday in November to choose one of two names submitted to him by the corporation as mayor. The two senior aldermen were magistrates, but one of them was decrepit and had been non-resident since 1794, and the other happened in 1833 to be the mayor, so that there was actually one magistrate only for a town with a population of well over 7,000. Quarter sessions had been totally discontinued since 1810. A court of record, which had formerly existed for the recovery of debts within the town, had also become disused. The town clerk, who acted as treasurer, as clerk of the peace at the Monmouth quarter sessions, as magistrate's clerk in petty sessions, as attorney and solicitor in the legal business of the corporation, obtained emoluments which averaged about £100 a year.[1] When the new Act came into operation, he refused to hand over any books of the corporation which were in his possession,[2] and this possibly accounts for their disappearance.

As soon as the Act was passed, an election was held to choose eighteen councillors. The town was divided into two wards, and at the head of the list for the west ward was John Frost, draper, with 171 votes. Prothero's influence was strong enough to get his nominee, Joseph Latch, appointed the first mayor, and the six aldermen also were 'substantial' men, among them Prothero's brother-in-law, William Brewer, and his fellow coal-

[1] *Merlin*, 27 July 1833; 6 June 1835.   [2] Ibid., 16 April 1836.

exporter, Thomas Powell.[1] The first meeting of the new council (12 January 1836) must have been looked forward to with great interest because of the clash of personalities which must ensue. Frost did not disappoint his supporters. He appeared with thirteen resolutions 'of a searching character' which he proposed to bring before the council in due course. But of more importance at the moment was the resignation of the town clerk and the appointment of Thomas Phillips to take his place. Very probably Prothero had retired because the Home Secretary had instructed the council to nominate magistrates, and one of his supporters immediately suggested his name. The nomination was for life, and it was probably thought that the matter could be rushed and settled, so that Prothero would be able to exercise in a new capacity as much influence as before. But Frost interposed and succeeded in getting the appointment deferred because insufficient notice had been given.[2] He then wrote immediately on his own responsibility to the Home Secretary, asking for his opinion on the basis of a clause in the Corporation Act which prohibited clerks to the justices from taking any part, directly or indirectly, in the prosecution of offenders committed for trial by such justices, and pointing out the position of Prothero and his partner, the new town clerk. At the next meeting of the council, a week later, he was able triumphantly to pro-produce Lord John Russell's reply to the effect that he thought it right to lay down the general rule not to recommend solicitors or attorneys for the office of justice of the peace.[3] This was, indeed, a 'slap at the lawyers' (the title of one of Frost's works in 1821 which did not see the light of day). But it did not end even there. At the fourth

[1] *Merlin*, 26 Dec. 1835.
[2] Ibid., 16 Jan. 1836, and Newport Library MSS., Corporation Minutes.
[3] *Merlin*, 23 Jan. 1836.

meeting of the council Frost himself was elected by a large majority, together with William Brewer, to act as magistrates, and their names were submitted to the Home Secretary.[1] This caused the utmost astonishment and consternation among Frost's opponents. They immediately wrote to Lord John Russell, enclosing copies of the pamphlets Frost had written, but the Home Secretary consulted the Lord Lieutenant of Monmouthshire who advised him to comply with the wishes of the council, and he does not seem to have replied to his correspondents. They then approached Lord Wharncliffe and asked him to bring the matter before the House of Lords, but he took the advice of Benjamin Hall not to do so.[2] John Frost, tradesman, thus became John Frost, Esquire, a fact which gave him great prestige among his later associates, the Chartists, who (democrats though they were) never omitted the title after his name. In the long-drawn-out contest with the 'prize-fighter', Thomas Prothero, which was his life, he may, at least, be said to have won this round, and nothing redounds to his credit as much as the impartiality and efficiency with which he carried out his magisterial duties, and to which his enemy, Thomas Phillips, generously bore testimony at his trial for treason.

Frost used the town council as an admirable sounding board for all his ideas and grievances, and soon the town clerk was complaining that every council meeting developed into an attack upon his partner and himself.[3] Frost got proceedings instituted in the Court of Chancery for the recovery of the land occupied by the Tredegar Wharf.[4] He appeared himself as plaintiff, at the request of the freemen, but the case was dismissed, and for the time being the question was allowed to lapse, the expenses

[1] *Merlin*, 6 Feb. 1836.
[2] *Merthyr Guardian*, 16 Nov. 1839; *Northern Liberator*, 16 March 1839 (Frost's own account); *Maidstone Gazette*, 26 Nov. 1839.
[3] *Merlin*, 6 Feb. 1833.   [4] Ibid., 30 Jan. 1833; 13 July 1839.

of both sides being paid out of the funds held by Frost. As much of local administration was still in the hands of the improvement commissioners, he called a public meeting which nominated him and a number of others to the board. The older commissioners did their utmost to prove the public meeting incompetent to elect new members, but they eventually gave in. They had, in fact, neglected their work shamefully. Although their number varied between sixty and eighty, and although only five were required to form a quorum, six consecutive meetings had been abandoned in 1834 and four in 1835 because an insufficient number attended.[1] Before he could function in his new office Frost had to take an oath that he was possessed of real and personal estate to the value of at least £1,500, an interesting indication of his fortune at this time, and this oath he took on 17 May. From that date until April 1838, he was constant in his attendance at the meetings of the commissioners, and almost invariably presided over them.

Frost had been described as 'the poor man's friend' by those who had supported his nomination as justice of the peace. He was soon able to render the poor even greater service in another capacity, for in August he was appointed a guardian under the new Poor Law Amendment Act. No office could appeal more to his undoubted benevolence and warm sympathy for the unfortunate. He ever bore in mind Cobbett's question and answer, 'What is a pauper? Only a very poor man', and strove ceaselessly to mitigate the effects of the new law. The reaction to it was of great significance not only in his own career, but in the growth of Chartism, for the Swansea *Cambrian* (the best-informed weekly newspaper in Wales during the period) went so far as to state that Chartism

[1] Newport Library MSS. Improvement Commissioners Minute Book, 1826–45.

was merely a continuation and development of the poor
law agitation.[1] It has been maintained that the evils
arising from the old poor laws were entirely unknown in
Wales, and that the hatred of the new law was largely due
to this fact. It is certainly true that the granting of out-
door relief to able-bodied men in work was not as common
in Wales as in many parts of England. No such relief was
given to single men in work or to married labourers with
no more than three children. But there were undoubted
abuses, and these usually took the form of paying the rent
of individuals out of the rates. In Llanidloes, out of the
£2,000 a year spent on the poor, £800 went in this way,
while in Anglesey the rents of 2,022 persons were paid—a
sum of about £3,557 a year. Paupers, indeed, were a very
desirable class of tenants, for the rents paid on their behalf
were easy to collect and were generally higher than could
be obtained otherwise. Speculators were known to lease
cottages from landowners, in order to let them to paupers
at a profit. Nor were the aged poor cared for satisfactorily. In some rural areas they were put up at the vestry
in a sort of Dutch auction, and let to whoever would take
them at the lowest amount. Sometimes they were let to
their own children, and sometimes even to other paupers.[2]
These abuses in the body politic the reformed Parliament
sought to remedy by the drastic surgery of the workhouse
system. It was the first important measure which showed
the distinct cleavage between the interests of the middle
and working classes, and therein lies its significance in
the Chartist Movement. Instead of being relieved in their
economic condition, as the latter had expected to be as a
result of parliamentary reform, they found their lot considerably aggravated. In bad times, whether they wished

[1] *Cambrian*, 15 Nov. 1839.
[2] Poor Law Commission Report, in *Land Commission Report* (1896),
Appendices, pp. 28–30; Third Annual Report of Poor Law Commissioners,
in *Merthyr Guardian*, 28 Oct. 1837.

it or not, they were forced to turn to the parish for relief. But it was a matter of deliberate policy to make life in the workhouses less attractive than that of the lowest-paid worker outside, and so they were faced by the alternative of which Dickens speaks in *Oliver Twist* 'of being starved by a gradual process in the house, or by a quick one out of it'. Moreover, life in the workhouse involved rigid confinement and such repellent tasks as oakum picking, and an intense hatred grew up against the new 'bastilles'. Attempts were made to destroy several of them, either during construction or after they had been erected, for example at Llanfyllin, at Narberth, and at Carmarthen. It became the policy of sympathizers with the poor, such as Frost, stubbornly to obstruct the operation of the Act, and in this they gained a considerable measure of success. In Merthyr Tydfil, for example, the Act had not been carried into effect as late as 1840.[1]

Frost's own attitude is clear enough, for he wrote constantly to the press on the subject, expressing, no doubt, the views which he put forward at the meetings of the board of guardians.[2] He believed the new system vicious in principle and likely to produce serious effects on society. It would inevitably tend to excite hatred of the rich, and would engender and keep alive a spirit which would sooner or later manifest itself in action. Poverty was punished as a crime; natural feelings were outraged by separating man and wife and parent and child; the allowance of food was barely adequate to sustain life; the treatment of the mothers of illegitimate children was brutal. Nevertheless, said Frost, the majority of the guardians were astonished that the poor did not admire the law, and he showed a penetrating appreciation of the real weakness of the system when he pointed out that the law was passed and

[1] Public Record Office, H.O. 40/57.
[2] *Merlin*, 6 Aug. 1836; 13 Aug.; 17 Dec.; 24 Dec.; 18 Feb. 1837; 25 Mar.

administered by persons who never expected to come under its operation themselves, and so had little reason to pay much regard to human considerations. On practical grounds, also, he raised objections to the system. He produced elaborate figures to show the cost of paupers per head under the old law, in comparison with the expense which would be involved in paying the interest on the cost of the new buildings, together with the salaries of the masters and matrons of the workhouses and of the relieving officers. He soon came into conflict with the poor law commissioner. As a justice he had insisted that the borough magistrates should meet in public, and this they did for the first time in May 1836. He sought to apply the same principle to the board of guardians, and succeeded in persuading his fellow guardians to admit the public. This was done for three weeks. The commissioner immediately asked that the public should be excluded, but the guardians refused, only to receive a peremptory order from him that his wishes must be obeyed. Frost sought to debate the matter with him (it was evidently a very lively debate) and when beaten he sought the support of the three members of Parliament for Monmouthshire and the boroughs in getting a ruling that the commissioner had exceeded his powers. He also tried to introduce the principle of the payment of the guardians for their services. Why, he asked, should the commissioners be paid (not to speak of grooms of the bedchamber and such people) and guardians not? He himself had to attend at Usk—a distance of about twelve miles—and the meetings were held on Saturdays, his principal day of business. He had not missed one meeting since his appointment. But this meant a serious financial loss to him, and unless guardians were paid, all the management would be thrown into the hands of a few rich men, the most improper persons to manage the affairs of the poor. He proposed that the salary of the guardians should be £20 a year.[1] It was the principle involved in the payment of members of Parliament, and Frost was quite consistent in his attitude, but it exposed him to much abuse and accusations of self-seeking.

In November 1836 Frost reached the peak of his authority when he became the second Mayor of Newport. He was proposed by the first mayor, Joseph Latch, who had been one of his opponents. Latch said that when Frost's name had been put forward as a magistrate, he had opposed it, for he feared that Frost was 'too warm a partisan' for that important office. But he had worked with him and found him so attentive to his duties, so uniformly dispassionate in his judgement and so efficient, that he now proposed him as mayor. Frost was seconded by one of his radical friends, and as there was no other nomination he was immediately proclaimed mayor. In the twelve months which had ensued since the Municipal Corporation Act had come into effect, Frost may well have thought that his star was in the ascendant. He had become progressively a town councillor, a justice of the peace, an improvement commissioner, a guardian of the poor, and now mayor of Newport, and a harbour commissioner in virtue of this office. He had therefore ample opportunity to fulfil his genuine desire to render public service, especially in the interests of the poor. His personal ambition, also, might well be satisfied, for he was a figure of importance in the public life of his native town, and held a position of authority which might well have erased the memory of the injuries he had suffered thirteen years before.

Early in the new year there occurred an incident which reopened all the old sores. It concerned Frost's stepson, William Foster Geach. This young man had qualified

[1] *Merthyr Guardian*, 25 Mar. 1837.

as a solicitor in February 1828, and for two years had practised at Bristol, then removing to Pontypool.[1] He was a small, keen man, meticulous in his appearance and methodical in his habits. He had apparently prospered, and had married a Miss Herbert, a member of one of the county families of Monmouthshire, who had brought him a considerable dowry. In the course of his professional duties he had lent some £800 to a widow of Pontypool. He wished to get the money repaid in January 1837, and in order to help his client he tried to arrange matters with a local banker. This was Reginald James Blewitt of Llantarnam Abbey, a descendant of the Morgan who had purchased the abbey in 1553. He had been educated at Rugby and called to the Bar, and it was he who had established the *Monmouthshire Merlin* in 1829 and had edited it for the first three years. By 1837 he had already started rebuilding the abbey. This had begun with a trivial repair, but Blewitt was led to make one structural alteration after another, until it had cost him nearly £60,000. This involved him not only in financial embarrassment, but in mental derangement, and he is said to have died in an asylum. Geach saw Blewitt at Llantarnam on behalf of his client, and all was satisfactorily arranged. On his return home he prepared an affidavit, and to save time he sent it to Blewitt already witnessed by himself, although Blewitt had not signed it. He evidently thought that he was acting in a friendly way with friends, but two days later he felt he had been indiscreet and wrote to Blewitt asking him to return the document so that he could prepare another. It was too late. Blewitt was a friend of Thomas Prothero (his brother, now dead, had married Prothero's daughter). He had immediately taken the irregular affidavit to Prothero's office, and

---

[1] Information kindly supplied by T. G. Lund, Esq., Assistant Secretary, Law Society's Hall.

already, without losing a day, the precious pair, Prothero and Phillips, had instituted proceedings in the Court of King's Bench to get Geach struck off the rolls. The *Merthyr Guardian* (the chief Tory paper in South Wales) declared openly before the trial that the dispute was a political one, and undoubtedly the motive behind it was to get at Frost. The case was not tried until 6 May, when Sir William Follett appeared for Geach. Blewitt had now withdrawn from it altogether, but Prothero and Phillips had continued with the case. The court, however, declared that nothing fraudulent had been intended, and dismissed the case. As Geach had admittedly committed an irregularity, he had, nevertheless, to pay the costs, and this may well have started the misfortunes which were to overwhelm him later on, and cause him to share his step-father's exile in the antipodes. For the present he was given a tremendous welcome when he returned to Pontypool.[1]

In his capacity as mayor Frost had meanwhile continued with his usual activities. He had brought forward the question of certain local charities where money was being withheld from the poor, and was instructed to communicate with the Charity Commissioner. He had had a committee appointed to correspond with the Anti-Corn Law League.[2] He obtained the passing of a resolution by the council petitioning the government to abolish church rates.[3] These rates (for maintaining church buildings and churchyards) were regarded as a great injustice by the Nonconformists, and were the subject of much agitation at the time. Curiously enough, the Newport council comprised twelve Nonconformists and only six churchmen (of whom, moreover, two were radicals), and so there was

[1] *Merthyr Guardian*, 11 Feb.; 18 Feb.; 13 May 1837.
[2] *Merlin*, 17 Dec. 1836.
[3] Newport Library MS., Corporation Minutes, 7 Feb. 1837, p. 83.

no difficulty in obtaining a majority on this question. Frost had already presided over a public meeting called to discuss church rates. He had expatiated on the immense wealth of the Church. No fond husband, he said, had ever guarded the charms of a beautiful wife with a more jealous eye and stronger hand than the Church had throughout the centuries guarded the loaves and fishes. He had no doubt that the bishops with their enormous incomes, their troops of liveried servants and gorgeous equipages, clothed as they were in purple and fine linen, and faring sumptuously every day, found it highly disagreeable to be disturbed, but he demanded justice for the poor. At the end of the meeting Nonconformist ministers paid high tribute to the mayor, 'the friend of the oppressed'.[1]

Once more there was talk of a general election, and on 18 January the mayor, by request, convened a meeting to discuss the matter. He praised Benjamin Hall and deplored the enormous expense and corrupt practices of the last election. The ballot, he said amid great applause, was the only cure.[2] But Hall had already decided not to offer himself again as candidate. He had fought three elections, and had had to withstand two petitions, and he had found that since the Reform Bill his expenses had not diminished, as he had hoped, but had kept increasing. He had therefore decided to seek a less difficult constituency elsewhere, and soon was to find one in Marylebone. To Frost's intense chagrin, the candidate chosen by the reformers was none other than Reginald James Blewitt of Llantarnam.[3] For the time being the election was postponed, but in June William IV died, so that an election must now take place. The duty of proclaiming the young queen fell, ironically enough, to John Frost. It was a very different scene from the jollification in 1830. There was,

---

[1] *Merlin*, 21 Jan. 1837.   [2] Ibid., 21 Jan. 1837.
[3] Ibid., 21 Jan.; 4 Feb. 1837.

indeed, a procession and a band, but there was only one 'miserable' flag (according to the *Merthyr Guardian*), and both the radical mayor and the conservative vicar commented on the marked absence of the gentlemen of the town. Frost presided at the dinner in the evening and proposed the health of the queen, but it was all a very half-hearted affair.[1] Serious business had already begun in preparation for the election. Frost could scarcely support an avowed enemy, such as Blewitt, and moreover he could no longer have any illusions about the motives of the Whigs. Lord John Russell had already declared (23 June) that he regarded the Reform Act as final—a statement which won for him the nicknames 'Little Finality' and 'Finality Jack'. Frost took refuge in the fact that, as magistrate, he was a returning officer for the boroughs, to take no open part in the election. But his enemies accused him of supporting Bailey, of accepting a bribe of £2,000 from him, and of abandoning the principles he had advocated for twenty years, on account of personal pique. Frost replied to this in a broadside. In a letter to the Home Secretary two years later he claimed that £10,000 was spent in bribery at this election. 'What's your price?' and 'What will you give?' were heard openly on all sides, he said, and the Whigs won because they bribed most.[2] So great, indeed, was the disturbance caused in Newport by the campaigning for this election that Frost had to swear in 150 special constables to preserve the peace.[3] But once more, although Bailey doubled the vote of his opponent in Monmouth and Usk, Blewitt's majority at Newport was sufficiently large to win him the seat (440 to 386).

[1] *Merlin*, 1 July 1837; *Merthyr Guardian*, 1 July 1837.
[2] Letter to Lord Normanby, 10 Sept. 1839. Reprinted *Western Vindicator*, no. 32, p. 4.
[3] Usk MSS. Treasurer's Vouchers. The cost to the shire of the constables on this occasion was £95. 8s. 6d.

From now on the antipathy between Frost on the one hand and Prothero and Phillips on the other developed into a bitter and relentless hatred, without appreciating which the activities of the Chartists two years later cannot be understood. In the first week of October appeared the last of Frost's pamphlets (as distinct from numerous broadsides), *To the Whig Magistrates of the County of Monmouth*. It was a most bitter attack on his opponents. If reform meant anything, he said, it meant honesty in public men, but this could not be said to be a characteristic of the reformers of Newport. Prothero and Phillips had charged £1,264. 14*s*. 7*d*. for getting the harbour bill passed (a sum which included three guineas a day for fifty-seven days for Phillip's attendance in London, in addition to the fees paid for the work done), and the details were now revealed to the public only because Frost as mayor had become a harbour commissioner. He further accused Prothero of misappropriating public money, for in the thirty years 1806 to 1836 no returns had been made of the fines imposed by the borough magistrates. Within a month of Geach's trial before the Court of King's Bench, Frost had applied to the same court through Sir William Follett for an order commanding the magistrates to render an account of all fines received. Mr. Justice Coleridge ruled that as no demand had been made to the magistrates, the order could not be granted, but if a demand were not complied with, then an order could be applied for later. Frost then tried to bring the matter before the Quarter Sessions at Usk, but failed, and his last action as mayor was to call a special meeting of the town council to discuss the matter. It was a very angry meeting, but Frost seems to have had his opponents on the run, for Phillips could only claim as an excuse that there were no instructions as to who should receive the fines, and that the person who had actually collected

them was honest, though possibly 'dilatory'—the dilatoriness apparently extending over thirty years. Nevertheless
Frost was defeated by ten votes to five (with two absten-
tions) on a resolution calling for an inquiry into the conduct of Prothero and Phillips.[1] Frost was also served with
notice to pay to the treasurer of the borough all the rent
from the Corporation Wharf, although nearly the whole
amount received by Frost had been spent in the suit to
recover the land occupied by the Tredegar Wharf, a suit
which he had undertaken at the request of the freemen.

It is probable that Frost's popularity towards the end
of his period as mayor had declined because of his conduct
during the election, and this may account for the turn
which things had taken in the matter of the fines and the
wharves. He decided nevertheless to stand for a second
period. He issued broadsides in support of his candidature,
pointing out, among other things, how Prothero and
Phillips were obstructing (in their own interests as lawyers) his attempt to revive the court of records for the
recovery of debts within the borough, which would
obviate the payment of lawyers' fees.[2] These drew broadsides from his opponents, one of them almost incoherent
with fury. Two others, which were particularly vindictive,
deserve attention. They were issued by *Detector* and
Vindex, and there is not much doubt as to their authorship. They included large extracts from Frost's letters
from Monmouth gaol, and for the first time, probably,
Frost realized how his attempts to arrange his bankruptcy in 1822 had become known. They also revived the
old accusation about Werndee. This interchange of
accusations must have kept Newport agog, but in the end
Frost was defeated by sixteen votes to seven. Moreover

[1] *Merlin,* 4 Nov. 1837.
[2] Newport Library MSS., Court of Record, show that the approval of the
judges for this court was obtained Dec. 1837 and Jan. 1838.

(perhaps in order to counteract Frost's influence more effectively) Thomas Phillips resigned his town clerkship, as a vacancy had occurred on the aldermanic bench, and the next day he was appointed alderman without ever having been elected councillor (15 December).[1]

For a time Frost seems to have withdrawn a little from public affairs. He still had a passion for reading and a desire to make a name as an author, and in 1838 a subject after his own heart turned up in the offer of a prize of 100 guineas by the Society for the Protection of Religious Liberty for an essay on the evils arising from the connexion between Church and State. This had always interested Frost, and he had spent six weeks in work on it, when one day his wife came into his study in tears, because a 'very near relative had got into trouble of a most serious kind'.[2] His project therefore had to be abandoned, and his draft was among the papers confiscated the following year. Was this near relative his son John? He was now twenty-four years of age, and nothing whatsoever is heard of him afterwards, except that during the period of his father's trial it was said that he was supposed to be in America. Frost never seems to have seen him again, even during the year which he himself spent in the United States. Probably, however, the near relative was Mrs. Frost's son, William Foster Geach, who was now in more serious difficulties. In 1837 he had arranged to admit into partnership a certain John Mauhan who had brought with him a capital of £2,000. But Mauhan came to the conclusion that Geach's assets were not what he had represented them to be, and during Geach's absence in London he had carefully examined his securities and come to the conclusion that the deed of a settlement on Geach by one of his wife's relatives was a

---

[1] Newport Library MSS. Corporation Minutes. 14 and 15 Dec. 1837.
[2] *Star of Gwent*, 2 Feb. 1861.

forgery. When he expressed his dissatisfaction on Geach's return, the latter repaid him his £2,000 and the partnership was dissolved. But Mauhan took his doubts to Prothero and Phillips, who immediately on their own account started proceedings against Geach for forgery. The matter came before three magistrates at Newport on 14 July, Phillips conducting the prosecution. Frost supported his stepson. So contradictory was the evidence that after fifteen hours' argument, the magistrates decided not to commit, though expressing no opinion as to the guilt or innocence of the accused. It was generally felt that Prothero and Phillips had gratuitously interfered in the affair again to get at Frost, and the welcome accorded to Geach on his return to Pontypool was extraordinary. (The Tory *Merthyr Guardian* describes it in full, while the Whig *Monmouthshire Merlin* is entirely silent.) He was met by 100 men on horseback and 3,000 on foot, and escorted into Pontypool with two bands playing, while fifty rounds of cannon were fired in his honour. The festivities continued well into the night.[1] It was, nevertheless, the beginning of the end as far as Geach was concerned.

In the autumn it became Frost's turn with two others to stand for re-election to the council. At the last minute it was decided to contest his place, and the west ward was strenuously canvassed. Frost, as usual, outlined his policy in a broadside. He was once more successful, though not this time at the head of the poll. For mayor there was only one nomination, Thomas Phillips (who had been on the council for only eleven months), and he was unanimously elected.[2] But of greater ultimate significance was a broadside issued by Frost some two weeks previously. In it, as a magistrate, he convened, by request, a meeting for 30 October to explain the principles of the Peoples' Charter. Frost's connexion with Chartism had begun.

[1] *Merthyr Guardian*, 21 July 1838.   [2] *Merlin*, 3 Nov.; 10 Nov. 1838.

IV

CHARTISM IN SOUTH WALES

'CHARTISM', said Carlyle, 'means bitter discontent grown fierce and mad. . . . It is a new name for a thing which has had many names, which will yet have many.' Undoubtedly the motive power behind Chartism was economic distress, and, political though its programme was, the purpose for which an extension of the franchise was desired was to remove this distress by reducing taxation. No doubt, also, distress was most pronounced in certain industrial areas. It was there that the existence of the two nations, of whom Disraeli wrote in *Sybil*, was most evident, two nations between whom there was no intercourse and no sympathy, who were as ignorant of each other's habits, thought, and feelings as if they were dwellers in different zones, or inhabitants of different planets. Nevertheless (whether this be a specifically Welsh aspect of Chartism or merely an accident), the motive power of Chartism in Wales seemed to come first from the countryside. It has been noticed that Frost in his many writings paid scarcely any attention to the condition of the industrial areas. While he was producing his first series of pamphlets there were strikes and serious disturbances in the Monmouthshire coal-field; immediately after he had recommenced writing there occurred the Merthyr riots of 1831. Yet in neither series does he make more than a passing reference to industrial conditions. He nowhere expresses a loathing for industrialism as such, as Cobbett did, but, like his master, he was more concerned with conditions in the rural areas, and he did not so much look forward to the future progress of the working class through the advancement of industry, as did most radicals, but back to the relatively prosperous days when he was a boy, days of whose prosperity he drew an idealized picture.

In keeping with this rural aspect of the movement is the fact that the first indications of any importance of the growth of Chartism in Wales are to be found not in the coal-field but in Carmarthen. It is true that Carmarthen was a town of well over 10,000 inhabitants, and the contrast between it and the industrial centres at the present day should not mislead one into over-emphasizing the rural nature of its life and activities in the early nineteenth century. It had, in fact, almost the same population as Newport. It had also a hat-making industry and a tinworks, and both trades at this time were in serious difficulties. The tinworks were being transferred to Aberavon, and even twelve years earlier (in 1826) a writer feared that this would throw hundreds of men 'on this parish', while 'Carmarthen as a trading and manufacturing town would sink into insignificance'. Moreover Carmarthen, was being displaced as a manufacturing town by Llanelly, still 'a miserable village' in 1798,[1] which was rapidly becoming an industrial centre owing to its position both on the coal-field and on the sea coast. There was, therefore, in Carmarthen an economic depression and unemployment, whose intensity should not be minimized because the numbers concerned were small. Nevertheless, it would be wrong to over-emphasize this as a possible cause of Chartism in Carmarthen. The town had, already, a long tradition of political agitation. Its parliamentary contests were renowned throughout Wales, and its inhabitants had a certain fractiousness not uncommon in country towns. The variety of their occupations preserved them from being cast all in the same mould, as might be the case in

[1] Sir John Lloyd (ed.), *The History of Carmarthenshire* (Cardiff, 1939), ii. 332.
[2] H. Skrine, *Tours Throughout Wales* (London, 1798), p. 72.

large cities, so they were intensely individualist and prepared to express their opinion on all questions. In the
autumn of 1818 discontent had developed into serious
rioting. There was distress in the town, and the crowd
tried to prevent the shipment of cheese to other parts.
The mayor called in troops, and his 'spirited and determined conduct' soon restored order.[1] In 1831 disturbances
occasioned by the agitation for the Reform Bill had neces-
sitated the enrolling of 200 Llanelly miners as special constables.[2] Discontent was now further aggravated by a
series of bad harvests after 1836, which particularly affected
a market-town such as Carmarthen.

Of considerable importance also in understanding the
growth of Chartism, especially in west Wales, is the attitude
towards it of Nonconformity. An anonymous writer in
the English radical newspaper, the *Sun*, noted the surprise
felt by many in 1839 that so religious a country should
have taken such an active part in the movement, and
maintained that for the Welsh it was a matter of religious
principle. The conduct of the government, he said, was
judged in Wales in accordance with the principles of
religion.[3] Certainly the Nonconformists in Wales were
now becoming politically conscious, and were radical in
their tendency. 'The old Dissenters', Hazlitt had said, 'I
look upon as the nursing fathers of our liberties.' Both by
temperament and by position they were rebels. The very
essence of their belief was their right of private judgement,
and this they maintained both in religious and in political
matters. Their agitation for liberty of conscience as the
natural right of each individual led them to demand
political liberty on the basis of the rights of man. Moreover, they were entirely devoid of any sentimental reverence

---

[1] *Bristol Mercury*, 5 Oct. 1818.
[2] *Land Commission Report* (1896), p. 153.
[3] Quoted in *Lovett Collection*, ii. 129; see also *Cymru* (1909), p. 104.

for the established order, and this supplied the disparagement of tradition which is a necessary element in the make-up of all radicals. Their active revolt against a Church established by the authority of the State and inextricably intertwined with it, also led them into revolt against the State itself. Further, they were subject to certain disabilities. It was only by the decision of Lord Mansfield in 1767 that Nonconformity itself had ceased to be a crime. Even yet a dissenting layman could be compelled to act as churchwarden, and Carmarthenshire was much agitated in December 1838 by the imprisonment for six months of a Nonconformist who refused to do so. But the chief source of discontent at this period was the enforced payment of church rates, which were applied to the upkeep of church buildings. This threw the Nonconformists into the ranks of the radicals, for they could scarcely hope for redress from a Parliament controlled by Anglican landowners. Their attitude was in striking contrast to that of the newer Nonconformists, the Calvinistic Methodists. The stress which the latter placed on predestination paralysed any desire for reform. Social inequalities to them were merely a means provided by providence for the development of character, and political reform they were not concerned with. They were therefore conservative in politics. They strenuously opposed Catholic emancipation; they even censured the growing movement for the disestablishment of the Anglican Church, while they excommunicated any of their members who joined trade unions. But Methodists were few in Carmarthenshire, which was essentially the shire of Independency, and the political education of this denomination was furthered in 1835 by the publication of a monthly periodical *Y Diwygiwr* (The Reformer), edited by David Rees of Llanelly. He took as his motto O'Connell's 'Agitate, agitate, agitate', and in the autumn of 1838 he

argued strongly that Chartism was consistent with Christianity, and urged the people of Wales to join the movement.[1] He was, however, averse to violence, and counselled
an alliance with the middle class. But this did not prevent
his being held responsible for the outbreaks which ensued.
This accusation was brought against him by an Anglican
periodical, *Yr Haul*[2] (The Sun), founded in the same year
in the neighbouring town of Llandovery. It had as its
editor David Owen, a brilliant journalist who had deserted
Nonconformity for Anglicanism. The polemics of David
Rees and David Owen were to enliven the controversies
of west Wales for many years.

The early appearance of Chartism in Carmarthen was
probably due, however, not so much to the depression in
its small industries or in agriculture, or to the influence of
Nonconformity, as to the presence in the town of an active
reformer, Hugh Williams. He was a native of Machynlleth,
where his father was a joint proprietor of lead-mines. His
sister was soon to become the wife of Richard Cobden, who,
in company with John Bright and some other share-
holders, eventually took over the mines. Hugh Williams
had apparently married a woman considerably older than
himself, who was possessed of some property. He now
lived at St. Clears, a village outside Carmarthen, and
practised as an attorney, 'a smooth-tongued and very
clever one', according to an opponent, the deputy mayor
of Swansea.[3] He had secured election as a guardian of the
poor, and used his position to resist the application of the
Poor Law Amendment Act. He induced the Carmarthen
Union to petition the government for the modification of
its more objectionable clauses.[4] He was thus active from

[1] *Diwygiwr* (1838), p. 372.   [2] *Haul* (1840), p. 122.
[3] H.O. 40/46; see also *Montgomery Collections*, xxviii. 143; A. H. Dodd,
The Industrial Revolution in North Wales (Cardiff, 1933), p. 180; R. T. Jenkins,
Hanes Cymru yn y 19 Ganrif (Cardiff, 1933), p. 127.
[4] *Swansea Cambrian*, 6 July 1839.

the beginning in the agitation which contributed so much not only to the growth of Chartism in West Wales but to the Rebecca Riots in which he played so prominent a part. Of more immediate importance, however, was his friendship with Henry Hetherington, the hero of the struggle against newspaper duties, to whom he had given financial assistance. It was Hetherington who later published Hugh Williams's *National Songs and Poetical Pieces*, an anthology dedicated to the queen and her countrywomen, and intended to convince them that the radicals were not quite the savages their enemies would have them believe.[1] It is more than probable, therefore, that when the London Working Men's Association, the parent body of Chartism, was founded in June 1836, with William Lovett as its secretary and Hetherington as its treasurer, Hugh Williams was aware of its existence from the start. Very soon a nucleus of a W.M.A. must have been formed in Carmarthen itself, for Williams claimed that he had 'got up the first radical meeting in South Wales' in the autumn of 1836, and on 11 February 1837 twelve inhabitants of the town wrote to J. A. Roebuck, the philosophic radical member for Bath, congratulating him on the fact that he was the first openly to claim 'equal rights' for the people.[2] This was two weeks before the 'birthday of the Charter' at the great meeting at the Crown and Anchor in London, when about 3,000 persons unanimously adopted the six points, equal representation, universal suffrage, annual parliaments, no property qualifications, vote by ballot, and payment of members, and requested Roebuck to present a petition embodying them to Parliament. Whether Hugh Williams was present at this meeting or

[1] This work, partly written and partly edited by Williams, is dated 1839, but the preface is dated 18 Feb. 1840.

[2] *Lovett Collection*, i. 22, 250; see also *Cymru* (1909), p. 171. The address from Carmarthen to Roebuck is not signed by Williams, but is evidently the work of an educated man.

not is not known (he was frequently in London, where his brother had chambers in Gray's Inn), but a few days later he addressed the Carmarthen W.M.A., an 'infant institution' of which he was the secretary, on the principles of universal suffrage, as well as on the evils of excessive differences in fortune, and on the state of Canada.[1] Early in January 1838 he was elected an honorary member of the London W.M.A.[2] In May the People's Charter (in the form of an Act of Parliament embodying the six points) was published, together with an address by Lovett and Hetherington explaining its principles, and in June a letter was received by the London W.M.A. from the branch at Carmarthen expressing its approval.[3] Williams then took it on himself to present the Metropolitan Association with a tricoloured flag, green, white, and blue, intended 'to replace the bloodstained standards of the world'. He seems to have been enamoured of this device, for he later presented flags to the associations at Carmarthen itself, at Merthyr, and at Pontypool, and composed a song, 'Freedom's Tricoloured Banner', to celebrate these occasions.[4]

Great meetings were now being held to support the workers' demands, particularly at Glasgow in May and at Birmingham in the first week in August. It is estimated that there were no less than 200,000 at the second meeting, and important resolutions were put forward. Attwood suggested a general strike for one week to impress the government, and Feargus O'Connor began his career of recklessness by exhorting his hearers, in the words of the poet Moore, to 'go flesh every sword to the hilt'. But more important was the decision to call upon the people to sign

---

[1] *Lovett Collection*, i. 48, 56, 194. The *Carmarthen Journal*, 25 May 1838, has a bitter attack on the Crown and Anchor meeting, and on the W.M.A. as a 'revolutionary faction'.

[2] British Museum, Add. MSS. 37773, W.M.A. Minutes, i. 90, 9 Jan. 1838.

[3] Ibid., p. 111, 26 June 1838.

[4] Ibid., p. 116; *Northern Star*, 26 Jan. 1839; see also *National Songs*.

a National Petition for the Charter, and to elect delegates to a General Convention to supervise its presentation. The London leaders, somewhat alarmed at the sentiments expressed at Birmingham, decided to call a meeting at Palace Yard, Westminster, to consider the Petition and the Convention, and invited the local W.M.A.s to send delegates. By this time the Carmarthen branch numbered about 250, and at a meeting held at their reading-room on 5 September, Hugh Williams was unanimously elected delegate. He addressed the branch for about an hour, dwelling at great length on the perfidy of the Whigs in connexion with the Reform Act, which had enfranchised a few paltry hundreds of the middle class while thousands of workmen remained without the vote. Instead of the prosperity which the Whigs had promised, the workers had received the sour porridge of the poor law institutions. He denounced the military despotism of the Whig government in Canada, the oppression favoured of those 'vile Whig traitors to liberty', O'Connell and Cam Hobhouse (the former friend of Byron). He urged the workers not to remain passive, but to organize themselves and convince their fellows. He himself had sent William Jenkins the previous week to hold meetings at Pontypool, Merthyr, Newport, Swansea, and Llanelly,[1] and had received cheering accounts from him. He gladly accepted their invitation to attend at Palace Yard.[2] The London meeting proved to be the last of importance held by the London W.M.A. About 30,000 were present, and the Petition and the Convention were decided upon. An attempt was made to counteract the unfavourable impression caused by the violence of the Birmingham speeches, yet several delegates spoke in a similar strain. They would not resort to violence

[1] The secretary of the Llanelly branch was Zechariah Williams, not to be confused with Zephaniah Williams, the Chartist leader. B.Mus. Add. MSS. 37773; *Lovett Collection*, i. 290.
[2] *Leeds Times*, 15 Sept. 1838.

until their enemies did, but once having put their hands to the plough, they would never turn back. Hugh Williams assured them that the radicals of South Wales would assert their rights at any time and in any manner they might be called upon, even to the extent of using physical force.[1] The London committee thought it prudent, nevertheless, to issue *An Address to the Irish People* (partly to reconcile O'Connor with non-violence, and to propitiate O'Connell) in which they declared that they would effect their object in peace, with no other force than that of argument and persuasion, and letters approving this address were received from associations at Carmarthen, Llanelly, Swansea, Newport, and Pontypool.[2]

In the summer of 1838 Chartism had become prominent in another part of Wales which might, at first sight, appear a rural area, that is, in Montgomeryshire. Here, however, it was a severe crisis in the flannel industry which was mainly responsible for its development. This industry had been carried on at Llanidloes for a very long time, and the town now had some 4,000 inhabitants. But in the last twenty-five years it had been outrivalled by Newtown—the home of Robert Owen—where a flannel of a finer texture was produced, and the population of the latter had rapidly increased to over 6,000. It had some fifty factories, employing in all about 3,000 persons. The third of the Severn towns, Welshpool, also had its flannel manufacture, but on a much smaller scale than Llanidloes and Newtown. It had in addition some small industries, and was the best market in Powis. Sheltering as it did beneath the walls of Powis Castle, it was naturally more conservative than its sister towns. Its population was roughly the same as that of Llanidloes.[3] In the

---

[1] *Carmarthen Journal*, 21 Sept. 1838; Add. MSS. 27819, p. 214; *Lovett Collection*, i. 250.

[2] Add. MSS. 37773, p. 126, 16 Oct. 1838.

[3] S. Lewis, *Topographical Dictionary of Wales* (London, 1833); also Dodd,

winter of 1837 these towns suffered the severest crisis in their history. This was due not so much to the introduction of machinery as to a financial crisis which led London banks to restrict credit and ruined several manufacturing companies. There was therefore much unemployment. Conditions of labour were also poor. The working-day varied between eleven and fourteen hours, yet weavers earned only eight to ten shillings a week, and spinners and slubbers twelve shillings, while a large number of children (ranging between the ages of nine and fourteen) were employed at half a crown a week. This economic distress unfortunately coincided with the attempt to apply the provisions of the new poor law and this produced intense discontent.

Dissent was also strong in the flannel towns. An anonymous writer, a 'Churchman', published a public letter (17 October 1838) to the Bishop of St. Asaph bitterly complaining that although the population of Newtown had increased to such an extent, no provision was made by the Anglican Church towards its spiritual needs, except in the totally inadequate parish church, which had only thirty free sittings. The Baptists, the Independents, the Wesleyans, the Welsh Calvinistic Methodists, and the Primitive Methodists, on the other hand, had in recent years spent over £10,000 in erecting chapels, and provided some 6,000 sittings of which 1,400 were free.[1] Yet the chief radical in Montgomeryshire was of good county descent. He was Thomas Powell, a personal friend of Hugh Williams and of Hetherington. He had lived in London but had returned to his native town, Welshpool, where he kept an ironmonger's shop. He was described as a 'fiery little Welshman, who had much of the rebel in

op. cit. For Chartism in Montgomeryshire, I am indebted to Miss Myfanwy Williams's unpublished thesis on the subject.

[1] Broadside in Place MSS. Add. MSS. 34245, B. 307.

him, albeit a sensible man, clever and wary'.[1] Possibly it was at his request that Hetherington appeared in the district in November 1837, and founded branches of the W.M.A.[2] But mid-Wales was in closer touch with the Midlands than with London, and it was mainly from Birmingham that Chartism was introduced into the three towns in the summer of 1838. Its exponent was one Richard Jarman, a native of Llanidloes, and political unions were formed there and at Newtown on the Birmingham model. These soon adopted the Charter and the Petition, which had now been translated into Welsh, and it was at Newtown that the first great Chartist demonstration in Wales was held. This was on 10 October. The number of the crowd was variously estimated at between 3,000 and 5,000, and they were drawn not only from the three towns but from the agricultural areas. They marched, in orderly fashion, through Newtown to their meeting place, where Pearce, a delegate from Birmingham, explained to them the principles of Chartism.[3] Among the speakers was Charles Jones, who stressed the need for peace and legality, and who was chosen as delegate to the National Convention.[4]

Peace did not seem likely to last long, for early in December a placard was posted calling upon 'sons of Gomer, Lovers of Freedom, Haters of Tyranny' to congregate on Christmas Day at Caersws, where a workhouse was being built. The magistrates feared that the building would be destroyed, and communicated with the Home Office. They swore in special constables and called out the yeomanry. Employers did their utmost to prevent

[1] R. Williams, *Montgomeryshire Worthies* (Newtown, 1894), p. 243.
[2] *Lovett Collection*, i. 140. Meeting at Newtown, 18 Nov. 1837.
[3] *Hull Saturday Journal*, 20 Oct. 1838; Place MSS. 27820, p. 269; *Lovett Collection*, i. 270, where the name of the chairman is given as Richard Janner (not Jarman), Dodd, op. cit., p. 409, calls him Jarvis.
[4] *Silurian*, 20 Oct. 1838.

the attendance of their workmen, and placards were posted entreating the people not to attend. Nevertheless, at eleven o'clock on Christmas Day, crowds numbering several thousands arrived to the strains of the Rechabites' brass band. But the meeting was peaceful. Powell and Jones urged them to avoid physical force until all constitutional means had failed, and to contribute towards the 'national rent' (for the expenses of the Convention). Lord Clive, of Powis Castle, who was present, had nothing worse to report to the Home Office than the desecration of the Saviour's birthday.[1]

It was towards the end of July or the beginning of August that a W.M.A. was formed at Newport.[2] Its founder seems to have been, not Frost, but William Edwards, a baker by trade. He was forty-one years of age and claimed that he had been a radical since 1816. He was a man of huge stature and colossal strength and was accused by his opponents of preaching violence. 'Mad Edwards, the baker' was how he was invariably characterized in the local press. Yet he himself claimed to be a moral force man, and the only literary production of his to survive, *An Address to the People* (written, it is true, within the sobering precincts of Monmouth gaol), is moderate enough. It is, however, full of scriptural allusions, and his style was no doubt that of the more ranting Nonconformist preachers. Early in the following year he devoted his whole time to mission work on behalf of Chartism in the Monmouthshire valleys and the west of England.[3] With him was associated Samuel Etheridge, like himself a veteran radical of the Hampden Club days. To begin with, the association differed little from the host of other friendly societies (both male and female) which

[1] H.O. 40/40; *Birmingham Journal*, 5 Jan. 1839; *Silurian*, 5 Jan. 1839.
[2] *Western Vindicator*, 20 April 1839; *The Charter*, 10 March 1839.
[3] *Western Vindicator*, 10 March 1839; 20 April 1839 (Life and Rambles of William Edwards); *Monmouthshire Advertiser*, 12 June 1841.

pullulated in Newport, as elsewhere, at this time, but in October it became very active, and on 23 October Edwards and Etheridge addressed a meeting of about 150 persons at the Bush Inn. They attributed the grievances of the working class to the lack of representation in Parliament. Another speaker then proceeded in Welsh to explain the principles of the charter, and it was decided to ask Frost, as a magistrate, to convene a public meeting for the same purpose. Frost, who was present, promised to do so,[1] and two days later he issued a broadside calling a meeting for 30 October. In this placard he made an appeal to the middle-class tradesmen of Newport. The object of the W.M.A., he said, was to put honest and industrious men into Parliament. This would benefit tradesmen as much as any, for their taxes would be reduced by half. The present members were the same as before the Reform Bill, and were elected by means of bribery, perjury, violence, and drunkenness. The tradesmen must choose; soon there would be no place for neutrals in the struggle for and against cheap government.

The meeting on 30 October at the Parrot Inn was attended by between 400 and 500 people, and Frost's speech was reported at great length in the press. It showed him a convinced supporter of Chartism. He reminded his audience how he had warned them to trust the Whigs no more than the Tories. The present Parliament differed in no way from the old rotten-borough Parliaments; the expense of royalty and of the administration had been increased instead of being reduced, and the Irish Coercion Bill and the transportation of the Dorchester labourers were the work of the reforming Whigs. The renewed demand for reform was due to distress, and this distress was caused by bad government. He then explained the points of the Charter, especially universal

[1] *Merlin*, 27 Oct. 1838.

suffrage. He denied that equality of property was aimed at; it was a calumny to call them Levellers. Differences in rank, circumstances, and property had always existed and always would; they were part of the order of nature. But inequality of property did not mean inequality of rights. He then argued for manhood suffrage on the ground that it had been the ancient rule of the land and that it was in accordance with the law of nature, and he brought in his favourite quotations from Blackstone to support his argument. But, in addition, he denied that it was inexpedient. It could not be expedient to withhold a right; moreover the workers who raised all the food, cut the canals and built the railroads were surely as proper persons to have the vote as the gamblers who now sat in Parliament. Women were excluded by the order of nature; in any case they had power enough already, and he himself would never think of acting against the advice of his wife. It was a closely argued speech in his best manner, and it showed a remarkable consistency in ideas over twenty years. The meeting closed with the adoption of the Charter.[1]

Frost, therefore, had thrown in his lot with the Chartist movement. However seriously or otherwise he may have considered becoming a candidate for Parliament, his chances of being adopted were now very remote. His personal enemy, Blewitt, was secure in the Monmouth boroughs, and his own conduct in the election of the previous year had alienated the reformers, while between him and their two leaders, Phillips, now mayor of Newport, and Prothero, there was bitter and implacable hatred. Possibly the opportunity of becoming a deputy to the Convention may have compensated him to some extent for his disappointment, but, in any case, it is hard to see how he could have kept out of the movement. For the

[1] *Merlin*, 3 Nov. 1838; *Silurian*, 10 Nov. 1838.

time being he was again embarrassed by local affairs. Two weeks after the meeting at the Parrot Inn the matter of the Corporation Wharf rents came before the Court of Queen's Bench. It was tried by Frost's old counsel of the Toby Mac Negus speech, now Lord Denman. Sir William Follett, for Frost, claimed that the rents belonged to the old freemen, and had been received by Frost at their request. Mr. Maule for his opponents claimed that the money should be handed over to the borough treasurer. Lord Denman ruled that the money should not remain in Frost's hands, but as it had not been shown that it had been demanded of Frost and refused, and as Frost had received the rent at the request of the freemen, Lord Denman would not make an order for its payment. Nevertheless he refused to grant Frost's costs.[1] Frost, however, had a brief respite, which he devoted entirely to Chartism. Two weeks after the decision at the Court of Queen's Bench, that is on 30 November, a meeting at the Devonshire House unanimously elected Frost as delegate to the Convention to represent Newport, Caerleon, and Pontypool. Later, on 17 December, he and Edwards addressed a meeting at Caerleon, and Frost was again adopted as delegate.[2] His visit to the third branch of his constituency, Pontypool, came on New Year's Day. It was by far the most important of the three meetings, and we shall return to it later. By now the *Address and Rules* of the Newport W.M.A. were published.[3] The purpose of the association was declared to be not only to remove unjust taxes and useless pensions 'but to probe our social evils to their source and apply effective remedies'. Members were warned against drunkenness—which is curious

[1] *Merlin*, 17 Nov.; 24 Nov. 1838.
[2] Ibid., 1 Dec., 22 Dec. 1838; *Silurian*, 8 Dec. 1838.
[3] *Working Men's Association for benefiting . . . the Useful Classes; Address and Rules*, Printed by J. Partridge, Newport. In Newport Museum, Miscellaneous Papers.

as nearly all W.M.A. meetings were held in public houses
—and caution was to be exercised in enrolling members,
in order to exclude the drunk and immoral. All members
paid one penny a week, and membership was confined to
the working class, since they must rely upon themselves
alone. Far from endangering property, they sought to
render it more secure, and life more sacred. Among their
objects were equality of rights, a cheap press and education. Their motto was: 'It is safe to do right', and by
January they numbered 430.[1]

A branch of the W.M.A. had been formed at Pontypool
as early as January 1838, for in that month an address
was issued by the branch advocating manhood suffrage
and the ballot, and urging the abolition of hereditary
distinctions, though admitting that property 'honestly
acquired' was to be held sacred. This address was signed
by Samuel Shell, whose son was to become one of the
'heroes' of the attack on Newport. But very little is heard
of the branch, and it may have lapsed a few months later
when Shell removed to Bristol.[2] It is remarkable that
Frost, even as late as his speech at the end of October,
made no reference to industrial conditions, and the
initiative in propagating Chartist ideas in the coalfield
would seem to have been taken by Hugh Williams. Yet
the motive power in the last stages of Chartism in Wales,
culminating in the outbreak of November 1839, came
from the industrial districts, and it therefore becomes
necessary to examine what the conditions were in those
areas.

No doubt the most important aspect of industrialism
in South Wales in so far as it affected Chartism was the
rapid growth in the population. In the thirty years

[1] Add. MSS. 37773.
[2] *Lovett Collection*, i. 160. Shell left for Bristol in July 1838. Newport
Museum MS. 379.

between the first and fourth censuses the population of Monmouthshire had increased by 117 per cent., the highest prcentage for any area in the British Isles, while Glamorgan came third on the list with an increase of 77 per cent.[1] This population, drawn in the first instance from the neighbouring districts, became eventually highly heterogeneous in character, and this made it particularly susceptible to radical agitation. Uprooted from the soil and herded together in unwonted surroundings, the workers lost the traditional conservatism of the countryman, and for some time found little to replace it. Besides, there was a fair sprinkling of undesirable persons among them. Fugitives from justice found that the works provided a convenient refuge against pursuit and detection, and it was customary in chapel circles to say that while the Lord knew the way of the just, the way of the unjust was towards Merthyr Tydfil. All this was complicated by racial strife. It has been estimated that about a sixth of the population was Irish, many of the immigrants being literally brought as ballast, free of charge, by empty ships returning from Cork and Waterford. The Irish were prepared to work for lower wages than the Welsh, and strife between them was endemic, breaking out into savage fighting on Saturday nights. It is particularly noticeable that the Irish took no part in the movements for social reform, and the *Dublin Review* was able to boast that of all the people indicted after the Newport riot, only one was an Irishman.[2] It would be true to say, therefore, that life on the coalfield, owing to the heterogeneous character of its population, bore many resemblances to that in the frontier districts

[1] J. H. Clapham, *An Economic History of Modern Britain* (Cambridge, 1926), i. 49.
[2] *Dublin Review*, viii (Feb. 1840), pp. 271–285; see also *Merlin*, 23 Nov. 1839.

of new countries, and produced its usual heritage of lawlessness.

The housing conditions of the people also resembled those on the frontier. The sordid details are familiar enough from the government reports of 1844 and 1845 on the health of towns and populous districts, and the report of 1847 on education in Wales, and they need not be repeated here. Immigration into a hitherto rural area had been so extensive that there had been no time to provide adequate houses. This was complicated by the geographical nature of the narrow valleys, especially in Glamorganshire, which involved difficulties in drainage and sanitation not yet entirely overcome, and which made it necessary that the houses should be built in terraces above each other. Living conditions in these areas were deplorable, yet it is at least doubtful whether the houses were worse than those of the old country towns, such as Carmarthen or Brecon, whose slums made up in intensity for what they lacked in extent, or for that matter, whether they were worse than the picturesque but insanitary mud cottages of the farm labourers. Yet the cumulative effect of congestion over large areas must have been much more pronounced than in the small country towns, and produced a spiritual malaise which was responsible for much of the drunkenness which prevailed.

Frontier conditions, also, produced the chief abuse of the coal-field, the truck system. Largely owing to difficulties of transport, the employers had to organize the obtaining of provisions for their men, and opened company shops. Even as late as 1838 the workers of Cyfarthfa petitioned their employer to establish a shop, as they thought they were being cheated by the shopkeepers of Merthyr, and the *Silurian* had to warn them that this might lead to abuses.[1] Abuses there undoubtedly were,

[1] *Silurian*, 25 Aug. 1838.

for the employers took advantage of their monopoly to charge 20 to 30 per cent. above market price for vastly inferior goods, and workers who attempted to deal elsewhere were dismissed. Often they were paid no wages at all, but merely received vouchers for food and other necessaries. Of all the abuses of the coal-field, truck caused most agitation, and the magistrates in their frequent petitions to Parliament attributed most of the rioting and discontent to it. In 1831 an anti-truck act was passed (becoming operative in January 1832), but nevertheless truck continued. Evidence was given before a commission of inquiry in 1842 by Thomas Jones Phillips of Newport. It was he who had arrested John Frost three years previously, so that he cannot be accused of bias against the owners. He claimed that truck had been the frequent theme of the Chartist agitators, and declared that the workers considered that they lost five to six shillings in the pound through truck. Owners still built butchers' shops and beer houses which they let out at a high rent on the understanding that their workers would be compelled to go there. Other employers received a percentage of the takings. If workers did not comply they would be given a hint of dismissal, which was usually sufficient, and he gave an authentic case of a worker whose child had died, and who had had to take goods from the company shop and sell them in order to get his wages so that he might bury his child.[1]

In addition to living conditions, conditions of labour took their toll of health and well being, and it must be remembered that these affected not only men but women and children. Hours of labour were long, and brutalized the workers, while there was an almost complete absence of safety devices or adequate ventilation, so that accidents and explosions were frequent. The mines report of 1842

[1] *Merthyr Guardian*, 17 Sept. 1842.

produced a picture of female and child labour in the mines, with which we have become so accustomed through constant repetition that it requires an ever greater effort of the imagination to realize its enormity. Little girls of five and six spent hours in the mines opening air-doors, terrified by the darkness and the rats, while young women of fifteen to twenty spent their day pushing wagons of coal, often unable to stand erect at their work. The harrowing details are familiar enough, but their effect on health and on the attitude of the workers towards social questions is incalculable. They make one infuriated at the smugness of the Liberal member for the Monmouth boroughs, who could report to the Home Office two days after the Newport riot: 'A more lawless set of men than the colliers do not exist. . . . It requires some courage to live amongst such a set of savages.'[1] Yet very few measures were taken to combat this lawlessness. In 1839 there were only seventeen police officers in the whole of Monmouthshire, and even in 1842, when the authorities had had time to profit by the experience of 1839, there were in the large industrial area which stretched from Rhymney to Hirwaun, and which included Dowlais, Merthyr, and Aberdare, also only seventeen police officers of all grades.[2] Nor did the Established Church do much to improve matters. In 1840, in the large parish of Trevethin (which included the town of Pontypool) there were only four Anglican places of worship as opposed to twenty-four non-Anglican.[3] In Merthyr, the largest town in Wales, the proportion was still more striking. The Anglicans remained contented with their

[1] H.O. 40/45.
[2] Usk MSS. give police officers for Monmouthshire: Abergavenny 3; Bedwellty 4; Chepstow 1; Monmouth 2; Newport 4; Pontypool 2; Usk 1. *Merthyr Guardian*, 23 April 1842, gives the following figures: Merthyr 10; Dowlais 3; Rhymney 2; Aberdare 1; Hirwaun 1.
[3] G. S. Kenrick, *The Population of Pontypool* (London, 1840), p. 41.

one parish church, while the Nonconformists had built twelve.[1] In fact, in the whole of the coal-field, from Aberdare to Pontypool, there were only thirteen Anglican churches, to serve a population of about 100,000, and although the mass of the inhabitants was Welsh speaking, in not one of these thirteen were the services conducted entirely in the Welsh language.[2] The late Archbishop of Wales found the cause of this dilatoriness in the poverty of the Church to which the landowners and iron-masters belonged, while the activity of the Nonconformists was due, he said, 'to the greed of groups of speculators, who saw the possibility of obtaining six or seven per cent. on their money by financing the building of new chapels'.[3] Thus, he argued, while the Anglicans should not be blamed, the Nonconformists should not receive any credit.

In the face of these conditions the workers themselves sought to combine, and early attempts at trade unionism were made. Lodges of Oddfellows (and Oddsisters, for that matter) were attached to several of the large iron-works,[4] and the Friendly Associated Coalminers' Union, founded in Lancashire in October, 1830, soon had branches, known as Union Clubs, throughout the Welsh coal-field. At first they abstained from politics, but they met in secret, a condition always conducive to the growth of violence. In June 1831 discontent in Merthyr broke out into serious rioting. The immediate cause was a reduction in wages at the Cyfarthfa ironworks, but the anger of the crowd found expression in an attack on the Court of Requests. Many tradesmen had availed themselves of the authority of this court to seize the furniture of workers to whom they had given credit. The crowd, therefore, demanded the surrender of his books by the clerk of the

---

[1] *Merthyr Guardian*, 8 Feb. 1840.

[2] E. Jenkins, *Chartism Unmasked*, Merthyr, 1840.

[3] A. G. Edwards, *Landmarks in the History of the Welsh Church* (London, 1912), pp. 214–15.　　　　　　　　　[4] *Merlin*, 25 July 1829.

court. He sought to save the situation by handing over old books, and when this deception was discovered, the crowd broke into his premises and utterly destroyed them. A troop of Highlanders was summoned and arrived next day at the Castle Hotel. Here the soldiers were hemmed in by a large mob and partly disarmed, whereupon they fired into the crowd with deadly effect. Some twenty-one were killed outright, and between seventy and eighty wounded. Nevertheless on the following day the yeoman cavalry which was escorting ammunition from Brecon found the road blocked and thought it judicious to retreat, while a detachment of cavalry from Swansea was surrounded and disarmed. Disturbances continued for some days, but eventually the workers surrendered and accepted the reduction in wages. Two men were condemned to death for their part in the riots, and one of them, Dic Penderyn, was executed in Cardiff gaol. Even to this day his name rouses a feeling of injustice among the workers of South Wales.[1] As they had obtained the upper hand, the employers of labour determined to crush the union clubs, to whose 'inflammatory tracts' they attributed the outbreak of the riots. The proprietors of six works therefore announced that they would employ no workman who was a member of a union club.[2] There ensued an almost complete lockout which lasted for about two months. The clubs tried to pay their members five shillings a week, but their funds soon dwindled, and the men, faced with complete destitution, were forced to return to work on the terms of their employers.

The collapse of legitimate unionism led to the strange outbreak of the 'Scotch Cattle', so called, apparently, because the red figure of a bull's head was used as a

---

[1] *Merlin*, 11 June 1831; see also contemporary account reprinted in C. Wilkins, *History of Merthyr Tydfil* (Merthyr 1908), pp. 407-21.

[2] *Merlin*, 17 Sept. 1831.

symbol. Their activities were most numerous in the Monmouthshire valleys. In April 1832 about 200 'Cattle' at Abersychan paid a visit to a blackleg's house at one o'clock in the morning, and then descended the valley to Pontypool, where they proceeded to destroy the houses of those who refused to join them. According to the *Merlin*, the cause of the outbreak was truck, the men being 'determined to be paid with current coin of the realm', and this was also the opinion of the magistrates. Rewards were offered for information, but the outrages continued. Blacklegs were beaten up and furnaces blown out, and order was restored only by the calling in of troops.[1] Then, for a year, disturbances subsided, and the peaceful aspirations of the workers found expression in the Grand National Consolidated Trades Union of Robert Owen. But this soon collapsed in March 1834 when the savage sentence of seven years transportation was passed on the Dorchester labourers by the fellow countryman of Judge Jeffreys, Mr. Justice John Williams. The unions met with the bitterest opposition. They were due, said the Lord Chancellor, to 'lazy, unprincipled and factious charlatans, opposed to the habits of industry themselves' who duped the people, and they were 'the worst things which could have been constituted for the interests of the country or of the workmen themselves'.[2] Crawshay and other iron-masters threatened to blow out their furnaces unless the men signed a declaration abandoning all connexion with trade unions, and once more the owners won.[3] But once more the 'Cattle' became rampant throughout the coal-field, especially in the Pontypool valley. Some of their leaders were transported and one was hanged. His death throes were described in detail inthe *Merlin*, which later published a letter from a

[1] Ibid., 10 March, 8 April, 12 May 1832.
[2] Ibid., 10 May 1834.   [3] Ibid., 26 July 1834.

correspondent highly commending it for this description, as it would have a very salutary effect on the people.[1] Such was the state of public opinion in Wales in 1835.

The Chartist doctrine, therefore, fell upon fruitful ground in the autumn of 1838. The Working Men's Associations quickly absorbed not only the respectable members of the old union clubs but also the 'Scotch Cattle', who brought with them habits of violence which were destined to become the determining factors in the late autumn of the following year. Nevertheless the fundamental element in the situation in South Wales in 1839 was the fact that wages were high. In comparison with the textile workers of Lancashire, Yorkshire, and Mid-Wales, the miners and ironworkers of South Wales were prosperous. Needless to say, this was the recurrent theme of the enemies of Chartism, but even the Chartists themselves admitted that this was so.[2] The figures supplied by Samuel Homfray to *The Times*, immediately after the outbreak, were no doubt authentic. He employed some 5,000 workmen at Tredegar, and their weekly wages were as follows: miners 22s. to 24s.; furnacemen 30s.; puddlers and heaters 35s.; rollers 50s. to 60s.; fitters and smiths 25s.; carpenters 21s.; moulders 24s.; masons 24s.; labourers (of whom there were very few) 12s. to 14s.[3] It is true that wages fluctuated, and that this was a boom period. Seldom had the coal and iron trade been so flourishing. Yet it is certainly true that as long as wages were high, working and living conditions, however bad, would not cause an outbreak, because they were in no way worse than they had always been. On the other hand, workmen who were reasonably prosperous would be more inclined to listen to a purely political appeal, such as that of

[1] *Merlin*, 2 Aug. 1834; 5 Apr., 12 Apr. 1835.
[2] *Western Vindicator*, 4 May 1839; *Merlin*, 11 Apr. 1840.
[3] *The Times*, 15 Nov. 1839; *Merlin*, 16 Nov. 1839.

Chartism, than if they had been sunk in the depths of misery.

The first of the great Chartist meetings of the coal-field coincided with the demonstration at Caersws on Christmas Day. It took place on the common at Penrheolgerrig, near Merthyr, where the Merthyr public meetings were generally held. A branch of the W.M.A. had been established there in October, with Morgan Williams as its secretary.[1] Placards in Welsh and English were posted to advertise the meeting and the National Petition was circulated in both languages. As Christmas Day was a holiday the magistrates feared the consequences, and wrote to the Home Office for advice. The number of the crowd was variously estimated. The *Merthyr Guardian*, which was attempting to decry the movement, stated that there were only 1,000 present, and that half of them attended from curiosity, but all the Chartist reports placed the figure at 10,000. They marched in procession to their meeting-place, with their green, blue, and white banner flying. Hugh Williams was the chief speaker. He strongly advocated moral force, yet his words were violent enough, bitterly attacking the aristocracy who had squandered the taxes of the country in warfare and then placed the whole burden on the shoulders of the people. He was unanimously elected delegate to the Convention, and in the evening 200 working men 'sat down to an excellent dinner, when many patriotic toasts were drunk and excellent speeches made.'[2]

It had not apparently been Williams's intention to become a delegate, but he accepted, and was soon elected by his own association as well. He had wished to hold a meeting at the Guild Hall, Carmarthen, but this had been

[1] *Lovett Collection*, i. 296.
[2] H.O. 40/40. *Silurian*, 29 Dec. 1838; *Northern Star*, 5 Jan. 1839; *Merthyr Guardian*, 19 Jan. 1839.

refused after a very stormy scene in the town council. The Chartists thereupon decided to meet by torchlight at General Picton's monument, in spite of the ban on such meetings which had been announced by royal proclamation on 12 December. The meeting of about 4,000 persons with lanterns and torches on a dark winter's night (9 January), in the badly lighted streets of Carmarthen, may well have inspired fear, but the demonstration seems to have been peaceful. Numerous speeches were made, in Welsh and English. A local schoolmaster made a stirring appeal to his hearers to support the cause for which their fathers had bled. He demanded the birthright of every man, political liberty, which he maintained would remove the poverty which existed in a land of plenty. He was followed by a young man who appealed to the young radicals and condemned the poor law. Then came William Jenkins, Hugh Williams's emissary to the coal-field. He was an old radical; formerly there had not been more than five or six in the town who agreed with him, he said, but now the Association numbered about 600. He spoke bitterly of the contemptuous terms, such as the 'great unwashed', applied to them by masters who lived at their expense. Lastly Hugh Williams spoke. He dwelt on the unrepresentative character of the House of Commons; five-sixths of the members were creatures of the House of Lords, and there was no more corrupt body in the world. The working class must be firm in its demands, for firmness and unity alone could succeed. Their poverty was due to the abuses which universal suffrage would remove, and together with them would go those 'leper blots on society', the workhouses. He advised them to study their motto, 'Peace, Law and Order'. The middle class, who had not shown much regard for the suffering of the workers, was now needlessly alarmed, he said, and, in fact, his speech was by no means as extreme in tone as many which had been delivered at Carmarthen during the agitation for the Reform Bill. He was unanimously elected delegate to the Convention.[1] The pressure of business led him to postpone his attendance at the Convention, and on the day of its opening a dinner was given in his honour at the Red Lion—at the time when the other delegates were celebrating in a similar way in London. But nevertheless he was active in propagating Chartist ideas in the three shires of West Wales, and in collecting signatures for the Petition. He hoped that Merthyr would supply 12,000 signatures.[2] He published a penny pamphlet *Exposition of the Principles and Objects of the Working Men's Associations*, written by himself, which was very widely circulated.[3] He sent William Jenkins around the villages of Carmarthenshire and even into Pembrokeshire. At Narberth the usual device of preventing the town crier from announcing the meeting was resorted to, but the inhabitants enthusiastically adopted the Petition. Already the countryside (the scene of the first Rebecca riots some months later) was in turmoil, for an attempt had just been made to burn down the new workhouse. From Narberth, Jenkins proceeded to Haverfordwest, Pembroke, Pater, and Fishguard.[4] In Cardiganshire, also, Aberayron was being reported 'a restless, radical town', and an attempt to hold a Chartist meeting at Adpar (Newcastle Emlyn) was prevented by the magistrates.[5] It was not until 10 May that Hugh Williams appeared at the Convention. He was introduced by Lovett, and took his seat as delegate for Carmarthen and Swansea only, for some misunderstanding

[1] *Silurian,* 19 Jan. 1839.
[2] Ibid., 16 Feb. 1839; Add. MSS. 34245 A. Letter from H. Williams, 4 Feb. 1839.
[3] *Silurian,* 19 Jan. 1839; H.O. 40/46.
[4] *Silurian,* 16 Feb. 1839; *Charter,* 24 Feb. 1839.
[5] H.O. 40/46, Letters 2 May 1839, 8 May 1839.

had arisen between him and the Merthyr Chartists.[1] He played very little part in the Convention, his services being already required elsewhere to defend the Llanidloes rioters.

The incident, however, in the winter of 1838–9, which was most far-reaching in its results, was the first appearance in Monmouthshire of Henry Vincent, the Chartist missionary. He was a young man, twenty-five years of age, and his astonishing eloquence had already earned him the title of the 'young Demosthenes', bestowed upon him by no less a judge than Sir William Molesworth. He obtained remarkable sway over the men of Monmouthshire—he never seems to have visited Glamorganshire—and undoubtedly it was his eloquence which led to the enormous increase in the Chartist ranks early in the new year, while it was his imprisonment which led the workers to extreme actions later on. Unlike most of the Chartist leaders, he was also a feminist, and his youth, good looks, and beautiful singing voice made him a great favourite with the women's organizations. His first appearance was at Pontnewynydd, near Pontypool, on New Year's Day, when Frost was adopted delegate from Pontypool. The meeting had been widely advertised by placards, and both Feargus O'Connor and Hugh Williams were included in the list of speakers, but neither seems to have been present. Some 7,000 marched in procession to the hustings erected near a beerhouse where the local W.M.A. met. Edwards the baker was voted to the chair, and expounded the points of the Charter. According to a hostile witness he declared that no doubt many lives would be lost before the Charter was gained, and that he was prepared to sacrifice his own. He was followed by Frost, whose theme, as usual, was the expense of the

[1] *True Scotsman*, 14 May 1839; Add. MSS. 34245 A, Letter of Morgan Williams, 15 May 1839.

administration. The 130 privy councillors received £630,000 a year in pensions and places—more than was paid in taxes by Monmouthshire, Glamorganshire, and Breconshire. The queen's income amounted to £510,000 a year. Among other expenses were £1,000 a year paid to each of the queen's twelve grooms of the bedchamber—twelve great strapping fellows about Her Majesty's bedchamber. And what did they do for their money? If you heard of a gentleman wanting a groom, said Frost, you knew he wanted some one to clean his horses, but what these chaps did for the queen he was at a loss to say. This sally was greeted with great applause. Vincent followed with an impassioned speech about the corruption of the drunkards, gamblers, money grinders, and tyrants in Parliament. Would not the men of Wales assist those of London, Yorkshire, Lancashire, and the West of England to get the Charter? The soldiers would not fire on them, for half of them were Chartists. The workers had been held down long enough. They had the shopkeepers on top of them, the shopkeepers had the farmers, the farmers had the parsons, the parsons had the lawyers, the lawyers had the army and the government, and on top of them all there was a pretty little bauble, the crown. But when the word 'now' was said in London the people would lay hands on its foundation, and the whole structure would totter and reel until down it would fall. With his incomparable oratory Vincent roused the crowd to a high pitch of enthusiasm and there was prolonged and tremendous cheering when he sat down.[1]

This meeting, in addition to the confirmation of Frost's appointment as delegate, had two important results, the one immediate, and the other delayed for some six months.

[1] H.O. 40/46; Newport Museum MSS. Depositions of David Jones and John Lewis Llewellyn; *Silurian*, 12 Jan. 1839; *Merlin*, 23 Nov. 1839; *Merthyr Guardian*, 4 Apr. 1840.

John Frost

The immediate result was Frost's controversy with Lord John Russell. On 16 January, Fox Maule, an under-secretary of State, wrote to Frost at Lord John Russell's direction asking him whether it was true that he was a delegate to a body calling itself 'The National Convention', and whether he had attended a meeting at Pontypool, at which 'violent and inflammatory language' had been used. If reports to this effect were true then it would be incumbent on the Home Secretary to recommend to the Lord Chancellor the erasure of Frost's name from the commission of the peace for the county of Monmouth. To this Frost produced a resounding reply which deserves quotation in full.

'Newport, Monmouthshire, 19 Jan. 1839.

'My Lord—In your lordship's letter of the 16th there is a mistake. I am not a magistrate for the county of Monmouth, but for the borough of Newport, in the county of Monmouth.

'In the spring of 1835, the council of the borough recommended me as a proper person to be a justice of the peace. I was appointed, and I believe that the inhabitants will bear honourable testimony as to the manner in which I have performed the duties of that office. Whether your lordship will retain my name or cause it to be erased, is to me a matter of perfect indifference, for I set no value on an office dependent for its continuance, not according to the mode in which its duties are performed, but on the will of a Secretary of State.

'For what does your lordship think it incumbent to get my name erased from the commission of the peace? For attending a meeting at Pontypool on the 1st of January? If the public papers can be credited, your lordship declared that such meetings were not only legal but commendable. But "violent and inflammatory language was used at the meeting". By whom? Not by me. I deny that violent and inflammatory language was used, and I call on your lordship to prove the truth of the charge. I will go further and say, that at no meeting at which I was present was violent and inflammatory language used. There was a time when the Whig Ministry was not so fastidious as to violent and inflammatory language uttered at public meetings.

'By what authority does your lordship assume a power over conduct of mine unconnected with my office? By what authority does your lordship assign any action of mine as a private individual, as a justification for erasing my name from the commission of the peace? Am I to hold no opinion of my own in respect to public matters? Am I to be prohibited from expressing that opinion if it be unpleasing to Lord J. Russell? If in expressing that opinion I act in strict conformity to the law, can it be an offence? If I transgress, is not the law sufficient to punish me? It appears from the letter of your lordship that I, if present at a public meeting, should be answerable for language uttered by others. If these are to be the terms on which Her Majesty's commission of the peace is to be holden, take it back again, for surely none but the most servile of men would hold it on such terms.

'Is it an offence to be appointed a delegate to convey to the constituted authorities the petitions of the people? Why! my lord, have we not had for many years delegates sitting in London during the session of Parliament to superintend the presentation of petitions to enact, alter, or repeal laws? Can it be a crime for a person appointed at a public meeting, to get laid before the House of Commons a petition, praying that the legislature will restore the ancient constitution of the country? I know of no body calling itself a convention. Your lordship is aware that a convention existed at one time in this country. Your lordship is aware what that convention did, and that its acts are called glorious.

'I was appointed a justice of the peace to administer the laws within the borough of Newport. Was the appointment made that the inhabitants might benefit by the proper exercise of the authority entrusted to me? Or was it made to be recalled at the will of your lordship, although the inhabitants might be perfectly satisfied with the performance of the duty? Your lordship receives a very large sum of money for holding the office of Secretary of State, paid, in part, out of the taxes raised on the inhabitants of the borough. Does your lordship owe them no duty? For what is your lordship invested with authority? To be exercised merely at the caprice of your lordship, regardless of the effects that may follow? I have served the inhabitants for three years zealously and gratuitously, and the opinions which I have formed as to the exercise of public authority teach me that they, and not your lordship, ought to decide whether I ought to be struck off the commission of the peace.

'Filling an humble situation in life, I would yield, neither to your lordship nor to any of your order, in a desire to see my country powerful and prosperous. Twenty years' reading and experience have convinced me that the only method to produce and secure that state of things, is a restoration of the ancient constitution. Deeply impressed with this conviction, I have laboured to obtain the end by means recognized by the laws of my country—petition; and for this your lordship thinks I ought to be stricken off the commission of the peace! Violent and inflammatory language, indeed! I am convinced that in my own neighbourhood my attending public meetings has tended to restrain violent language. Does your lordship wish that the peace should be preserved? I have always been a preserver of the peace, and of this your lordship may be convinced by applying to the duke of Beaufort and Lord Granville Somerset.

'Probably your lordship is unaccustomed to language of this description; that, my lord, is a misfortune. Much of the evils of life proceeds from the want of sincerity in those who hold converse with men in authority. Simple men like those best, who prophesy smooth things.

I remain yours,
JOHN FROST.'

Certainly Lord John Russell was unaccustomed to language of this description, and his reply to Frost was almost an apology. He disclaimed any intention to interfere with Frost's opinions, but still held that Frost should have intervened to discourage the use of violent language by others. He welcomed the assurance that the Convention was merely a committee to watch over the presentation of a petition to Parliament, and concluded by stating that no immediate steps would be taken with

regard to Frost's position as a magistrate.[1] But the correspondence was published in the newspapers and created
a sensation. No minister of State had been addressed in
such terms before by a mere justice of the peace. Lord
John's diminutive person and squeaky voice rendered
him at all times open to ridicule, and this was now
poured upon him. The Tories were delighted by the
encounter, and spoke of the Home Secretary as being
'frost-bitten'.[2] They enjoyed the allusions to Whig
violence in the agitation for reform, to the Glorious
Revolution of 1688, which the Whigs so often referred to,
and to Lord John Russell's address at Liverpool in
September in defence of freedom of speech and of public
meetings. Frost's letter found an echo even in Court
circles, but his notoriety there did not last long, for it was
quickly displaced by the greatest Court scandal of the
century. This was the case of Lady Flora Hastings, a
maiden lady-in-waiting to the Duchess of Kent. She was
suffering from a complaint which gossip wrongly dia-
gnosed as pregnancy, with the result that the Virgin Queen
refused to allow her to appear at Court without a medical
examination, and of the complaint and the calumny the
poor woman died. The matter first became generally
discussed towards the end of January, and in comparison
with it the affair of a magistrate of Newport lacked
piquancy, so that Frost's name was quickly forgotten.

[1] The whole correspondence is to be found in *Annual Register*, 1839
(Chronicle), pp. 22–6.
[2] *Merthyr Guardian*, 16 Feb. 1839.

V

THE CONVENTION

IF Frost's fame at Court did not last long, the reputation he had gained amongst his new associates was enormous. At one leap he had reached the forefront among the Chartist leaders. He was now in demand as a speaker outside his own area, and towards the end of January he accompanied Vincent to a great demonstration at Brandon Hill, Bristol.[1] But the time had come for him to take his seat at the National Convention, and he travelled up to London in time for the opening meeting on 4 February. Here he was received with éclat. Fifty-three deputies had been elected, although some of them never took their seats, and, in fact, fifty was the maximum number which could have met without rendering the Convention liable to prosecution for seditious meeting. Most of the delegates were, of necessity, men with no experience in public matters, so that Frost, quite apart from his sudden fame, would have been destined to play a prominent part in the proceedings of the Convention in view of his knowledge of municipal government. Moreover he was a magistrate (the only one among the delegates apart from Bailie Craig of Kilmarnock), and this conferred dignity upon the Convention itself. He regarded his duties with great seriousness. He was constant in his attendance and spoke at most of the meetings. As early as the third day he was appointed chairman for the day, and he was elected immediately to committees to draw up rules and regulations for the procedure of the Convention, to consider the course of action to be taken, and for various other purposes. No doubt much time was wasted, as it was at the beginning of the National Assembly in France, in discussing footling

[1] *Merthyr Guardian*, 2 Feb. 1839; *The Times*, 5 Feb. 1839.

questions, such as the pay of the doorkeeper, and this was due both to the inexperience of the delegates and to the lack of a sense of humour. Frost, himself, never seems to have followed his colleagues in imitating the silliness of members of Parliament by placing M.C. (Member of the Convention) after his name.

At the opening meeting Frost reported that 5,500 signatures to the Petition had been obtained in his area, and he handed over £10 as a contribution towards the national rent.[1] He was thanked by the assembly for the 'manly and spirited rebuke' he had administered to the Home Secretary. He was no doubt elated by all this, and was still somewhat excited when he proceeded in the evening to a three and sixpenny dinner at Marylebone, arranged for members of the Convention by the West London Democratic Association. The great Feargus O'Connor himself took the chair, and Frost responded to the toast: 'The people is the only source of political power.' He had now been a reformer, he said, for twenty years, and at last the people of Wales were stirred up to demand the right of making their own laws. In the last three months twenty branches of the W.M.A. had been formed in Monmouthshire alone, with a membership of between 15,000 and 20,000. A few days ago he had received a letter from Lord John Russell to the effect that if he should perform his duties as a delegate, his name would be erased from the commission of the peace. 'However, here I am, a delegate and a magistrate,' said Frost, amid great applause, 'and if Lord John Russell takes my name off, the people will put it on.'[2]

Without any doubt what Frost had in mind in making this statement was that magistrates ought to be, and soon would be, popularly elected, a reform which he had

[1] Add. MSS. 27821, p. 143.
[2] *Merthyr Guardian*, 9 Feb.; *The Charter*, 10 Feb.; *Merlin*, 16 Feb.

advocated for a number of years.[1] But the remark was obviously capable of a revolutionary interpretation, and the Home Secretary was forced to act. He was still smarting from the taunts of Tory members who had urged him to publish the previous correspondence, and to whom he had replied that Frost had admitted attending meetings at which violent speeches had been made, but had stated that he was not answerable for such language and did not approve of it.[2] On 12 February, therefore, his under-secretary wrote to Frost requesting information as to whether the above words had been used by him. Frost's reply was even more cavalier than his previous one. He again denied the authority of the Home Secretary to question him as to language which he might or might not have used as a private individual. But he, in his turn, would put a question to Lord John Russell. Was it true that Lord John had said in Parliament that Frost had admitted being present at meetings where violent language had been used? When he received his Lordship's reply he would, himself, admit or deny that he had used the language attributed to him.[3]

On the day when he wrote this reply (14 February) Frost used still more questionable language. The subject of discussion in the Convention at the time was the competence of the body itself—how far it was merely a body to supervise the presentation of a Petition to Parliament, and how far it was a Parliament in its own right. And further, should its Petition be rejected, was it entitled to defy the law and adopt 'ulterior measures', as they were called, to secure its objects? This all-important subject had been raised on the second day of the Convention, but had been deferred, and now came up for full discussion. J. P. Cobbett moved that no measures should be

---

[1] e.g. *Welchman*, 1832, p. 4.   [2] *Merlin*, 16 Feb.
[3] *Annual Register*, loc. cit.; *Merlin*, 2 Mar.

adopted which might be in contempt of the law. Vincent strongly opposed this. He ridiculed the faintheartedness of those who supported the motion. The slightest reference to the Attorney-General seemed to give them a paralytic attack. He himself had no such fears; he cared for no Attorney- or Solicitor-General. Frost, also, spoke in the same strain. Reason, he said, amidst cheers, would have no weight with the House of Commons; unless the Convention could make use of weapons other than reason, no good would be effected for the people. As for himself, he added, the authorities could not send him to any gaol in London where he had not been already, and he was willing to give the delegates the benefit of his experience. This was greeted with laughter, and Frost was evidently still vain enough to relish a reputation for diablerie. Cobbett was defeated by thirty-six votes to six, so that the Convention, together with Frost, was pledged to illegal measures. Cobbett thereupon resigned his seat.[1] He was the third son of Frost's old 'master', and to him had been written the *Letters to his Son* which formed Cobbett's *English Grammar*, the book which had commenced Frost's political education, so that his defection must have caused Frost some pain.

It was obvious that there was already a distinct cleavage in the ranks of the Chartists, and Frost's tendency was towards the extremists. Yet for a time the adherents of moral force had the upper hand, and the missionaries who were chosen by ballot at the end of February to visit the country for three weeks in order to obtain signatures for the Petition, were instructed 'to refrain from all violent and unconstitutional language, and not to infringe the law in any manner by word or deed'. Among those chosen was Frost, but he declined to serve.[2] Early in March there was

---

[1] Add. MSS. 27821; *Charter*, 17 Feb.; *Cambrian*, 23 Feb.; *Merlin*, 23 Feb.
[2] Add. MSS. 27821.

still more dissension. At a meeting of the London Democratic Society, a much more violent body than the
Working Men's Association, Harney and two other
delegates carried resolutions urging the Convention to
present the Petition without delay, and to meet all acts of
injustice and oppression with resistance. This caused
great discussion in the Convention, and only three spoke
in defence of Harney and his associates. One of these was
Frost. He claimed that the Convention had no right to
interfere with the proceedings of the Democratic Society,
and that delegates should be free to express what opinion
they pleased in a private capacity, although as delegates
they should do nothing to compromise either their constituents or the Convention.[1] This was a reasonably
moderate standpoint, and Harney and the two others
apologized.

His association with the extremists did not prevent the
W.M.A. from arranging for a dinner in honour of Frost,
'as a testimony of our approbation of his splendid rebuke to
the Secretary of State for his unconstitutional interference
with the free expression of his political opinions'.[2] But
before this took place, a still more important meeting was
held on 16 March, at the Crown and Anchor in the
Strand. At this Frost took the chair, and he announced
that its purpose was to explain to the Londoners why the
presentation of the Petition was being delayed, and to
obtain their support for the Convention. All the speakers
who followed, without exception, advocated the use of
physical force. O'Brien reported that the men of Yorkshire and Lancashire had already procured arms; if the
people of the rest of England followed their example, the
Charter would soon be won. O'Connor warned them

[1] *Charter*, 10 Mar. Cf. M. Hovell, *The Chartist Movement* (Manchester,
1918), p. 127.
[2] Add. MSS. 37773. W.M.A. Minutes, 5 Mar. and 12 Mar.

that millions of petitions would not dislodge a troop of dragoons, and that there would have to be martyrs for the cause. Harney declared that before the end of the year they would have universal suffrage or death, and many others spoke in a similar strain.[1] The sensation caused both in the press and in the Convention itself was enormous, and three Birmingham delegates immediately resigned. Two days later Frost had his dinner at the White Conduit House. The tickets cost three shillings, and there were some 200 present. It proved, said the *Northern Star*, 'a good dessert after the feast of the Crown and Anchor'. William Carpenter was in the chair, with Frost on his right hand, and the descendant of Irish kings, O'Connor, on his left. The chairman first toasted 'The People'. He attacked the Whigs and said their time was soon drawing to a close, for the people were determined to get the Charter—by moral means if possible, but, if not, then at all hazards. The second toast was 'John Frost'. They all knew of his manly conduct towards Lord John Russell. Might men in office profit from his independent example, and men in power be taught prudence from the lesson he had given them. This was drunk 'with three times three'. Frost thanked them for the honour they had done him. He still held the commission of the peace, and would hold it freely and independently or not at all. He recounted the circumstances of his appointment as a magistrate, and the service he had rendered in that capacity. He then proceeded to deal with what was now to become the chief topic of his speeches, the manner in which the Russell family had acquired its property, for Lord John now seemed to have displaced Thomas Prothero as his *bête noire*. He could promise his lordship that within less than three months every collier in Wales would know the history of Woburn Abbey and Tavistock

[1] Add. MSS. 27821; *Charter*, 24 Mar.

Priory, and every victim of the new poor law should know what obligations had been attached to these vast estates when they were acquired. O'Connor also dealt with the same subject. The poor had a right to be clothed and fed out of the produce of the lands of Woburn Abbey, for these had been bestowed on the Abbey only for purposes of hospitality. O'Connor went on to deal with the question of physical and moral force, and produced a paradox which seemed to satisfy his listeners, that they should use physical force morally. Others spoke of the battle which was approaching, but Lovett managed to introduce a more moderate note, and the evening closed with Frost proposing the health of the ladies, which also was drunk with 'three times three'.[1]

As Frost said, he was still a magistrate, but he remained so only for another three days. The Home Secretary had hesitated to take action, for to have dismissed Frost because he was a delegate would have been to pronounce the Convention illegal, a matter on which the government had not made up its mind. Moreover, he did not want to make Frost appear a martyr. But on 27 February he was again questioned in the House, and so laid the matter before the Lord Chancellor, who wrote on the next day to Frost giving him an opportunity to explain his remark on 4 February about the people's replacing him in the magistracy. For some time Frost delayed replying, and when he did so (7 March) he denied using the language attributed to him, and complained of Lord John's false statement in the House. This reply the Lord Chancellor considered far from satisfactory, but he thought it not necessary to comment on it in view of what was reported to have taken place on 14 February (the speech on 'ulterior measures') and at the Crown and Anchor two days before the date on which he was writing. Of the former the Lord

[1] Add. MSS. 27821; *The Sun*, 24 Mar.

Chancellor had authentic information; for the latter he relied on the report in the *Morning Chronicle*. He had therefore directed the commission of the peace to be sent for from Newport, but would attend to any explanation Frost might give before 12 March. If this was not satisfactory his name would be removed. Frost received this letter the day after his complimentary dinner. He immediately replied at length, denying categorically that he had used the language attributed to him on 4 February (with regard to the magistracy), accusing the Lord Chancellor of relying on a spy's report of what had taken place in the Convention on 14 February, and declaring that the *Morning Chronicle* report was false. He asked what it was he had to explain, and said that his real offence was that he had opposed a system of government which had bribery, drunkenness, and perjury for its foundation. He presented to the Lord Chancellor resolutions passed at a meeting of his fellow citizens a few days previously, and said that he valued their good opinion more than holding power under a set of men of whose conduct he would not trust himself to speak.[1]

At the first rumour of the possibility of Frost's dismissal, a memorial had been sent from Newport to the Home Secretary, highly commending Frost's personal character and public services. When the matter was raised again, some 120 persons had signed a request to the mayor to call a public meeting, but Phillips had refused to do so, stating that the purpose of the meeting was not clearly explained, and that some one might propose that 'weapons other than reason' were justified. The Chartists, therefore, held their own meeting on 5 March, and among the principal speakers were Edwards the baker, Dickenson, a butcher, and William Townsend, Junior, the son of a wine merchant, all three soon to

[1] *Merlin*, 2 Mar., 30 Mar.

135

figure very prominently in the Chartist movement. But the most striking speech of the evening was that of Benjamin Byron, minister of Hope Chapel, where Frost's family worshipped. He had known Frost for a long time, he said, and knew him as a conscientious and honest man, incapable of a mean or dishonest action. He was far better than those who vilified him, and anything in his character which they might wish to see reformed had been produced by the persecutions of which he had been the victim. Byron maintained strongly that no objection could be raised to his remark about being restored to the magistracy by the people, for all he contemplated was making the magistracy elective. Another Nonconformist minister spoke of Frost's struggle for the people, and the meeting passed resolutions, copies of which they sent to the Home Secretary, the Lord Chancellor, and to Frost.[1] These were the resolutions which Frost included in his letter of 20 March to the Lord Chancellor, but they did not help him, and on the next day he was removed from the commission of the peace, having held the office for just three years.[2] The Convention immediately presented a petition to Parliament for his reinstatement, on the ground that no charge had been distinctly assigned, apart from presiding over a meeting at which it was alleged (and that only on the authority of a newspaper notorious for its misrepresentation) that improper language had been used. The Convention stressed that this was a purely arbitrary action comparable to the interference of kings with the judges in the past, and that it was likely to reduce all magistrates to being pliant tools in the hands of the ministers. The Convention had little hope of success in presenting this petition and some opposed it as a waste of time, but it was decided to present it in order to call public attention to the affair and to force the Home

[1] *Merlin*, 9 Mar.; *Charter*, 24 Mar.   [2] *Merlin*, 23 Mar.

Secretary to publish the correspondence between him and Frost, which he seemed very reluctant to do.[1] Memorials also came from Wales and from Scotland, but without effect.[2] Frost's activities as a magistrate, in which he had taken such a pride, were at an end.

In the meantime Edwards, Etheridge, and others had toured the Monmouthshire villages to explain the Charter, and had held a demonstration at Blackwood,[3] soon to become an important centre of Chartism because of its geographical position, half-way between Newport and Merthyr. They had even captured an anti-Corn Law meeting at Newport, presided over by the Mayor. Here they had produced an amendment to a resolution in favour of repeal, declaring that the agitation against the corn law was a delusion, likely to produce more harm than good, that what was necessary was universal suffrage, and, amid considerable uproar, they had carried the amendment by an overwhelming majority.[4] On 23 February, also, had appeared the first number of the *Western Vindicator*, edited by Henry Vincent. Its publisher, Payne of Bristol, had already served two years' imprisonment for selling unstamped newspapers. It obtained a large circulation among the workers of South Wales and the west of England, who took great pride in having a paper of their own, and eagerly looked forward to every issue. To comply with the law it had to avoid dealing with 'news and occurrences', though from the third issue onwards this was obviated by publishing weekly 'The Life and Rambles of Henry Vincent' (facetiously dedicated to Queen Victoria), which incorporated much Chartist news. Most of the articles, however, were

---

[1] Add. MSS. 34245 B 214; *Charter*, 31 Mar.

[2] *True Scotsman*, 6 Apr. (Frost's reply 21 Mar. to address of Chartists of Dalkeith); *Western Vindicator*, 13 Apr. (memorial from Pontypool); *Charter*, 28 Apr. (dinner given to Frost in this connexion).

[3] 4 Feb., see *Silurian*, 16 Feb.   [4] 14 Feb., see *Merlin*, 16 Feb.

of a general nature, and there were many extracts from the writings of Volney and other liberal writers. Occasionally articles appeared in Welsh. The early issues all contained contributions from Frost. He expounded the principles of the Chartists, and dealt, as usual, with the evils of taxation and the enormous emoluments of the Royal Family and the Privy Councillors. The widow of William IV had just been granted £100,000 a year at a time when the new poor law was being stringently applied. Security of person and property did not exist for the working class who paid half their earnings in taxes, but Frost was at pains to allay the suspicions of the farmers and tradesmen of Monmouthshire that any attack would be made on their property. Yet the uselessness of petitioning Parliament to reform itself led him to become more and more heated in his expressions. Vincent was even more tendentious. He declared that unless an immediate political and social change were effected, 'a bloody revolution' must take place, and commented on the defensible nature of the South Wales valleys, which a few thousand armed men could hold.

As early as the beginning of March, the mayor of Newport was reporting to the Home Secretary that arms were being distributed, and the government was prepared to draft soldiers into the area. A few days later the mayor admitted that these reports were exaggerated. Nevertheless he noted the sullen discontent of the people, who were being incited to violence and told that they need fear no bloodshed as the soldiers would not act against them. There was nothing to cause apprehension as yet, he thought, but sooner or later this incitement would lead to illegality, which might even take the form not of isolated acts but of widespread insurrection.[1] There was considerably more excitement on 16 March when Vincent,

[1] H.O. 40/45, Letters 3 Mar. and 12 Mar.

as the official missionary of the Convention, arrived in Monmouth, on his second visit to the shire. He had come via Stroud, Lord John Russell's constituency, and had there facetiously proposed Frost as a candidate at the next election, which had been received by the people with 'deafening acclamations'.[1] At Monmouth an attempt was made to prevent him from holding a meeting, but he succeeded in forming the nucleus of a W.M.A. His fellow-missionary Burns then went on to Pontypool (nothing further is heard of his mission), and Vincent proceeded to Newport (19 March). In the evening some 3,000 to 4,000 people listened to him in an open space in the town.[2] His main theme was a denunciation of the aristocracy, and he quoted to them a whole chapter from what might seem an innocuous source, viz. Paley's *Moral Philosophy*.[3] A number of pigeons, he said, were engaged in gathering corn which they piled up into a heap. Amongst the company was one fat, lazy fellow who would not work; he sat in a corner while all the rest increased the heap, and all he did was to eat and grow fat. His fellows, however, were not content that he should fatten in idleness upon the fruits of their industry and endeavoured to get rid of him; but he called to his assistance a number of equally overgorged companions, and drove away the industrious birds, and if any poor starving pigeon dared to take a grain of his own corn he was punished with death; the fat pigeon and his helpmates feasted upon the corn and gave the labourers they drove away nothing but the chaff. That, said Vincent, was just how the working class was treated. He then referred to

[1] *Western Vindicator*, 9, 16, 23 March.

[2] Ibid., 30 March; *Silurian*, 30 March gives figure 5,000. Thomas Phillips at trial of Vincent, J. Macdonnel, *State Trials*, iii (1831–40), p. 1054, gives the figure 300, but this may be a misprint for 3,000. *Cambrian*, 29 March gives 400–500.

[3] Book III, Part 1, Chapter i, William Paley, *Works* (London, 1838) pp. 50, 51.

the growing snowball of Chartism and called upon their oppressors to beware lest it should roll down and crush them. As the barons had got Magna Charta by marching against the king, so would they obtain the Charter.

In the morning Vincent addressed one of the women's gatherings at which he was so popular, before leaving, by packet, for Bristol. But five days later (25 March) he was back again. Once more the women arranged a 'tea meeting' for him, at which he sang democratic songs, and then went in procession through the town, cheering Mrs. Frost as they passed her house. But this time his object was to go among the hills, and the next two days were devoted to meetings at Pontllanfraith and Blackwood. On the evening of 27 March he held yet another open-air meeting at Newport. Edwards the baker marshalled his forces in the town, and Vincent addressed them from a wagon placed beneath a gas lamp. He called upon them to be ready for 6 May when the petition was to be presented, and when, if their demands were not conceded, every hill and valley should be prepared to send forth its army, at the call of the Convention. He was answered by cries from the crowd of 'We will, we will', and Edwards held up his powerful arm, crying out, 'Here's the stuff'. Vincent then spoke of the mayor, and of his partner Prothero, whom he should like to see hanging from the lamp-post behind him. The next morning he left for Stroud, taking with him young William Davies of Blackwood, who was destined to play such a dubious part in the movement.

At Stroud he was met by Frost, who had, apparently in earnest, decided to oppose Lord John Russell at the next election, and had obtained a fortnight's leave of absence to visit the west country. He wrote a highly enthusiastic letter to Lovett describing his reception.[1]

---

[1] Letter dated 2 April. Add. MSS. 34345 A 195. See *Charter*, 31 March, 7 April; *Merlin*, 6 April; *Western Vindicator*, 6 April; *Cambrian*, 13 April.

There were, he said, some 10,000 present, and he had dealt at length with his dismissal from the magistracy, with the origin of the poor law, and the history of the Bedford estates. He had given the little fellow such a hammering that he was sure there was no bone left unbroken in his body, and because of the grammatical errors in the Home Secretary's letters to him, he had induced the crowd to make a farthing subscription towards presenting Little Finality with a copy of Cobbett's *Grammar*.

From Stroud, Frost came home. He found that there had been a change in his family since his departure, for on 20 March his daughter, Sarah, had been married at St. Woollos Church to Harry Fry, a surgeon of Newport, formerly of the 14th Light Dragoons. The groom was eighteen years older than his bride, and, if Frost's enemies are to be believed, his reputation was none too savoury. He had, they said, become involved with the wife of a Somersetshire attorney, and had had an action brought against him, in which the attorney had been awarded £1,000 damages. He was also, they said, a notorious gambler, and had been known to win £50 in a night—always the most difficult form of gambling to forgive.[1] In the following December, when her father was already in prison, Sarah gave birth to a son, and three years later to a daughter.

But Frost did not remain more than a week at home, and on 6 April he once more left for London. The situation was getting critical, and he felt he must be at the centre of affairs. 'These are times', he said in his letter to Lovett, 'to try men's souls', and he condemned the Birmingham delegates who wished to dissolve the Convention because of the language uttered at the Crown and

[1] Newport Museum MSS. 839. Analysis of possible witnesses for the defence.

Anchor. If people had no nerve for the coming struggle, he said, let them resign. A resolution condemning the Birmingham seceders also came from the Carmarthen W.M.A. At a public meeting the Carmarthen Chartists declared openly that oppression justified resistance, that what was right warranted all expedients adopted to secure it, and that any force which could be conjured up should be used.[1] An incident had just occurred which greatly embittered the Chartists. This was the first riot in the west in connexion with the movement, and it was caused, it should be noticed, not by the Chartists but by their opponents. Vincent had left Stroud for Devizes, accompanied by W. P. Roberts, a Bath solicitor, who five years later became the standing legal adviser of the Miner's Association and became popularly known as the 'Miner's Attorney-General.' A great demonstration had been arranged at Devizes for Easter Monday (1 April), and there was great excitement in the town, as it was rumoured that the Chartists would be armed. The magistrates had issued notices forbidding the meeting, but in spite of this, and although it was a very wet day, the Chartists arrived in the afternoon with their banners flying and their band playing. Special constables together with the Yeomanry and the 14th Lancers were there to greet them, and no sooner had Vincent and Roberts mounted their wagon than the attack began. Vincent was struck on the head with a stone which knocked him clean out of the wagon, and it was with difficulty that the leaders retreated to the Curriers' Arms. The crowd then threatened to burn down the inn, and Vincent had to ask the high sheriff for an escort to leave the town, but he 'did not consider it prudent to comply'. Eventually, however, they managed to leave without further molestation. Vincent complained bitterly that accounts of the affair had

[1] Report of 15 April meeting in *Charter*, 5 May.

been distorted. The Chartists, he said, were not armed, but
the lesson of Devizes was plain; they must provide themselves with arms for self-defence, and he recommended them
to carry constables' staffs.[1] Vincent was seriously injured.
He was therefore not able to return immediately to Wales
to address, with Frost, a meeting at Pontypool on 5 April,
and as Frost decided to hasten his departure for London,
William Edwards proceeded alone to Pontypool, where
he delivered a very violent speech.[2]

The growing seriousness of the situation was indicated
by the appearance of the first issues of the *London Democrat*
edited by the firebrand, Harney, and containing articles
on military service by a mysterious Polish refugee in
London, Major Beniowski. From mid Wales, also, there
came reports of arming. At the opening meeting of the
Convention, Charles Jones, the delegate from the three
towns, had handed over £37 towards the national rent,
a fairly large sum when compared with the £10 from
Newport, Caerleon and Pontypool.[3] He had immediately
returned to his constituency, and, on 1 April, had asked
the Convention to send a missionary to the district.[4] The
choice very naturally fell upon Hetherington, for he was
a staunch disciple of Robert Owen of Newtown, and a
personal friend of Hugh Williams and of Thomas Powell.
At Welshpool he found that the cause was not flourishing;
the influence of Powis Castle was no doubt too strong.
The people of Newtown were far more enthusiastic, and
he reported with some anxiety to the Convention that they
were all physical force men. He had been told that an
order for 300 muskets had been sent to Birmingham, and
that one man had been prosecuted 'for having carried on

---

[1] Add. MSS. 34245 A 228; *Western Vindicator*, 6 April; *Cambrian*, 13 April.
[2] *Western Vindicator*, 20 April.
[3] Add. MSS. 27821, p. 143; 34245, B. 219.
[4] Add. MSS. 34245, A. 185.

an extensive manufactory of pikes in the town'. When his report was given in the Convention (Frost being in the Chair) this was greeted with cheers, but Hetherington himself was a moral force man, and he seems to have tried to curb the violence of the textile workers. Not so Charles Jones. At the Newtown meeting (9 April) he made a most violent speech. 'If Lord John Russell, and those with whom he acts will by their perversity drive us to the edge of the precipice', he said, 'and if we must take the leap, then, by Heaven, we will take it.'[1] Others advocated a run on the banks, and a refusal to pay taxes. All were convinced that 'it must end in a fight' and were prepared to support the Convention in any way that was required. From Newtown Hetherington proceeded to Llanidloes, where he found 600 men enrolled in the Association, half of whom were well armed. The men of the villages nearby were equally enthusiastic, and Hetherington was told that they all regarded affixing their signature in the same light as the shilling which the recruit received when entering the king's service. This, again, was greeted with cheers in the Convention, but Hetherington had thought it necessary to repeat to the people the instructions given to the missionaries to discourage everything illegal. He had then proceeded to Rhayader, where he found the people engaged in dedicating a new Baptist chapel, a ceremony lasting over two days. But the Baptist minister had allowed him to announce his meeting in the chapel, and had postponed the evening service for his benefit. He then held another very crowded meeting at Newtown (12 April). At Welshpool he once more failed to get a public room, through the intervention of the mayor, and the Tories tried to break up an open-air meeting, though without success. Hetherington then left for Shrewsbury and London, where

---

[1] *Shrewsbury News*, 13 April, quoted in Miss Myfanwy Williams's unpublished thesis.

he presented his report to the Convention on 25 April.[1]
Four days later the outbreak at Llanidloes had begun.

In Monmouthshire the opponents of Chartism were
taking measures to defend themselves. On 12 April
a widely advertised meeting of the Yeomanry of twenty
parishes was held at the Royal Oak, Christchurch, some
three miles from Newport on the Chepstow road. Its
purpose was to present an address of loyalty to the queen,
indicating the attachment of the yeomen to the monarchy
and the constitution, and their determination to show this
attachment by upholding the institutions of the country,
at the hazard, if necessary, of all that was dear to them.
The chairman was William Phillips of Whitson, a magistrate of the county, but the prime mover was the mayor
of Newport, Thomas Phillips, and when the address of
loyalty had been carried it was he who moved the second
resolution. He did not wish to proscribe any one's opinions,
he said, but the yeomen were not going to be dictated to,
and the present state of things, when resistance to the law
was inculcated as a duty, and the settlement of property
was threatened, could not be tolerated. Those who had
a stake in the country, men who had property to lose,
the fruits of honest industry, were not to be deterred from
protecting it by the fear of a pike in the heart or a halter
round the neck. He therefore moved an address to the
Lord Lieutenant offering to enrol themselves in any form
of which the government might approve in defence of the
constitution, and this was carried unanimously. The vote
of thanks to the chairman was seconded, surprisingly
enough, by Harry Fry, the son-in-law of John Frost, and
the chairman responded by 'recommending them to keep
their powder dry, and to make their horses stand fire'.[2]

---

[1] The report is given in full in *Charter*, 28 April; *Lovett Collection*, ii. 2.
[2] *Merlin*, 6 April; *Cambrian*, 19 April; *Charter*, 21 April; *Western Vindicator*,
27 April, 3 Aug.

This was as tendentious a remark as ever Frost had made while he was a magistrate, and it is no wonder that the *Merlin* omitted it from its report. This address, the Lord Lieutenant, Capel Hanbury Leigh, forwarded to the Home Office on 1 May, and he immediately received a reply that the gentlemen might form themselves into an association, and that arms would be supplied to them. This was undoubtedly a most unstatesmanlike action, for at the very time when complaints were being made that one class was arming, the government deliberately supplied arms to its opponents. The class struggle was thus intensified, although the only rioting so far had been that of the anti-chartists at Devizes. It would have been far wiser to have used the regular troops to preserve order, and the Lord Lieutenant wisely kept the arms for some time after they had arrived at his office, in order not to inflame the feelings of the workers. But the history of the association was not a happy one, for several members withdrew in disgust when they found that they were to be only armed special constables, and not cavalry acting under Her Majesty's commission, and William Phillips of Whitson (as Blewitt spitefully reported to the Home Office) 'retired to the continent for protection against the sneers liberally dispensed towards him in consequence of his failing to be invested with the title of Major Commandant to which he had been elected'.[1]

By 18 April Vincent was sufficiently recovered from his injuries to resume his mission in South Wales. He arrived by the packet from Bristol, and was met on landing by his faithful henchmen Etheridge and Edwards. At an open-air meeting in the evening Townsend took the chair, and Vincent delivered a bitter attack on the aristocracy. They looked upon the Chartists with contempt, he said, but when the time arrived for the Chartists to rise, such

[1] H.O. 40/45, several entries.

a blow would be struck as in twenty-four hours would decide their fate. He then went on to declare that the workers were not bound by the laws, as they were made by men in the election of whom they had no voice. On the next evening Edwards rounded up his men, and Vincent delivered another stirring speech. He once more assured his listeners that the soldiers would not act against them, and ended with the words: 'When the time for resistance arrives, let your cry be, "To your tents, O Israel" and then with one voice, one heart, and one blow perish the privileged orders! Death to the aristocracy! Up with the people and the Government they have established!' As was usual when Vincent was present, the meeting closed peacefully with three cheers for their sweethearts, their wives and themselves,[1] but the excitement in Newport was now enormous. The people knew their Scriptures well enough to realize that the biblical quotation (1 Kings xii, 16) referred to the revolt of the tribes against their king. The mayor reported to the Home Office that he did not as yet fear violence unless an accidental collision occurred. Some 200 householders, however, had signed a requisition to him to adopt measures to preserve the peace of the town. He thought that Vincent's concluding remarks were illegal, but doubted if he could get witnesses to swear to them, and thought that it would be necessary in future to employ reporters who came from a distance. To this, the Home Office replied that the meetings were undoubtedly illegal, and that Vincent could be apprehended if sufficient evidence could be obtained. At the same time the Home Office issued orders for the despatch of troops into the area.[2]

Vincent, accompanied by Edwards, had proceeded to Pontypool (20 April). Here the chair was taken by another

[1] *State Trials*, loc. cit.; *Merlin*, 20 April.
[2] H.O. 40/45; *Merlin*, 27 April.

147

Chartist agitator—Jones, 'the watchmaker'. William Jones was a young man of thirty. He was the illegitimate son of a Bristol tradesman, and claimed that he had been harshly treated in his youth (he frequently compared himself to Richard Savage). He had abandoned his trade of watchmaker, and taken to the stage, but without much success. So, in 1833, he settled in Pontypool, once more as a watchmaker, and there he married and set up a business of his own. His late employer indicted him for embezzlement, but agreed to the matter's being settled as a debt. Jones was an early exponent of Chartism. The local W.M.A. met at the Bristol House Beer Shop which he kept in addition to his business, and he was in the habit of addressing other branches in the neighbourhood. The only letter of his which has survived is full of long words, wrongly spelt, and this is probably indicative of his rhetorical style of speaking. It is difficult to avoid thinking that he was a misfortune to the Chartist movement.[1]

The Pontypool meeting was on a Saturday. On Sunday Vincent was back at Newport, and he and the leading Chartists attended divine service at St. Paul's Church. The sermon which they heard from the Reverend James Francis was especially for their benefit. Those who attempted to use force to alter the laws, he told them, differed little from those who entertained ideas of wilful murder. To resist the power of the State was to resist the ordinance of God. As long as men firmly believed that there was a hell where the wicked should be eternally damned, and a heaven in which the contented Christian should be everlastingly rewarded, so long those who desired to spread popular discontent knew they could make no progress,

[1] Dowling, *Rise and Fall of Chartism in Monmouthshire* (Newport, 1840), p. 89; *Merlin*, 27 April; Newport Museum MSS., 582; Jones's letter is reproduced in *Merlin*, 25 July 1840.

and so they had had recourse to the daring expedient of shaking the religious faith of the people. Wild beasts, he said, were gentle compared with those who had lost all religious hope and fear. And not only was resistance to the law contrary to divine will; so also was discontent with one's lot in society. It was God's decree that the situation should be such as it was, and he cited for them the fortitude of a boy who was both deaf and dumb, and who had managed (in spite of his affliction) to convey to others his belief that it was the will of God. He called upon the working class to ponder seriously on the evil courses into which wicked and designing men were hurrying them. In spite of the nature of this sermon, which friends urged the Reverend Mr. Francis to publish, the Chartists conducted themselves in a highly decorous manner.[1]

On Monday Vincent and Edwards were at Blackwood. Here their chairman was an extraordinary person, Dr. William Price, of Newbridge (i.e. Pontypridd), who delivered a lengthy speech in Welsh, which was loudly cheered. According to Vincent, it was full of eloquence and argument, and of quotations from Thomas Paine.[2] Dr. Price (who was to play a mysterious part in the November rising) was then thirty-nine years of age. He was, without question, a remarkable surgeon, but he was an eccentric. He had long, flowing black hair and a beard which he never cut, and it was rumoured that he had exhumed the body of his father and decapitated it, to prove that the old man had received an injury to his skull in his youth, which had rendered him *non compos mentis* and therefore incapable of making a will. Forty-five years later he attained wide notoriety. To his son by his housekeeper he gave the name of Jesus Christ, and when the infant died he attempted to burn its body. An enraged crowd interfered, and Price was indicted at

---

[1] *Merlin*, 27 April.   [2] *Western Vindicator*, 4 May.

the next assizes, but Sir James Fitz-James Stephen ruled, after full consideration, that a person who burned instead of burying a dead body did not commit a criminal act, and cremation was thus legalized.[1] That, however, was in the distant future, and before then Dr. Price had experienced many and varied adventures.

From Blackwood Vincent and Edwards went to Nantyglo in north Monmouthshire, the site of Crawshay Bailey's great ironworks. On the way they met Bailey himself, who threatened to have Vincent thrown into a pond if he dared to speak to 'his' men, but the flippant Chartist routed him by asking him whether he was a physical force conservative.[2] A mile or so lower down the valley, the missionaries held another meeting at the Royal Oak Inn, Coalbrookvale (Blaina), whose landlord, Zephaniah Williams, was the third leader in the November rising. He was, said Vincent, 'one of the most intelligent men it has ever been my good fortune to meet.[3] He was a native of Argoed (Bedwellty), and was now forty-four years of age. His elegant handwriting seems to indicate that he was a well-educated and even fastidious man,[4] and the letters which he wrote from his exile show a very remarkable sense of style. His occupation (in addition to innkeeping) was that of a master collier or mineral agent, a fact which was to prove of the utmost importance to him in Van Diemen's Land. But he had gained great notoriety as a free-thinker, and was the most hated of the Chartist leaders. His enemies repeated on every available occasion the story that he kept in his house a picture of the crucifixion, with the enigmatic words written beneath it: 'This is the man who stole the ass.' This accusation he never seems to have taken the trouble to refute, but in 1831 he

[1] Obituary notice in *Cardiff Weekly News*, 28 Jan. 1893.
[2] *Western Vindicator*, loc. cit.; *Merlin*, 27 April.
[3] *Western Vindicator*, loc. cit.
[4] H.O. 40/45, Petition to the Queen, 21 Dec. 1839.

had published a letter to a Reverend Benjamin Williams who had attacked him for leading the people astray. This pamphlet shows him to have been a good controversialist. He pointed out how his opponent's accusation was inconsistent with his belief in predestination, and he produced a very capable defence of the rationalist standpoint. Moreover, he was not averse to having a thrust at his enemies. 'Those who distrust reason in matters of faith', he said, 'deem its free and unshackled exercise, notwithstanding all their concessions in their pious moods, as of essential importance in worldly matters, in which they forget not to use the wisdom of serpents, however wanting in the innocence of doves.' Like Frost and Jones, he had figured in the law courts. He had been charged at the Usk Quarter Sessions in 1832 for having assaulted a petty constable, and hindered him in the execution of a warrant and the performance of his duty, but had been acquitted. Like Frost, also, he had crossed swords with Thomas Prothero, who had indicted him and three others with 'unlawfully and riotously demolishing a certain erection and a waggon way used in a mine', but the judge had ruled that there was no justification for such a serious charge and had dismissed the case.[1] It was at his house that the local W.M.A. met, as well as the Female Chartist Society, and here it was that Vincent spoke. Young Joseph Bailey (the candidate for the Monmouth boroughs) tried to trap him into admitting that he was a republican, presumably in order to make it possible to bring a charge of sedition against him, but Vincent replied that what he desired was

---

[1] *A Letter to Benjamin Williams*, 1831; Newport Museum MSS., Solicitor General's Brief, and description for reward for capture; Usk MSS., Recognisances Epiphany Sessions, 1832, gives charge re assault—he was charged with two others, one of whom was sentenced to two months' hard labour; in July 1824 he had charged a servant for misdemeanour (July Sessions)—he was then described as coal agent; *Merthyr Guardian*, 13 Apr., 1839 for Prothero's charge.

to extend to the people the power of making their own laws, so that then they could choose what form of government they liked. The crowd threatened to manhandle Bailey, and Vincent had to interpose to prevent his being hurt.[1] The following day (24 April) Vincent and Edwards were again at Pontypool before returning to Newport.

Here the mayor was making active preparations in view of the probability that Vincent would hold another meeting on the 25th. On the 24th he called together both the borough and county magistrates to the King's Head, and a notice was immediately issued signed by the mayor and his two Newport colleagues. This declared that meetings had been held in the town where resistance to the law was advised, and that large numbers of people had attended them late in the evening and had paraded through the streets in circumstances likely to endanger the public peace. Such meetings were therefore declared illegal, and publicans were also enjoined not to allow them to be held in their houses. Special constables were then sworn in at the office of the clerk to the magistrates, Thomas Jones Phillips. Nevertheless Vincent had an address printed calling a meeting for the evening of the 25th, and, according to his account, some 8,000 attended. (The mayor put the figure at about 1,000, with 'spectators' in addition.) They first paraded through the streets, singing 'Britons never will be slaves'. Then Dickenson took the chair, and Vincent proceeded to question the legality of the mayor's injunction. He declared that the only illegal meeting had been that of Christchurch where the yeomen had been admonished to keep their powder dry. The injunction was merely an expedient, because the Whigs and Tories had not been able to find anything illegal in the actions of the Chartists, and he challenged the magistrates to arrest him. Even the very hostile

[1] *Merlin*, loc. cit.

Merlin had to pay tribute to his remarkable oratorical powers on this occasion. But the magistrates did not arrest him, and on the next day he addressed the crowd again from a window in Frost's house and on the quay, before departing with Townsend for another moonlight demonstration at Brandon Hill, Bristol.[1]

Frost regarded the magistrates' handbill as a 'declaration of war'. He denied that any violence had been contemplated, or any attack on property, and quoted his favourite authors to show that resistance to the law had been justified by some of the greatest lawyers.[2] The attitude of the Home Office was curious. The depositions of witnesses had been forwarded by Thomas Jones Phillips, but much of the evidence the Home Office's legal adviser rejected out of hand as 'of no use', 'much too general', mere 'hearsay', and 'not sufficient to prove sedition'. He strongly advised against calling one witness because his evidence proved that the purpose of the Chartists' weapons was 'to protect themselves'. He concluded that the evidence as to seditious and inflammatory speeches was 'very loose and weak', while that as to the use of offensive weapons was 'weak and scanty', but he believed there was sufficient ground for declaring the meetings illegal, and therefore for apprehending Vincent. Yet he did not think it prudent to direct such a proceeding when there was great danger of not having sufficient evidence to support a prosecution, and he wished to have the opinion of the law officers of the Crown as to the legality of the meetings. In view of the class feeling which had been roused in Monmouthshire and which made it almost impossible to conduct a fair trial, this considered opinion of a detached legal adviser is of the utmost importance, but actually

---

[1] H.O. 40/45; *Rise and Fall*, p. 25; *Merlin*, loc. cit.; *Merthyr Guardian*, 27 Apr.; *Cambrian*, 3 May; *Western Vindicator*, loc. cit.; *State Trials*, loc. cit.
[2] *Western Vindicator*, 27 Apr.

some days before it had been obtained, the mayor had been informed by the Home Office that the meetings were illegal, and authorization to prosecute was now sent in spite of it.[1]

The situation was becoming more and more serious. Rumours of the manufacture of pikes, and of hawkers who made a profitable trade out of selling arms among the hills, found their way into the newspapers,[2] although they were violently denied by the Chartists.[3] To counteract Vincent's influence a great anti-Chartist demonstration was held at Coalbrookvale on 29 April. Both the Whig and Tory newspapers, in agreement on this matter in spite of their bitter rivalry on all others, estimated that there were as many as 5,000 present. Crawshay Bailey, very naturally, was voted to the chair. He delivered a truculent speech. His property, he said, was the result of his own industry, and he would sacrifice his life rather than lose it. What, he asked, had the valley been fifty years before, and how much capital could Vincent and the Newport baker lay out to develop it? The argument about taxation he considered erroneous, for the taxes returned in benefits to the working class, just as the tide flowed up the rivers. There were many speakers, both in Welsh and English, among them Zephaniah Williams's opponent, the Reverend Benjamin Williams. Much was made of the fact that the agitators were Englishmen who had come among the Welshmen of Monmouthshire, and who were paid three or four pounds a week for their work. Poverty was due, it was claimed, not to taxation, but to the improvidence of the poor. The gentlemen on the platform, said the Reverend Benjamin Williams, were the best friends of the working class; the Chartists were their worst foes. There were, in addition, many references to Zepha-

---

[1] H.O. 40/45. [2] *Merlin*, 20 Apr.; *Cambrian*, 26 Apr.
[3] Etheridge in *Silurian*, 11 May.

niah Williams's blasphemy and Frost's bankruptcy, and the day closed with a resolution to support the just prerogative of the Crown and the constitutional privileges of Parliament.[1] Two replies to this demonstration were forthcoming. One was a very lengthy address from the radicals of Merthyr Tydfil. The return of the taxes to the working class in the way of benefits, it described as hypocritical cant. A few weeks' sickness made a workman liable to get the bed on which he lay taken away from him, or to be separated from his family in a bastille. Opposition between the employers and their workers, it said, was growing. They had suppressed the torch-light meetings of the latter, but the workers still had burning torches in their hearts; would they put these out?—'Let the plague spot, Lord John Russell, answer.'[2] The second reply was a very able one from Zephaniah Williams. Abusive speeches had been made about him, but he could not see how his difficulty in accepting a belief in revelation invalidated the argument for universal suffrage. He believed that there had existed a historic person, Christ, so good, pure, and disinterested that had he lived in Coalbrookvale his house would have been pulled down over his head long ago. He himself could easily have passed off as a Christian if he had not been imprudent enough to advance his opinions, and he noticed that his opponents had not drawn attention to the fact that God made his Son poor, and yet a *representative* of all mankind. He accused the employers of secretly prompting violence and hoping for disturbances, so that they might make the place a second Devizes.[3]

[1] *Report of Anti-Chartist Meeting, Coalbrookvale* (Monmouth, 1839); *Merlin*, 4 May. (These two reports are identical, although the *Merlin* frequently made scurrilous references to the *Monmouthshire Beacon* which printed the separate report.) *Cambrian*, 13 May, notes presentation of the address to the queen by Joseph Bailey, junior.

[2] *The Operative*, 12 May; Add. MSS. 27821, p. 112.

[3] Letter in *Silurian*, 15 June.

On the day of the Coalbrookvale meeting, Hugh Williams forwarded the signatures to the Petition from South Wales, in preparation for 6 May. They were 27,147 in all, and their distribution is interesting. Glamorganshire accounted for 18,884, of which 14,710 were from Merthyr Tydfil, the remainder being mainly from Swansea. The number for Carmarthenshire was 6,144, but of these only 1,043 were from the borough. Pembrokeshire and Cardiganshire accounted for 1,103 and 1,026 respectively.[1] The deputy mayor of Swansea, an ex-army man, had informed the people that if there was a disturbance, he would use fire-arms 'to pick Hugh Williams off', and he now wrote to the Home Office to ask for troops or a sloop-of-war with marines.[2] But the disturbances, which occurred with unexpected suddenness and violence, took place not in West Wales but in Montgomeryshire. There, 3,461 had signed the Petition.[3] Hetherington's report that they were arming (read to the Convention 25 April), seems to have been quite accurate. Young Chartists at Llanidloes began to visit neighbouring farms to 'borrow' muskets ostensibly for a shooting-match, and the farmers dared not refuse them. Secret drilling was also taking place. The magistrates therefore wrote to the Home Secretary for troops, and he, pestered with similar demands from all parts of the country, contented himself with sending down three London policemen, to arrest the ringleaders, thus combining 'the maximum of irritation and the minimum of security'. These arrived on Monday, 29 April (the day of the Coalbrookvale meeting), in company with the police officers of Newtown and Welshpool, Blinkhorn and Armishaw, and stayed the night at the Trewythen Arms Hotel. News of their purpose quickly spread, and the next morning Lewis Hum-

---

[1] Add. MSS. 34245, A. 352.   [2] H.O. 40/46; Letter 19 May.
[3] Add. MSS. 34245, B. 219.

phreys, the Chartist 'bugler', with his 'Horn of Liberty' (celebrated by Hugh Williams in a broadsheet poem), summoned a meeting at the Severn bridge. While this was in progress, the magistrates hastily summoned special constables, and Humphreys and two others were arrested as they passed the Trewythen Arms and taken inside. Immediately the storm broke. The crowd rushed the hotel and reduced it to a complete wreck. Somewhat unaccountably they stove in the ends of the beer barrels and poured the beer and wine down the gutters. The prisoners were rescued and their handcuffs sawn off. Blinkhorn, who had continually interfered with the Newtown Chartists, was badly mauled, and he and Armishaw were only rescued by the intervention of Thomas Powell, who took Armishaw part of the way home. Of the London policemen one was found in a potato cellar, and the other two in a hay loft. It was they who had arrested Joseph Raynor Stephens and other Chartist agitators, but the fury of the Welsh exceeded anything they had ever seen. By midday the riots were over, and the attack on Caersws workhouse, which the authorities feared would immediately follow, did not take place.

Until the end of the week the Chartists ruled Llanidloes. There were no disturbances, for the Political Union, meeting at Llandinam, had urged its members not to destroy any more property. At last, after five days, the magistrates plucked up sufficient courage to intervene, and on Saturday afternoon a detachment of infantry from Brecon arrived, followed by the Montgomeryshire Yeomanry Cavalry, which was pelted with stones on its way through Newtown. But the Chartists had been forewarned, and most of the leaders had fled to Merthyr. Large rewards were offered for information, including one of £50 for the apprehension of Lewis Humphreys, and eventually thirty-two of the Llanidloes Chartists were arrested and twenty of those of Newtown. Among them was Thomas Powell. The greatest efforts were made to secure Charles Jones. Officers were sent to Manchester and to Birmingham, but without success, and he seems to have disappeared completely. Rumour had it that he had died of tuberculosis, but this may well have been a device to cover up his tracks.[1]

After these riots, Chartism in Montgomeryshire ceased to be of much importance, and although the trial did not take place until 17 July it may conveniently be considered at this point. Hugh Williams immediately appeared on the scene and gratuitously undertook the defence of the prisoners. An appeal was made to the Convention for support, but by this time there were several Chartists in need of defence, and a general fund was established. To this Merthyr Tydfil contributed £100 and Frost's district £50[2]—an interesting indication of the relative strength of Chartism in the two areas—but of this only £20 seems to have reached Llanidloes.[3] The prosecution had great difficulty in procuring evidence, and it was thought prudent to keep the chief witness in safe custody in Montgomery gaol, lest he might be tampered with or 'conveyed away'. Constant opposition was raised to Powell's bail, in order to keep him in prison, and he was not released until 25 June. Thirty-three persons were indicted, and of these thirty-one were found guilty. A man who was said to have stabbed a policeman was sentenced

---

[1] For the Llanidloes riots I am largely indebted to Miss Myfanwy Williams's unpublished thesis and to Professor Dodd, op. cit. Press accounts differ very considerably, e.g. *Shrewsbury News* (reproduced *Northern Star*, 11 May) denies the destruction of the hotel. There is a very lengthy account in *Merlin*, 18 May, also 1 June, 20 and 27 July; see also *Leeds Times*, 11 May, and Add. MSS. 34245, B. 35 and 49; H.O. 40/46, letter 25 May, gives arrest of Humphreys and claim for reward; accounts of solicitor for prosecution, MS. in Cardiff Library, indicate search for Charles Jones and difficulties put in the way of Powell's bail. The lawyer's expenses amounted to £225. 18s. 1d.

[2] *Silurian*, 6 July.   [3] Add. MSS. 34245, B. 49.

to fifteen years' transportation, while the bugler and one other received a similar sentence of seven years. The authorities evidently had difficulty in finding a charge to bring against Thomas Powell. At first they indicted him for assault, but this was dropped, and a charge of using seditious language was brought against him. Even so, to find language which could be called seditious, they had to go back to the Newtown meeting of 9 April, when he was reputed to have said 'that moral force would avail the Chartists nothing'. If he did use these words, it is remarkable that they should have passed entirely unnoticed in the press, which paid much attention to the remarks of Charles Jones on that occasion. Powell produced witnesses to prove that he had advocated moral force only, but the jury found him guilty, while recommending him to mercy. The judge concurred with their verdict, and while admitting that Powell had protected the police on 30 April, declared that the riots showed the effects of such language as Powell had used. He therefore sentenced him to twelve months' imprisonment in Montgomery gaol, after which he must find securities (himself in £400 and two others of £200) to keep the peace for five years, and remain imprisoned until such securities were found.[1] After his release, he seems to have emigrated to Trinidad.

The Newport magistrates hesitated to arrest Vincent and his associates, possibly waiting until the troops arrived. These came by packet from Bristol on 2 May— a division of the 29th regiment, eight officers, a surgeon, seven non-commissioned officers, and 105 of the rank and file. They were billeted in public houses, but the commanding officer complained that he could not answer for their efficiency under such conditions, presumably because the Chartists were tampering with them, and so they were

[1] *Charter*, 23 July.

removed to the workhouse.[1] Frost was still convinced that 'a great part of the army' were Chartists. In a letter dated 6 May he wrote: 'If one regiment of soldiers were once to refuse to obey the orders of such justices as Thos Phillips Jnr., what would then, I ask you, be the consequences?'[2] It was a delusion which was to cost him dear. Yet in spite of all injunctions the Chartists continued to hold their meetings. The day before the arrival of the troops a widely advertised demonstration took place, at the request of the Merthyr Chartists,[3] at Dukestown, Sirhowy. Both Dr. Price and Hugh Williams were included in the list of speakers, but neither seems to have been present. Jones the watchmaker delivered what seems to have been, for him, 'a temperate speech', explaining the principles of the Charter, and Edwards followed with 'one of his raving farragos, . . . tearing away for a couple of hours', according to the *Merlin*.[4] Even Etheridge seems to have grown tired of Edwards's violence, for on 7 May he circulated an address in Newport, in his capacity as secretary of the W.M.A., denouncing the violent language used by Edwards and others, yet defending the Chartists against the accusation of the *Merlin* that they aimed at the destruction of property.[5] Yet in Newport also, in spite of the presence of the soldiers, two large meetings were held in the open air in the first week of May, at which Dickenson and Townsend spoke. But on Tuesday, 7 May, the day of Etheridge's circular, the magistrates at last carried out their threats.

They had issued warrants for the arrest of Vincent, Edwards, Dickenson, and Townsend. The two latter were arrested in Newport, and at midnight on the same day Vincent was arrested in London by an officer sent up

[1] *Merlin*, 4 May. [2] *Western Vindicator*, 11 May.
[3] Newport Museum MSS., letter 25 Apr. 1839 from Morgan Williams, secretary, seized with Etheridge's papers.
[4] *Merlin*, loc. cit. [5] Reproduced in *Silurian*, 11 May.

from Monmouthshire for that purpose. He was not allowed to see any one in London, and on Thursday evening he started on his way to Newport, handcuffed for the first fifty miles. At Newport the excitement was enormous. On Friday 300 miners appeared in the town, although they had taken care not to carry even walking-sticks, so that the magistrates should not be able to formulate any charge against them, yet in the afternoon there was a skirmish when Edwards arrived by boat from Bristol and was immediately taken before the magistrates. At three o'clock, when Vincent arrived, there was still more uproar. Evidently the affair had been planned with some care, for there were no less than eleven magistrates present, and 300 special constables had been sworn in. The four men were charged with being present at the meeting of 19 April (the occasion on which Vincent delivered his 'To your tents O Israel' speech) and at other times, with having conspired to produce discontent, and having unlawfully assembled in breach of the peace. Exorbitant bail was demanded of them (Vincent in £500 and two others of £250 each; the three others £300 each with two others of £150 for each of them), together with sureties to keep the peace for twelve months. These conditions obviously could not be complied with (it is evident that the magistrates never intended them to be) and on the next day the four prisoners were removed to Monmouth gaol.[1]

Frost had immediately been sent to South Wales by the Convention to prevent a repetition of the Llanidloes rioting.[2] He travelled via Bath (possibly to consult W. P. Roberts) and found Newport in considerable uproar when he arrived at seven o'clock on Friday evening. He immediately addressed the crowd 'begging and praying'

---

[1] *Western Vindicator*, 18 May, 25 May; *Cambrian*, 17 May; *Star*, 18 May.
[2] Add. MSS. 27821, p. 133.

them to offer no resistance to the law, and although he got no promise from them he claimed that it was his presence alone which prevented an outbreak.[1]   He advised against giving the bail demanded, and it was decided to test its legality. Eventually this question was brought before Mr. Justice Pattison, in chambers, and he ruled that the magistrates had no right to demand sureties for good conduct before a prisoner was convicted. But this was not until 25 June, when Vincent and the others had been at Monmouth nearly seven weeks.[2] The arrest of Vincent evidently caused Frost anxiety. He wrote to Lovett that he feared one of two things would happen: the people would become entirely dispirited or there would be an outbreak, and either would be fatal to the cause.[3] At the same time he wrote a letter to Lord John Russell, bitterly accusing him of arming the middle class against the workers. He told him plainly what advice he had given to the people at Newport. He had urged them once more to try judges and juries, who would surely afford them protection. But 'if their attempt should fail', he had said, 'if it appears that person and property have no security from courts of law, I will then give you other advice and be ready to follow it'.[4] Moreover, his own position was by no means certain. When he arrived in Newport on 9 May it was expected that he would be arrested immediately, and it is probable that the magistrates intended to do so. Their policy evidently was to get the Chartist leaders safely in prison, at least for a time (for the Assizes did not take place for nearly three months), and the comment of Thomas Phillips on this in a letter to the Home Office after Vincent's trial is significant:

Although Frost was not committed for trial by the magis-

---

[1] Add. MSS. 34245, A. 430.   [2] *The Charter*, 30 June.
[3] Letter dated 15 May in Add. MSS. 34245, A. 445, reproduced *True Scotsman*, 25 May.   [4] Letter dated 16 May in *Charter*, 19 May.

trates, the Council for the Crown determined that he should be included in a second indictment on the ground that he was the real author of the movement in the county, and being the most guilty party they could not justify either to the public or the government his escape from prosecution.[1]

The authorities therefore considered Frost 'a guilty party', and this merely on the grounds of his being a Chartist leader. For it is an extraordinary commentary on the situation that, in spite of Frost's numerous speeches in the meantime, when the magistrates wished to find something on which they could base a definite charge of illegality, they were forced to go back to his remark about the grooms of the bedchamber on 1 January, and it was with using seditious language on that occasion that he, together with Vincent and Edwards, was charged.

A crisis had thus been reached in the Chartist movement in Wales. An outbreak had occurred in Montgomeryshire, and in Monmouthshire the great favourite of the miners had been arrested. For the time being their energies were directed towards providing for his defence, the women's associations (the Female Radicals of Newport, the Female Patriotic Society of Abersychan and the others) being particularly active.[2] Yet at any moment the men might take matters into their own hands and attempt to rescue him. A crisis had also occurred in the Convention itself. On 6 May the Petition, with 1,280,000 signatures, was taken to Attwood's house, but he was now wavering in his allegiance to Chartism (Frost, indeed, had proposed that some one else should be asked to present it), and because of the expected resignation of the ministry (which occurred the next day) Attwood doubted the possibility of being able to bring it before the House of Commons. The great day had, therefore, arrived, the day towards which the expectations of the working class

[1] H.O. 40/45, letter dated 3 Aug.   [2] *Western Vindicator*, 20 July.

of the whole country had been stimulated, and it was obvious that nothing could be done. The Charter 'would not be the law of the land in less than a month' as had so often been said. Therefore the Convention felt that it must get further assurance of support from the people, and find out how far they were prepared to adopt 'ulterior measures' if the Petition were rejected. So it was decided on the proposal of O'Connor, seconded by Frost, that great 'simultaneous meetings' should be held all over the country, at which these 'ulterior measures' would be submitted,[1] and, in preparation for these meetings, the Convention (which had removed to Birmingham only two days previously) adjourned on 15 May.

[1] Add. MSS. 27821, p. 88.

VI

'ULTERIOR MEASURES'

With the arrest of Vincent a distinct stage in the history of Chartism in Wales was reached. The authorities had, at last, decided to take the initiative and to suppress the movement, and this they attempted to do by depriving the Chartists of their leaders. Moreover, there was always the possibility (except in July, when Vincent was released on bail) that the miners would attempt to rescue their favourite. It was not only Frost who feared that this might happen. The mayor of Monmouth expressed his fears to the Home Office, and asked for troops; as many as 1,500 special constables were enrolled at Pontypool, and at the request of the Lord Lieutenant troops were stationed at Abergavenny.[1] The content of the Lord Lieutenant's letter leaked out and was published in the press, thus considerably aggravating the situation. This was a serious blunder, and involved him in some bother with the Home Office, but he declared himself completely ignorant of how it had happened, and disclaimed all responsibility.

This was the atmosphere in which the 'simultaneous meetings' were held. For the Glamorganshire and Monmouthshire coal-field, Blackwood was chosen as a convenient centre,[2] and as the day was a public holiday (Whit Monday, 20 May), no less than 30,000 people seem to have been present.[3] Four magistrates attended, and a careful note was taken of all the speeches made. As was usual with Chartist meetings in Wales, the proceedings

---

[1] H.O. 40/45, letters 11 May, 13 May, 14 May.
[2] The Chartist demonstration planned for the same day at Llandaff fair does not seem to have taken place. Lord Bute to Home Office, H.O. 40/46, 22 May.　　　　　　　　　　　　　[3] *Charter*, 26 May.

opened with prayer in Welsh. Jones the watchmaker then spoke. He seems to have attained more prominence after the imprisonment of Edwards, and he devoted his speech to castigating the magistrates who had committed the four Chartists. This was also Frost's theme. He questioned the legality of the magistrates' action, as usual quoting lengthy passages out of Blackstone's *Commentaries*. He then elaborated the 'ulterior measures' which the Convention proposed: (1) withdrawing all savings from the banks; (2) converting all paper money into gold; (3) adopting the proposal for a 'sacred month', that is a general strike, at the same time abstaining from all intoxicants; (4) preparing themselves with the arms of freemen to defend the laws; (5) adopting Chartist candidates for the next election, such candidates to be decided by a show of hands, and, if elected, to consider themselves representatives and meet in London shortly; (6) dealing exclusively with tradesmen who favoured Chartism; (7) abstaining from agitation for anything less than the Charter, and (8) obeying all the just and constitutional requests of the majority of the Convention.

Thus the Convention proposed three main expedients to attain its purposes—precipitating a financial crisis, the sacred month, and exclusive dealing. The first had always been a favourite topic of Frost, and it was generally thought in the summer of 1839 that a financial crash was imminent. Frost's ideas at this time on the sacred month are nowhere clearly expressed, but he seems to have adopted a cautious attitude from the start. Exclusive dealing he wholeheartedly supported. He had continually advocated an alliance between the workers and the middle class, but he had come to realize that the latter would not support their cause, that they were the 'enemies of Chartism'. He therefore urged the workers to deal only with those who were sympathetic to them, and this was fairly effectively carried out in Merthyr, where the attitude of the shopkeepers was tested by asking them to contribute to the Vincent defence fund.

Frost invited the magistrates present at Blackwood to speak, but they declined. They were, as he informed Lord John Russell in a lengthy account of the demonstration which he sent him, without the courage or the ability to reply, not having the knowledge necessary to refute the arguments of those whom the 'higher orders' deprived of the franchise on the assigned reason that they were too ignorant to use it. All the 'ulterior measures' were adopted, and Frost was reappointed delegate. Jones then read an address of loyalty to the queen, which expressed a hope that she had not authorized the use of troops against the workers (a reference to the Lord Lieutenant's letter). After a concluding prayer, and cheers for Vincent, for Frost, and for Crawshay (one of the magistrates present who seems to have been popular with his workmen) the Chartists re-formed their ranks and marched from the field.[1]

This meeting seems to have given an impetus to Chartism. As a result of it the men of Merthyr Tydfil were said to be joining at the rate of 100 to 120 a week,[2] and Hetherington came down to address them.[3] Other branches were formed, including Chartist Youths' Associations, among them one at Newport, of which young Henry Hunt Frost was the first member.[4] But the opponents of Chartism were also active. Although disgusted with the refusal of the government to establish a yeoman cavalry, the gentlemen of West Monmouthshire nevertheless decided to form themselves into an armed

---

[1] *Charter* loc. cit.; Add. MSS. 27821, p. 330; *Merlin*, 25 May; *Western Vindicator*, 29 June.   [2] *Northern Star*, 15 June.   [3] *Silurian*, 25 May.
[4] *Merlin*, 16 Nov., which gives Henry Hunt Frost's card: 'Newport Youths' Democratic Association. Union is Strength, Knowledge is Power. Henry Hunt Frost. Entered 4 June 1839. No. 1. John Bull, Secretary.'

association, with two corps, cavalry and infantry. This they did at the suggestion of Lieutenant-Colonel Sir Digby Mackworth, who declared that the real object of the Chartists was plunder and the division of property, however much they denied it in public. He had an assurance that the government would supply the yeomen with sufficient arms. It was obvious, therefore, that the queen's circular of three weeks previously (3 May), prohibiting arming and training, had been directed against one class only. Even the Duke of Beaufort saw the unwisdom of this, and raised the question in the House of Lords on 11 June. He deplored that any one but the regular forces should be allowed to carry arms.[1]

On 3 June Frost left Newport to attend a great demonstration at Glasgow, in accordance with a resolution passed at the Convention in his absence. He travelled via Liverpool, going on from there by packet. According to his own estimate, he addressed a crowd of 150,000 on Glasgow Green on 10 June. The advice he gave them, he said, was the same as he had given to his countrymen in Wales, but it certainly included a startling suggestion. They were to keep the law rigidly. The members of the Convention had never yet broken the law, and were not likely to do so. Consequently if the government attempted to lay hold of its members (which they certainly were doing) the Chartists were determined to seize some of the leading men in the country and hold them as hostages. If their enemies were going to do as James II did, it would be their duty to see that those who broke the law did not do so with impunity.[2]

This suggestion of taking hostages seems to have originated entirely with Frost, and it was greeted with

[1] *Merlin*, 18 May, 25 May, 15 June.

[2] *Charter*, 19 May–16 June; *Western Vindicator*, 22 June; R. G. Gamage, *The Chartist Movement* (London, 1894), pp. 118–19. Full account in Add. MSS. 27821, p. 233.

'immense cheering'. It throws a lurid light on a placard dealing with Vincent's arrest which he had published just before leaving Newport. In it he contrasted the attitude of the Whigs towards public meetings in 1832 and in 1839. 'One of the most noisy brawlers for Reform', read the broadside, 'was Thomas Phillips, and this insolent man, sprung from what he is pleased to call the lower orders, is now the most bitter persecutor of those who advocate a real Reform of the House of Commons.' Witnesses had been refused a hearing, said Frost, and exorbitant bail demanded from Vincent. Then came this passage: 'We seek for justice; in doing so we keep within the limits of the law. If others exceed the limits, if our leading men be imprisoned, no violence having been committed, why then we shall consider that a coal-pit is quite as safe a place for a tyrannical persecutor as a gaol for an innocent Chartist.' Evidently, therefore, Frost contemplated using coal-pits to hold people as hostages for the safety of the Chartist leaders. This was an outrageous suggestion, and although the broadside ended, 'Be firm, be peaceable, and our righteous cause will succeed', it is small wonder that the Attorney-General considered it a direct incentive to violence. Consequently, two days before the Glasgow meeting, the Attorney-General moved at the Court of Queen's Bench for leave to file a criminal information against Frost and John Partridge (the printer) for libel on the mayor of Newport, and this leave was granted by Frost's old counsel, Lord Denman. The case did not come up for consideration until 6 November, two days after the Newport riot, and as there was then a much more serious charge against Frost, it was not proceeded with.[1] It is, however, of the utmost importance to appreciate that when Frost led his

[1] *Merthyr Guardian*, 15 June; *Northern Star*, 15 June; H.O. 40/45; *Cambrian*, 16 Nov. On 6 Nov. the 'rule was held over for argument'.

men to Newport there were already two charges against him, on either of which he was likely to get a long term of imprisonment. He had already burnt his boats.

Frost heard of the libel action while visiting his friend Bailie Craig at Kilmarnock. He immediately returned to Newport, where he found that his presence was required for another reason. This was the perennial question of the Corporation Wharf. It will be remembered that Frost had been requested by the freemen to receive the rent of the wharf on their behalf, and that he had obtained their acquiescence to spending most of it on an action to recover the land occupied by the Tredegar Wharf, but that his suit in Chancery had been dismissed and the matter allowed to drop. In November 1838 an application had been made at the Court of King's Bench to recover the whole of the rent from Frost, but Lord Denman had ruled that as no request for the surrender of the money had been made to Frost and refused, he could not issue an order. Seven months later this had now been raised again by the mayor, in Frost's absence. It met with some opposition on the town council and was deferred until the following month.[1] It placed Frost in an embarrassing position. The Convention was due to reassemble at Birmingham on 1 July and it was important that Frost should be present, as the whole question of 'ulterior measures' would be raised. He decided that he would attend at any cost, but before he went, he made a rapid tour of his constituency. On 25 June he visited Merthyr, apparently for the first time, and addressed some 8,000 at Penrheolgerrig. He was given a great welcome, with the usual procession, and his entire theme seems to have been the likelihood of a financial crisis. On the following day he was at Nantyglo, afterwards proceeding to Abersychan and Pontypool. Jones the watchmaker was also

[1] *Merlin*, 15 June.

going around the area. On 16 June he and Morgan
Williams, now the chief leader in Merthyr, had held a
meeting on the mountain between Aberdare and Hirwaun, also attended by about 8,000 people, and on 1 July
he addressed an audience of between 6,000 and 7,000 at
Coalbrookvale, after a great procession from Brynmawr.
Frost had been advertised to speak on this occasion, but
he had already left for Birmingham.[1]

There he took the chair on 2 July, and reported that
the meetings which he had attended in Wales had been
numerous and enthusiastic, and that the people were
fully determined to carry out the 'ulterior measures' of the
Convention.[2] The all-important question, however, was
that of the sacred month, and on this he shared the
hesitation of the Convention itself. It had been raised
at Blackwood on Whit Monday, but Frost afterwards
denied that he had then recommended the miners to stop
work for a month.[3] He was by no means above quibbling
about the form of words he had used (as we have seen in
his correspondence with the Lord Chancellor), and his
denial may not amount to much. He now declared himself in favour of the sacred month, though he did not
think that the Convention was in a position to advise the
workers when it should take place.[4] But he was forced to
ask the Convention for leave of absence in order to be
present at the Newport Town Council on 10 July. There
he scored a partial victory. He recounted the history of
the Corporation Wharf in great detail, and complained
of the use which was being made of the matter to harass
him. Eventually it was decided that Frost should be
indemnified for his expense, even to the extent of being
allowed his costs in defending the action brought against

[1] *Silurian*, 29 June, 6 July; *Northern Star*, 6 July; *Merlin*, 13 July.
[2] *Charter*, 7 July.
[3] *Western Vindicator*, 27 May.   [4] Add. MSS. 27821, p. 278.

him in the Court of King's Bench, as well as the costs of the action he had brought against Sir Charles Morgan in the Court of Chancery, and that the affair should be closed by his handing over to the Treasurer of the Council the sum remaining in his possession. This was as favourable a settlement as he could have expected, but it is hardly likely that he would have agreed even to this, had his whole time not been occupied with the Chartist movement, for he still claimed that the money belonged to the freemen of the old borough.[1]

Frost was unable to return to the Convention for some weeks. He had, first of all, to come to the rescue of his friend, W. P. Roberts, the Bath solicitor who had been present with Vincent at the Devizes riot. Together with two others he had been arrested (again at Devizes,) on the charge of attending illegal meetings, but they had been acquitted. Immediately, however, another charge had been brought against them, that of having used indictable language as far back as the previous November. Roberts was required to give bail, himself in £500 with three sureties of £250, and application was made to Frost to become bail for him. He immediately proceeded to Devizes and with two others offered himself as bail, but the magistrates objected that he was not known to them. Another bail was then found, but the magistrates then objected to having two old and one new bail. Therefore, with some difficulty, three new bail were found, but they arrived in the court just in time to see the three prisoners being taken handcuffed to Salisbury gaol. It is difficult to justify the conduct of the authorities on any grounds. As Frost complained, their policy was obviously to bring indictments against the Chartist leaders, even with no chance of succeeding, merely to involve them in enormous expense. They issued warrants against them, treated

[1] *Merlin*, 13 July, 10 Aug.; *Western Vindicator*, 20 July.

them as if they were convicted, and held them to bail for outrageous amounts, so that they could keep them in prison, and then often abandoned the charges against them. It is no wonder that this caused feelings of extreme bitterness.[1]

Events had also taken a serious turn, for on 4 July the first riots in Birmingham had occurred. The magistrates had forbidden the holding of meetings in the Bull Ring, where so many of the Reform meetings had been held without interference, and on the evening of the 4th they ordered a detachment of metropolitan police to disperse a crowd which had gathered there. A bloody struggle ensued which ended only when dragoons arrived. Lovett issued a declaration characterizing this as 'a wanton, flagrant and unjust outrage', a verdict with which most historians agree, but for this he was arrested, and pending the production of £1,000 bail was kept in Warwick gaol, and treated as a felon. The Convention thereupon left Birmingham and reassembled in London, partly in order to be near the centre of things when the financial crash, which they thought imminent, would occur. But two days later, on 12 July, the Petition was at last presented to the House of Commons, and was rejected by 237 votes to 48. It was now evident, even to the most sanguine, that the Charter would never be obtained by peaceful means, and the only subject for discussion in the Convention was the sacred month. Complaint was made that O'Connor, O'Brien, Dr. Taylor, Craig, and Frost were absent, though they had 'forced the subject on the Convention'. Craig had indeed deserted the cause, and was back at Kilmarnock 'ensconced behind his counter'.[2] But Frost claimed that he and the three others had been 'the most cautious of the members in discussing a subject involving such tremendous consequences'. He explained

---

[1] *Charter*, 28 July.   [2] *Saturday Journal*, 27 July.

his absence as due to the matter of the Corporation Wharf, his exertions on behalf of Roberts, and the trial of Vincent which was about to take place. He declared his conviction that the people of Wales were not prepared to strike, neither would those of Bristol, while at Bath a strike would be quite ineffective, as the city was dependent upon the gentry who could leave it at their pleasure.[1] Hugh Williams, also, believed that before the sacred month should be decided upon, another request to be heard at the Bar of the House of Commons should be made, and another address sent to the queen. He reported that the Llanidloes workers were prepared for the strike, come when it would, but he believed it should not in any case take place until the end of August or the beginning of September.[2] The more extreme elements were taking a stronger line. The Abersychan W.M.A. declared that 'if an attack were made on them as at Birmingham, they would repel force by force',[3] and at the same time the neighbouring W.M.A. at Pontypool declared that they were ready to defend the Convention to death. 'We most earnestly request all who are able, to provide themselves with arms immediately', ran their declaration.[4] The opponents of Chartism, also, were prepared to go to extremes. The *Merthyr Guardian* in a leader on the Birmingham riots advised calling in troops whenever there was a likelihood of their being necessary, and should there be any opposition to the military power, it said, 'it will be met with the word of command FIRE, and that word of command will neither convey the meaning that blank cartridge are to be used, or that the firing

---

[1] *Charter*, loc. cit.; Gamage, op. cit., p. 147. The statement in the *Charter* that a meeting had taken place (at Newport, the *Charter* believed) which had pledged itself to support the sacred month is garbled.

[2] Add. MSS. 34245, B. 49, letter dated 19 July.

[3] Resolution 20 July, in *Western Vindicator*, 27 July.

[4] Resolution 22 July, in *Northern Star*, 3 Aug.

is to be over the heads of the people but *at the mob*, and if possible, at those who are evidently *leaders of the mob*'.[1]

Frost thought that his presence in Wales pending the trial of Vincent would be of greater service than at the Convention. In the meantime he visited Cardiff, 'a miserably enslaved town', and there spoke to the 'navigators' who were digging the new docks, but they 'were from lack of education unable to see the true and false' in any argument, and were, moreover, mostly Irish, so that it was impossible to interest them in Chartism.[2] The case of Vincent, Edwards, Dickenson, and Townsend eventually came before Baron Alderson at the Monmouth Assizes on 2 August. They were charged not only with unlawfully assembling at various times, but with an overt act of conspiracy on 19 April, and with riot. Serjeant Talfourd, the great friend of Dickens, appeared for the Crown. He gave an account of the various meetings from 19 March until 26 April, and, in general terms, accused the Chartists of setting one class in society against another. The workers, he maintained, could not claim exclusive right to the term 'the useful classes'. 'I should like to know whether those who produce all the graces and ornaments of life are not useful too,' he said, 'and whether they have not their sufferings and their cares, from many of which the working classes are exempt.' He maintained that the meetings, held in the manner in which they were, constituted a breach of the peace, and he attempted to forestall an argument for the defence by declaring that what other people might have said or done on other occasions had nothing to do with the case. It is significant of the atmosphere in which the case was tried that this speech was greeted with applause, and the judge felt

[1] *Merthyr Guardian*, 27 July.
[2] *Cambrian*, 26 July. For Chartism in Cardiff see *Western Vindicator*, 6 and 13 July, 4 Nov.

constrained to rebuke the audience. The defence was conducted by Roebuck, and it must be admitted that the Chartists in Wales were invariably fortunate in their counsel. Roebuck elicited from Thomas Phillips, the chief witness for the Crown, three damaging admissions: first that he had repeatedly heard Vincent tell the crowd to keep the peace; second, that there had occurred no breach of the peace to his knowledge, and, third, that no riot had taken place at all. In his concluding speech Roebuck produced a masterly defence not only of the prisoners but of Chartism. As Talfourd had expected, he made reference to the turbulence of the Reform meetings, by which the rest and peace of every large town in England had been disturbed. You cannot teach men to-day, and unteach them to-morrow, he said. The Whigs had clamoured for 'the Bill, the whole Bill and nothing but the Bill'; the Chartists now said: 'We will have the Charter.' Then Roebuck continued in these words:

'Aye,' says the Whig government, 'now you sing a different song. It is true we sang "nothing but the Bill". But we do not allow you to sing "nothing but the Charter". No, we will let you know a different thing from that. It is true the Tories did not put us down. They have some regard for law and order, and common sense and decency. They did not put us down. But you have got into different hands now. We have got our Bill and we will take exceeding good care that you shall not have your Charter.'

Roebuck referred to O'Connell, 'the man upon whose breath the stability of the present ministry rests', who claimed that he could call upon 500,000 fighting men. Why was he not prosecuted? He had been far more guilty than any one of the prisoners. Roebuck sought to prove not only that the object of the Chartists was legal, but also their means. Working men must meet in the evenings if they are to meet at all, and if it was their

intention to break the peace, then how did it come about
that the peace was not broken? 'Some applause and some
hisses followed the delivery of the speech of the learned
counsel', reads the official account, 'upon which Baron
Alderson said, "I am waiting till people come to their
senses". Silence was at length restored.' In this tense
atmosphere the judge summed up briefly, and the jury
retired. However much doubt there had been in the
minds of the legal advisers to the Home Office, there was
none in those of the Monmouth jury, for in less than a
quarter of an hour they had returned into Court. They
found all the defendants guilty of attending illegal meetings, but acquitted them of conspiracy, and further found
Vincent and Edwards guilty of uttering violent and
seditious language. Baron Alderson then passed judgement, and dealt severely with Vincent as a missionary of
the National Convention. He made the important pro-
nouncement (for the first time) that this was an illegal
body, and that the Government might think it right to indict
its members at some future time. Should any of them use
language which induced their followers to attempt to
obtain the Charter by force, they would lay themselves
open to the charge of high treason. He sentenced Vincent
to one year's imprisonment, Edwards to nine months, and
Dickenson and Townsend each to six months.[1]

The trial had aroused intense interest in the neighbourhood, and the Grand Jury box was filled with 'elegantly
dressed ladies'. The hissing of the counsel for the defence,
presumably by these 'elegant ladies' and their 'gentlemen'
friends, which was sufficiently startling to be recorded in
the sober official report, shows that it was impossible for
the prisoners to have a fair trial. As it was, Thomas

[1] John Macdonell, *Reports of State Trials*, vol. iii, 1831–40 (London, 1891),
1038–86; *Rise and Fall*, pp. 19–22; *Merlin*, 3 Aug.; *Cambrian*, 10 Aug.
Northern Star, 10 Aug.; MSS. (245 pp.) from shorthand account in H.O.
40/45.

John Frost

Phillips reported to the Home Office that 'the gentlemen thought the punishment of Vincent and Edwards far too lenient'.[1] There was, however, some revulsion of feeling. A witness for the prosecution wrote to Baron Alderson urging the extreme youth of Townsend as a reason for remitting the sentence, and even the *Merlin* (possibly thinking of the effect its opposition to the popular cause might have on its circulation) pleaded for mercy in a leading article, stating that the release of Dickenson and Townsend, in particular, would give pleasure to the townspeople.[2] Even the counsel for the prosecution was embarrassed by Lord John Russell's complete refusal to be subpoenaed by Vincent,[3] for the Home Secretary had less than twelve months previously justified the holding of public meetings, and his refusal contrasts strangely with the action of Pitt when, as Prime Minister, he was subpoenaed by Erskine in the famous trial of Horne Tooke.

For the Chartists of Monmouthshire the sentencing of Vincent was an event of capital importance. He was their idol, and whatever may have been the sentiments in the Grand Jury box, the large crowd outside greeted the prisoners as they were removed to gaol with cries of 'Vincent for ever'.[4] Frost had advised them 'once more to try judges and juries' and their trial had proved a failure. Frost's own case was transferred to the next assizes, but he found rising within himself 'a spirit most difficult to repress'. 'If power were placed in my hands', he wrote, 'I should be afraid of myself'—afraid that revenge would overpower his understanding. He reflected that the beginners of the French Revolution were moderate men, and that the aristocracy had learned to regret that they

---

[1] H.O. 40/45, letter dated 3 Aug. [2] *Merlin*, 17 Aug.
[3] H.O. 40/45, letter from Talfourd dated 31 July.
[4] Newport Library. Broadside, printed Crawley, Bath.

178

had not listened to them. Was he perhaps feeling that the situation was already slipping from his grasp? But for the moment, at any rate, he enjoined the workers to be firm. Steady was the word. No petty ebullition of passion, but a cool, steady determination to obtain that liberty which is the noblest gift of God to man.[1]

But the activity of the government was having a very sobering effect on the Chartist leaders. Lovett, the noblest member of the Convention, had also been sentenced, and three men who had been connected with the riots which had broken out again in Birmingham on 15 July were in Warwick gaol under sentence of death. Moreover the terrible words 'high treason' had been uttered, and the Chartist leaders well knew that if any outbreak now occurred it would lay them open to this charge, with its barbarous consequences of hanging and quartering. What then was to become of the national strike, fixed provisionally for 12 August? Such a strike would very likely lead to rioting, and moreover it was found that certain industries were suffering from a crisis of over-production, so that the employers might welcome the 'national holiday' rather than otherwise. Consequently O'Connor performed one of his frequent tergiversations, and the Convention rescinded its own order, substituting for it a recommendation to cease work for two or three days—a kind of token strike—'in order to devote the whole of that time to solemn processions and solemn meetings'. For 12 August, therefore, the Monmouthshire Chartists arranged a great demonstration to be held at Dukestown (Sirhowy), and thither Frost went accompanied by his son, Henry Hunt. According to Frost, it was one of the largest meetings ever held in Wales, although the *Merlin* (always inclined to disparage the

[1] 'To the Workingmen of Wales and the West of England', in *Western Vindicator* 10 Aug.

Chartists) fixed the number at 2,500. The magistrates, as usual, had taken precautions, and several were present. One of them, Samuel Homfray, was even invited to preside, but he declined, and the chair was taken by Dr. Price, whom Frost reported to be 'a gentleman of talent and great influence in the neighbourhood'. Jones the watchmaker spoke first, and, if the *Merlin* is to be believed, he said that 'they would try by fair means to get Vincent and the others out of prison, but were determined to get them out at any rate'. The principal speaker was Frost, whose theme was the sacred month. He explained why he opposed the suggestion, stating that if the workers carried out their threat, the masters might close their works for another six months—no doubt a reference to the crisis in the iron industry. He referred in complimentary terms to Samuel Homfray, a man more honest and with more good sense than the majority of their legislators, and he suggested that Homfray might be adopted as parliamentary candidate—though only after the Charter had been obtained, for if he were returned for seven years he would soon be as bad as the others. The meeting resolved to petition the Queen for mercy towards the three Warwick prisoners, and Frost was asked to wait on Lord John Russell to request him to remit the sentence on Vincent and the others.[1] At the same time a similar petition 'respectably and numerously signed' was forwarded on behalf of the Warwick prisoners by the Carmarthen Chartists, who held 'that sanguinary punishments were more in keeping with barbarous and unenlightened times'.[2]

Frost's speech at Dukestown was a surprisingly moderate one, and he was evidently concerned with restraining the extreme elements. He was loudly cheered, so that at least

[1] *Merlin*, 17 Aug.; 16 Nov. (evidence of Morgan Jones); Newport Museum MSS., 414, 417, 434; Add. MSS. 34245, B. 137 (Frost letter, 13 Aug.).
[2] *Cambrian*, 17 Aug.

a certain section of the Chartists supported him, but that
there was a cleavage among them is evident from resolutions sent to the Secretary of the Convention at this time.
It should be noticed that these, like the July resolutions,
came from Pontypool, always the most violent section of
the coal-field, and the scene of Jones the watchmaker's
activities. They said that the people 'must assume a
menacing aspect', and 'strike terror in the hearts of the
shopocracy and aristocrats'. The workers were determined to try the experiment of a general strike, and called
upon the Convention to fix a date. 'Fortune', they concluded, 'favours the brave'.[1] The deciding factor, however, was to be the treatment of Vincent and his fellow
prisoners in gaol, about which there were many un-
pleasant rumours, and much would depend upon whether
Frost could secure an amelioration in their condition.
On 22 August, indeed, a petition from the prisoners,
which was issued as a broadside, was presented to the
House of Commons by Hume, and to the House of Lords
by Lord Brougham. It declared that although Baron
Alderson at the trial had expressed an opinion that they
should suffer no inconvenience except confinement, they
were treated as convicted felons. Their diet was two
quarts of gruel, a pound and a half of bread, and a pound
of potatoes per day, while they were deprived of the use
of fire, pens, ink and paper, and were allowed only
theological books. It complained that they, as members
of the working class, had been selected for prosecution,
whereas wealthy individuals in Ireland and elsewhere were
encouraged and patronized. It concluded by asking for a
discharge, or if that were not possible, an abatement of
the rigour of their confinement, and the privilege of
purchasing their own food.[2]

[1] Add. MSS. 34245, B. 91 (letter dated 2 Aug.).
[2] Place Collection, lvi. 194.

John Frost

Frost left for London on Saturday, 24 August, to be ready for the reopening of the Convention on the following Monday, and to wait on the Home Secretary in accordance with the request made to him at Dukestown. There ensued a prolonged correspondence between him and Lord John Russell and Lord Normanby, who succeeded Lord John at the end of August. Lord John would not see Frost, but would present a petition to the Queen if it were properly worded. Frost then re-opened the whole question with Normanby. He declared that punishment did not produce a good effect on the community unless the people were convinced that a wrong had been done. He claimed that the jury had been prejudiced, for a juryman had been heard to say at the end of July that Vincent deserved to be hanged without judge or jury. Frost concluded by forwarding the Dukestown resolutions. Normanby's only reply was that the resolutions of a meeting could not properly be laid before the queen. Frost then asked him to receive a deputation, only to be asked in turn what the deputation wished to place before the Home Secretary, and when Frost replied by giving details of Vincent's treatment, Normanby informed him that the prisoners were 'allowed such indulgences as were consistent with the ends of justice and the regulations of the prison in which they are confined'. This infuriated Frost. 'Your answer, my Lord,' he wrote, 'is unworthy of . . .' an epithet which even the *Northern Star* thought best to omit. Yet he once more repeated his previous arguments, but all in vain, and two days later he reported his failure in a 'Letter to the workingmen of Glamorgan, Monmouth and Brecon' which he may well have regretted, for in it he said, 'It will be for you to consider what other means you will take either to obtain their discharge or to get some alteration made in these inhuman regulations.'[1]

[1] *Sun*, 13 Sept.; *Northern Star*, 14 Sept.; *Western Vindicator*, 28 Sept.

Vincent's cause was being prejudiced by his best friends. The *Western Vindicator* continued to appear, each issue bearing an article signed Henry Vincent. Thus, while the Chartists were complaining of Vincent's treatment, their enemies were furious that he was still able to issue the paper from gaol.[1] Actually he was not even aware of the existence of these articles, for they were written by his partner, Francis Hill, who, in a letter to Vincent dated 16 September, explained that he had been urged by friends to use Vincent's name because of the 'wonderful influence' it had on the people. This 'little bit of diablerie', as Hill called it, cost Vincent dear, for the letter, intercepted by the prison authorities, was sent to the Home Office only on 25 November, when the visiting magistrate had to explain how it was that Vincent appeared to have obtained news of the Newport riot, and was able to continue the *Western Vindicator*, and had to assure the Home Office that the 'strictest prison discipline' was enforced. Vincent, he said, did not know that Frost was in the same prison as himself for several days, and even then thought that it was in relation to the forthcoming prosecution of Frost, Edwards, and himself.[2] It may well be that the severity of Vincent's confinement, at least at the beginning, was due to an attempt to stop the leakage which seemed to be taking place.

It was on 12 September that Frost wrote to the workers of South Wales, confessing his entire failure to procure any concessions for Vincent; two days later the Convention itself was dissolved. The energetic measures taken by the government and its systematic repression of the Chartists had had their effect, for the Convention which had reassembled on 26 August was a very attenuated body. Twenty-one of its members had resigned, and several

[1] Thomas Phillips to H.O., 12 Aug., in H.O. 40/45.
[2] Charles Marriott to H.O., 25 Nov., in H.O. 40/45.

others were in prison. There followed an exhibition of weakness even more painful than was shown in the discussion of the sacred month. Within three days the Convention, under Frost's presidency, had made a special request to the constituencies to send up their delegates to a meeting on 4 September to consider what their future policy should be. On that day one of the members moved that the Convention should declare itself dissolved, and should pass a self-denying ordinance to the effect that no delegate to the existing Convention should sit in a new assembly, which should now be called. This naturally was displeasing to O'Connor's vanity and ambition, and there ensued a far from amicable discussion. This was resumed two days later, under Frost's presidency once more, and an amendment was brought forward that the Convention should adjourn only, and a committee be appointed to sit in the interval. This received ten votes for and ten against, and Frost was called upon to give his casting vote, which he gave in its favour. But in spite of this, more desultory discussion followed, and once more it was decided to vote on whether the Convention should dissolve or adjourn on 14 September. This time eleven voted for dissolution and eleven for adjournment. It therefore fell again to Frost's lot to give the casting vote, and nothing better illustrates the uncertainty and hesitation with which the Convention acted than the fact that Frost who had earlier given his casting vote for adjournment only now gave it for dissolution. It was in this undignified way that the Convention of the working classes came to an end.[1]

Thus at one and the same time the workers had failed to get the release of Vincent by peaceful means and had been deprived of any leadership. They were both thrown on their own resources and convinced that peaceful

---

[1] Add. MSS. 27821, p. 310; E. Dolléans, *Le Chartisme* (Paris, 1912), i. 408–411.

means would avail them nothing. Frost had again had occasion to 'entreat' them to be careful and to avoid a premature outbreak. He informed them that there were rumours of spies among the hills, whose object was to incite them to acts of violence, and declared that he had good reason to believe that these rumours were correct. In the same letter he thought it wise to insert the remark that the prisoners in Monmouth gaol were in good health and spirits, evidently hoping to counteract the effect which stories of their ill-treatment were having on the people.[1] He now tried to explain to them why the Convention had failed. Too much had been expected of it, he said, and they must not be disappointed because they did not get the Charter by asking for it in Parliament. One reason why the Convention had not contained more talent was because men in public positions who were competent to become candidates, had been faced with certain ruin if they were chosen. Still the Convention had proved itself as competent as the House of Commons, but its business had to be transacted by talking, and how few, he reflected (possibly thinking of O'Connor on the one hand and himself on the other), how few combined fluency of speech with solidity of judgement. But Chartism, he assured the people, was not defunct. The calm which prevailed was quite natural, for men could not always be in a state of agitation, nor was it wise to preserve them in that state. In the recess they should have time to consider what would be the best course to pursue in favour of the Charter.[2]

During these weeks of calm in August and September the Chartists adopted the extraordinary procedure of attending divine service in a body in their local parish churches. This caused some amazement and apprehension to the devout, who were unable to explain its

[1] Letter dated 27 Aug. in *Western Vindicator*, 31 Aug.
[2] Letter dated 23 Sept. in *Western Vindicator*, 28 Sept.

purpose, but on all occasions the Chartists were said to have behaved themselves in a highly decorous manner. The attitude of the churches towards them had not changed much. The Baptists in their annual association meetings at Risca had presented an address to the Queen deploring the prevalence of disaffection and insubordination, and expressing an opinion that it was not 'native to British soil'. A Wesleyan minister had accused the Chartists of being levellers, thieves, and robbers.[1] Why then did they attend church? Whatever may have been the reason, on the morning of 11 August they marched in orderly fashion up Stow Hill, Newport, to the parish church of St. Woollos, and in the evening attended the service conducted by their friend Benjamin Byron in Hope Chapel. On 18 August the Merthyr Chartists crowded out the parish church there. The curate, Thomas Williams, who had been notified of their intention, preached for their benefit from the text (1 Peter ii. 13–17): 'Submit yourselves to every ordinance of man for the Lord's sake: whether it be to the King as supreme; or unto governors, as unto them that are sent by him for the punishment of evildoers and for the praise of them that do well. For so is the will of God, that with well doing ye may put to silence the ignorance of foolish men: as free, and not using your liberty for a cloak of maliciousness, but as servants of God. Honour all men. Love the brotherhood. Fear God. Honour the King.' At Pontypool the following Sunday, also, the text was a promising one: 'For I have learnt in whatever state I am therewith to be content.'[2] The animadversions of the reverend gentlemen on these texts can easily be imagined, and need not be reproduced. On the other hand the Chartists of Aberdare and Hirwaun specially requested an Inde-

---

[1] *Western Vindicator*, June 15, July 6, 13, and 20.
[2] *Merlin*, 17 Aug.; *Merthyr Guardian*, 24 Aug.; *Silurian*, 31 Aug.

pendent minister to preach to them. Before consenting
he insisted upon a public assurance that there were no
physical force men among them, but having obtained this
assurance he produced a scriptural justification of the
doctrine of the rights of man. Oppression, he claimed,
was inherent in Toryism. He admitted that God had
ordered the social arrangement which existed, but he
stressed not only the equality of rights between master and
man but also the equality of duties. He implored his
listeners to eschew physical force and not to raise the
sword against their fellow men.[1]

To all appearances, therefore, the Chartist movement
seemed moribund. Hugh Williams had reported that the
Chartists of the rural areas were 'depressed' by the prosecution of their leaders and were awaiting events in the
industrial areas.[2] From Glamorganshire the magistrates
reported that the miners of Newbridge (Pontypridd) were
all Chartists, and that arms were being sold to them with
which they practised firing at targets, but soon afterwards
the Lord Lieutenant, the Marquis of Bute, assured the
Home Office that Chartism was on the decline.[3] The
Lord Lieutenant for Monmouthshire thought it unnecessary any longer to keep troops at Monmouth town.[4] Even
Frost wrote to a neighbouring magistrate, the Reverend
James Coles, and to the Lord Lieutenant, urging as a
reason for altering the severe conditions imposed on Vincent that 'the agitation has now subsided'.[5] But is it possible that this calm was deceptive, that even the attendance
of the Chartists at church was a cloak to cover nefarious
designs? It is certain that at the beginning of October
Frost urged the men to organize themselves and to form

[1] John Davies, *Y Ffordd Dda* (Merthyr, 1839), preached 9 Sept.
[2] Add. MSS. 34245, B. 140, letter dated 14 Aug.
[3] H.O. 40/46, letters dated 6 Sept. and 17 Oct.
[4] H.O. 40/45, letter dated 30 Sept.
[5] Gurney, op. cit., pp. 515, 516., letters dated 28 Sept.

'tithings' in each parish, every ten men selecting a leader for themselves who would both organize his section and be answerable for its conduct. It is certain, also, from the evidence produced at the trial, that the men who marched to Newport were organized in this way. Moreover among the papers seized in Etheridge's house after the riot was a manuscript which gave details of such an organization,—each five leaders to choose a head officer; three groups of fifty to form a company and three companies to form a brigade. But Etheridge claimed that this paper had nothing to do with the Chartists, that it concerned the Irish Rebellion of 1798, and that it had been in his possession for over twelve months. It is quite possible that the idea was taken from the Irish Rebellion, when this 'cell' system had been adopted, yet it is important to notice that Etheridge had relinquished his secretaryship of the Newport W.M.A. in June, and had ceased to be connected with the Chartists in any way, because he disapproved of their violence, and it is unbelievable, if Frost's tithings were meant as a revolutionary organization and not merely as a means of uniting the Chartists for peaceful purposes, that he should have published an account of them in the pages of the *Western Vindicator*.[1]

However this may be, on 3 October, Frost hurried from Newport in considerable perturbation, and addressed a meeting of some 500 men at Zephaniah Williams's beer house, the Royal Oak, in Coalbrookvale (Blaina). It was a particularly riotous gathering, and Frost was frequently interrupted. He explained that the cause of his appearance there was a report which had reached him that a rising had already commenced, and that the working men of the hills were all under arms and in full march for Monmouth for the purpose of liberating Vincent and the

[1] *Western Vindicator*, 5 Oct.; Newport Museum MSS. 830 (copy of Etheridge's paper); *Merlin*, 23 Nov. (examination of Etheridge).

others from gaol. He was, however, pleased to find that
the further he came from home the more peaceable the
country seemed, and he exhorted them, as they valued
the success of their common cause, not to commit themselves to any premature outbreak. They were not all to
expect to be generals, each acting as he thought proper.
They were to wait with patience until he, as their commander, when the proper time came, should give the word
of command, when he expected every man to be found at
his post, fearless of danger. He said that no other parts of
the country were yet prepared. The people of Scotland
were anxious to join them, and those of Lancashire and the
West of England, but the time was not yet come. This
remark caused some tumult, but Frost insisted that they
must have the co-operation of all, and therefore they
must not be precipitate. When the time came he would
be at the post of danger ready to lead them (if the report
of his words in the *Merthyr Guardian* is correct) 'in crush-
ing the vile plunderers of their liberty'. Frost had been
speaking for some twenty minutes when Jones the watchmaker arrived. He was loudly cheered and called upon
to speak immediately. He had been on a missionary
expedition to the Forest of Dean, he said. Difficulties had
been placed in his way; the parson of Coleford had refused
to allow him to speak without three days notice, and elsewhere he had been refused victuals at a public house.
But the Foresters were ready to help them, and he knew
that the workmen of Britain were quite capable of thwart-
ing the 'matchinations' of their enemies. He was willing
to sacrifice the last drop of his blood. He hoped that all
would keep peace with their enemies, but if their enemies
broke the peace, they should take sword in hand, and
trample their heads under their feet. He could answer
for himself and his brother Frost, who stood there by him
as they had stood from the beginning, and would stand

till the last struggle. This rigmarole was greeted with loud cheers, and then Frost spoke again. He called upon them to stand together and organize themselves. He shortly expected a dissolution of Parliament, when he would offer himself as a candidate for the county of Monmouth, and he expected to be supported on the day of election by the presence of 30,000 men. He did not want more than 30,000, but they must march to Monmouth, organized in sections of ten men, each section with a commander. This was evidently a reference to one of the ulterior measures which had been suggested—the election of representatives 'on the old plan' by show of hands. He was sure that they would secure his election, and if they did not obtain universal suffrage within a month after that, he would no longer argue for Peace, Law, and Order. This was greeted with applause, apparently it was the first remark of his which had pleased them throughout the evening. But he again begged them not to ruin the cause by one false step. He was as anxious as they were to get Vincent out of prison, but they must wait. Vincent, he insisted again, was not as badly used as was said; he was getting fat in prison. There was a movement throughout Europe among working men; they were longing for the time when they would free themselves from their oppressors, and remove the intolerable burden of labour which was heaped on their shoulders. There would be a time when two or three days labour would place within their reach every comfort of life. But the day of election would soon arrive and he should meet them at Monmouth, not to have a halter put round his neck, for he should not like that (shouts of 'You shan't') but to be elected their representative in Parliament, where he should labour whilst he had breath for the restitution of their rights.[1]

[1] *Merthyr Guardian*, 19 Oct.; *Charter*, 10 Nov.; Newport Museum MSS. (Deposition of Thomas Maddock).

'Ulterior Measures'

This was the last public meeting of the Chartists in the hills before the riot, and it would be difficult to over-estimate its importance. Evidently they were bent upon releasing Vincent, and Frost was doing his utmost to dissuade them by telling them that Vincent was getting fat in prison, and by warning them that they would ruin their cause. Even as late as 19 October (that is, only two weeks before the actual outbreak) Frost wrote in a letter 'my object in attending [at Blaina] was to soothe and not to irritate. I understood that the men were going to liberate Vincent, and happy was I to find that the report was incorrect.'[1] He attempted to gain a little time, a month or two, by concentrating their attention on the coming election, and he even tried to soothe them by holding before their eyes visions of a future utopian state—the first, and last, indication in all his speeches and writings of a socialistic standpoint. But his reception had been almost a hostile one, and the firebrand, Jones, had been much more loudly cheered.

Moreover the public meeting was followed by a secret one at the King Crispin beer-house, Brynmawr, some two miles away. It lasted until two o'clock in the morning, and some indication of its nature may be gathered from the fact that the 'hooting and yelling' of the Chartists on their way home 'caused so much terror in the minds of some of the inhabitants that they left their beds and kept on the watch till daybreak'.[2] What, one wonders, happened at this secret meeting? Of this the only indication we have comes from the reminiscences of Dr. William Price. It is true that these should be used with great care, but nevertheless they bear marks of authenticity. According to Dr. Price, Frost summoned a meeting of delegates from the various branches about this time, at which he himself

[1] Extract of letter from Frost 'to a magistrate' given in *Charter*, 8 Dec.
[2] *Merthyr Guardian*, loc. cit.

represented the Merthyr and Aberdare districts. Dr. Price locates the meeting at Twyn y Star, Blaina, and not at the King Crispin, Brynmawr, but as Price related his experiences some forty years later, a slight error between two beer shops a mile or so distant from each other is not of much importance, and the meeting which he describes may well be that of 3 October, for he, also, comments on the fact that it lasted 'until two or three o'clock in the morning'. Characteristically, also, Price says that he did not have a high opinion of Frost, but that Jones was a 'thorough good fellow'. If it is true, as Price states, that Frost called a meeting of delegates, it adds point to his remark in his letter of 19 October, that he had heard that a rising was in full preparation and had sought to prevent it. Moreover, as the secret meeting lasted for hours there was undoubtedly great difficulty in reaching an agreement, and much violent argument. Price states that Frost, who occupied the chair, asked them if they were prepared to rise at his bidding—a question which may well have come late in the proceedings, after the men had expressed their determination to rise, and may have been intended to find out how many were agreed to that course. The answer which Price gives was that of the delegate of Abersychan, and it will be remembered that Abersychan was the home of the 'Scotch Cattle' and of the extreme Chartists. The delegate was himself an old soldier, who had served twenty-five years in the army and had fought at Waterloo.

'I will tell you, Mr. Frost,' he said, 'the condition upon which my lodge will rise, and there is no other condition as far as I am concerned. The Abersychan Lodge is 1,600 strong; 1,200 of them are old soldiers; the remaining 400 have never handled arms, but we can turn them into fighting men in no time. I have been sent here to tell you that we shall not rise until you give us a list of those we have to remove—to kill.'

192

This, allowing for some verbal exaggeration on the part of Dr. Price, may well have been the attitude of the extreme Chartists—a determination to rise, but to do so not for any half-measures, such as a peaceful demonstration of force or useless parade of 30,000 men at Monmouth on election day, but to accomplish their object even at the expense of the bloodshed which must necessarily take place, and according to Price, every delegate gave a similar reply. It was, in fact, a more logical attitude than that of Frost, who seemed to contemplate a kind of 'token' revolution, which Dr. Price characterized, with more good sense than he is generally given credit for, as putting a 'sword in my hand and a rope around my neck at the same time'.[1]

But whatever may have been the outcome of the secret meeting, Frost still persisted in his idea of a show of strength at the election at Monmouth—20,000 marching ten abreast, and proposed a new petition for the prisoners, though he admitted that 'thousands thought there was no purpose' in petitioning.[2] The landlord of the King Crispin tried to carry the torch of Chartism to Brecon, but found little welcome there (21 October). He promised the small group of Chartists which was formed that Frost and O'Connor would come to speak to them, which if it means anything (and probably it does not) suggests that he did not at that time contemplate the possibility of an outbreak in less than two weeks.[3] On October 22 Frost wrote his last public letter. It was a last appeal to the farmers and tradesmen of Monmouthshire. He once again defended the Chartists against the charge of wanting to take away their property, and warned them that unless the Charter became the law of the land, and that speedily, there would be no security for person or property. The country, he thought, was fast approaching the state of

---

[1] *Cardiff Times*, 26 May 1888.   [2] *Western Vindicator*, 12 Oct.
[3] *Merlin*, 26 Oct.; *Cambrian*, 2 Nov.

France before the first revolution. There were spies everywhere, and the people were in a state of sullen discontent. There was possibly a depth of feeling in his concluding remark, that the government in France had thought it could suppress the revolution by destroying its leaders, but the only result was that leaders ten times more violent had appeared.[1] But to all appearances Chartism was dead. It disappears almost completely from the pages of the *Merlin* and the *Merthyr Guardian*. At the end of October the Attorney-General, Sir John Campbell, in addressing his constituents, said that Chartism was extinct. The government had left it to the good sense of the people to put it down. The Tories, he claimed, would not have acted in that way; they would have repeated the Manchester Massacre of 1819. To this his audience responded with cheers, and the only reference to Chartism in the *Merlin* for Saturday, 2 November, was an echo of his words in a very brief paragraph (headed 'Extinction of Chartism') which stated that the forbearance of the government was rapidly destroying Chartism without making victims of the deceived or martyrs of the deceivers. But the complacency of the Attorney-General was misplaced, for, as the Tory wits soon were quoting from Shakespeare's *Henry VIII*:

'The third day came a frost, a killing frost,
And—when he thought good easy man, full surely
His greatness was a'ripening—nipped his root.'

The day after the *Merlin* had declared Chartism to be extinct the Chartists commenced their march on Newport.

---

[1] *Western Vindicator*, 26 Oct.

VII

THE ATTACK ON NEWPORT

Nothing is more remarkable about the attack on Newport on Monday morning, 4 November (except, perhaps, the difficulty of discovering any satisfactory motive for it), than the secrecy with which it was planned. It has been seen that the *Merlin* of 2 November was convinced that Chartism was extinct. Still more striking is the evidence supplied by a letter from the manager of the British Iron Company at Abersychan to his London office, dated 3 November. He had been told on the Saturday that 'something serious was being contemplated', yet although he lived in one of the most radical sections of the coal-field, and had every opportunity of observing any unusual development, he dismissed the information given to him as an idle rumour. Within twenty-four hours of the time he had received it, he and his family had left their home and were hiding in a shed a quarter of a mile away. The Chartist *Western Vindicator* itself seems to have set up the issue for even the following Saturday, 9 November, without any indication of a possible outbreak, and that number included only a brief letter from a correspondent at Newport stating what had taken place.[1]

This secrecy was very much commented upon at the time.[2] In attempting to account for the success of the workers in keeping their plans from the authorities, one reason was found in the inaccessibility of the mining valleys. It is certainly true that there were very few justices in the coal-field, but it is also true that the employers of labour still, at this time, lived among their workmen in these valleys. Absentee ownership was a later

---

[1] Letter dated 3 Nov. in H.O. 40/45; *Western Vindicator*, 9 Nov., 23 Nov.
[2] e.g. H.O. 40/45, Lord Lieutenant to H.O., 6 Nov.

development in South Wales. Yet the masters and their agents, although they lived among their men, had very little contact with them, for the division between them was not only one of class, but of race, language, and religion. The iron-masters of Wales had come from across the border, and they placed in positions of trust only their fellow countrymen. 'In the works, the Welsh workman never finds his way into the office', states the Welsh Education Report of 1847. 'He never becomes either clerk or agent. He may become an overseer, or subcontractor, but this does not take him out of the labouring, and put him into the administering class.'[1] Is it then possible that the secrecy was due to the fact that the planning was done through the medium of the Welsh language? The mayor of Newport, in his book on Wales published ten years later, specifically denied this.[2] It should, perhaps, be remembered that he was then concerned with refuting other aspersions cast upon his countrymen on account of their language, and also that he was convinced that the Newport riot was to have formed part of a general insurrection if it had been successful. In the planning of such a revolt involving other areas as well, the Welsh language would hardly have had any place. But even if his theory is not correct, even if the riot was an isolated affair, the use of the Welsh language can scarcely be considered a satisfactory explanation of the secrecy which preceded it, for Jones the watchmaker and many of the minor leaders spoke no Welsh. It may be that the planning of an insurrection, even of a local character, existed only in the minds of the authorities, that there was scarcely any planning, and that the affair was suddenly decided upon only a few days before it took place. Yet it has to be admitted that it is very difficult to reconstruct the activities of the

[1] Quoted T. Phillips, *Wales* (London, 1849), p. 54.
[2] Ibid., pp. 52–3.

Chartist leaders during the month of October, whether they were intentionally keeping their movements secret or not.

It is undoubtedly true that there was considerable activity at this time. There is evidence, for example, of tampering with the soldiers. A company of the 45th regiment had just been drafted to Newport. Its members were nearly all raw Irish recruits with less than two years' service. They were treated to drinks in the beerhouses, and, according to the evidence given by some of them later, were promised half a crown a day if they deserted. Two actually did desert, and made their way into the hills, but they reconsidered their decision and returned. A Chartist who was said to have aided them was committed for trial at the next Quarter Sessions, although it was admitted that he was 'half drunk' when he did so. When the riot had taken place and the Chartists had come to be the scape-goats for everything, other soldiers pleaded an inducement by them as a reason for having deserted, but by this time this had probably come to appear a very satisfactory excuse.[1] There is also evidence that pikes were being made at forges in Newport and elsewhere, and that bullets were being cast in rough moulds. As for powder, its use by the miners in their daily work made it very easy to procure; one Newport firm sold no less than one thousand barrels a year. Guns and pistols, on the other hand, presented much more difficulty, yet a number of these were procured.[2]

Frost's movements at this period are difficult to trace with any definiteness, and yet they present a most important problem. On 3 October he had been at the Coalbrookvale (Blaina) meeting. In the following week, according to a letter of 8 October, he went around the

---

[1] *Merlin*, 16 Nov., 7 Dec.; *Charter*, 15 Dec.
[2] Museum MS., evidence of several persons; Gurney, p. 403.

hills, and, according to evidence taken by the magistrates before the trial, he addressed a large meeting at Blackwood, giving an account of his delegateship, and contrasting his attitude in doing so with that of the members for Monmouthshire, who had never felt it necessary to account for their actions to their constituents.[1] We know that he was at Newport on 8 October, for on that date he wrote a letter from Newport to the *Western Vindicator*. He announced in this his intention to visit Merthyr and Pontypool, but there is no evidence to show whether he did so or not. On 14 October he was expected to attend a dinner at the People's Hall, Bury, given in honour of the delegate from Bury to the Convention, but, again, there is no evidence that he did so.[2] It was five days later (19 October) that he wrote the letter in which he explained his reason for attending the meeting at Coalbrookvale. He was then at Newport, and it was from Newport that he wrote his last public letter on 22 October. If reliance can be placed on Dr. Price's reminiscences, he met Frost again on 27 October, presumably at Newport. On 31 October he was probably at Blackwood; he was certainly there the following day. Is it possible, therefore, that he could have visited London during this month? The only possible times were between 8 and 19 October, and after 22 October. It would be very unlike Frost not to have commented upon it, if he had recently returned from London when he wrote his letter of 22 October, yet a visit on his part to London about this time is an essential element in the most generally accepted theory of the riot, while a visit after 22 October scarcely allows the necessary time for the activities involved in the theory.

The theory is that of William Lovett. He was in prison during the riot, but he claims that as soon as he came out

---

[1] Museum MS., evidence of Job Tovey.
[2] *Northern Star*, 28 Sept.

he made inquiries and obtained information from a person who had taken an active part in it. According to him, the chief cause of the outbreak was the treatment of Vincent. Frost did all he could to get this altered, and, having failed, came to London. (Frost's last letters to the magistrates on this subject were written, it will be remembered, on 28 September.) Frost mentioned to two or three members of the Convention that he had great difficulty in restraining the Welsh from attempting to release Vincent by force, and was told that if the Welsh rose to release Vincent, the people of Yorkshire and Lancashire were ready to join in a rising for the Charter. It was then decided that Frost should go back to consult the chief leaders among the Welsh, and that Peter Bussey should consult the people of Yorkshire and Lancashire. A meeting was convened in the north at Heckmondwick (between Leeds and Huddersfield), where about forty delegates attended from the surrounding districts, among them three members of the Convention, including Lovett's informant. This meeting was informed of the intention of the Welsh to rise, and although several delegates thought the rising premature, it was decided to aid it by an outbreak in the north. According to Lovett's fellow prisoner, Collins, who also claimed to have obtained his information from one of the persons involved, a messenger was sent to O'Connor to request him to lead them as he had so often promised to do. The following conversation, at which Collins's informant was present, then took place:

Delegate: Mr. O'Connor, we are going to have a rising for the Charter in Yorkshire, and I am sent from —— to ask you if you will lead us on, as you have often said you would when we were prepared.

O'Connor: Well, when is the rising to take place?

Delegate: Why, we have resolved that it shall begin on Saturday next.

199

O'Connor: Are you well provided with arms then?

Delegate: Yes, all of us.

O'Connor: Well, that is all right, my man.

Delegate: Now, Mr. O'Connor, shall I tell our lads that you will come and lead them on?

O'Connor (indignantly): Why, man! when did you ever hear of me, or of any of my family, ever deserting the cause of the people? Have they not always been found at their post in the hour of danger?

O'Connor's bluster convinced the delegate that he would be ready to lead them, although he later denied that he had made any promise at all. But when he found that the people were in earnest, O'Connor is said to have sent a messenger to Yorkshire to assure the people there that no rising would take place in Wales, and sent Charles Jones to Wales, to assure the Welsh that there would be no rising in Yorkshire, and that it was all a government plot. When Jones arrived at Frost's house, he found he had already left for the country for the purpose of conferring with the leaders in different districts, and was directed where to find him. When he found Frost he was told that O'Connor's message had come too late, that the people were resolved on releasing Vincent from prison, and that Frost might as well blow out his own brains as try to oppose them or shrink back. He then urged Charles Jones to go back to Yorkshire and Lancashire to tell the leaders what the Welsh had resolved on doing. As Jones was short of money he gave him three sovereigns to aid him in getting back as soon as possible. But before anything could be done in the north, the Welsh had risen and been defeated. The men of the north were exasperated when they found that they had been misinformed. They, therefore, decided to rise the following Saturday, with Peter Bussey as their leader. Peter, however, was suddenly taken ill. The Bradford Chartists were resolved to see for themselves how ill

he was, and searched his house, but could not find him, as
he had gone, it was said, to the country for his health.
His little boy, however, in chattering with the customers
in his father's beer-shop some days later, let out the truth.
'Ah,' said the boy, 'you could not find father the other
day, but I knew where he was all the time; he was up in
the cock-loft behind the flour sacks.' On account of this
contretemps Bussey soon had to wind up his affairs and
depart for America. O'Connor in the meantime, says
Lovett, thought it a timely opportunity to visit Ireland,
and did not return until the outbreak was over.[1]

If Lovett's account is to be taken as strictly accurate,
then the conversation with O'Connor took place on or
after Saturday, 26 October. This would mean that the
Heckmondwick meeting had taken place some days previously, and Frost's visit to London some days before that.
But on 19 October he wrote expressing his relief that the
miners were not going to liberate Vincent, and three days
later he was still in Newport. In any case O'Connor had
arrived in Dublin on 6 October, some three weeks before
the date on which the conversation is supposed to have
taken place, and did not return until 6 November. Lovett's
account cannot therefore be accepted as authentic. His
antipathy for O'Connor was such that he sought to disparage him on all occasions. Still less tenable is the elaboration of Lovett's theory, that O'Connor could have saved
Frost if he had wished, but preferred to sacrifice him out
of jealousy.[2] Frost would certainly have known if O'Connor had betrayed him, but his letters, both immediately
after the trial and twenty years later, show that throughout his life he retained for O'Connor's memory not only
friendship but affection. Very curiously, Lovett did not
incorporate in his memoirs information he had derived

[1] William Lovett, *The Life and Struggles of William Lovett* (London, 1876),
pp. 238–41. [2] Hovell, op. cit., p. 181.

from Dr. John Taylor. The latter was a prominent member of the physical force party, but he retired from the movement after his imprisonment in 1840. In May 1841 he wrote to Lovett to congratulate him on the revival of Chartism, and apparently Lovett asked him for information about the incidents of 4 November. Taylor, in reply, supplied him with an eight-paged manuscript, evidently made enigmatic in order to delude the police if it fell into their hands, and sent in four sections for the same reason. Taylor declared that the riot was a complete mystery to him. Yet on the Tuesday before the riot Hetherington had brought a messenger to him, who mentioned that an outbreak was likely to take place in Wales. Taylor immediately proceeded to Yorkshire, and there he heard that the rising was to take place on Saturday, but that a messenger had been sent to Wales to put the affair off for ten days. He then proceeded to Newcastle, and tried to organize his men, but this had been made difficult by the opposition of O'Connor, and, before he had succeeded, the disastrous news came from Wales. He had heard of a dinner in Yorkshire 'some months previously' (possibly this was an echo of Heckmondwick), but he knew nothing about it, and, also, he declared that O'Connor had sent a person called George White around the Yorkshire towns on the Saturday, to say that there would be no rising, as it was all a government plot. This account obviously does not agree entirely with Lovett's own version, and Taylor evidently was not the 'informant' of whom Lovett spoke in his memoirs, for he was not present at Heckmondwick. Lovett must have had some reason for rejecting his evidence, and with regard to O'Connor the story is obviously inaccurate, as O'Connor had not returned from Ireland on the Saturday. Yet Taylor's account proves that there were rumours of projected risings in various parts of the country. And, moreover, although Lovett's story must be rejected on the evidence available to those historians who have accepted it, it contains an element of truth, for further evidence is now available that a messenger did come to Frost on Saturday, 2 November, that Frost did tell him that it was now too late to stop the rising, although the messenger thought it premature, and that it was from Bradford (Peter Bussey's home) that he came.[1]

What then were the movements of the Welsh leaders at this time? According to Dr. Price, Frost sent a certain Isaac Morgan to him on Saturday, 26 October, to ask Price to see him on the following morning. He then informed Price that the Chartists would rise that night week. Price immediately asked for the plan of the outbreak, and was told that it was still in Etheridge's office. A curious confirmation of this is that the plan for the organization in groups of ten was actually found (as we have seen) in Etheridge's office when his papers were seized. Price declared that he would only rise on the conditions laid down at the secret meeting of the delegates, but Frost remonstrated that this might mean killing a thousand soldiers. Price agreed that it would, possibly a hundred thousand, to which Frost replied, ' I cannot do it; I cannot do it', and wept like a child and talked of heaven and hell. It was then that Price told him that he was not going to have a sword put in his hand and a rope around his neck at the same time. 'If I take a sword in hand,' he said, 'I will use it, and no one shall take it from me but at the cost of my life.' Price, if his story is true, evidently felt that a rising was worthless, unless the Chartists were prepared to fight.

---

[1] Taylor's account is in *Lovett Collection*, ii. 211. Dolléans accepts Lovett's story in its entirety; Rosenblatt accepts it while admitting Lovett's enmity for O'Connor; West believes that O'Connor's conduct at this time 'appears in an extremely unfavourable light' and says of Lovett's story that it was 'characteristic even if not true'; Hovell argues that O'Connor's denial of knowledge of the affair 'is absurd on the face of it', although he does not commit himself as to the authenticity of Lovett's story.

He even professes to have suspected Frost of wishing to destroy the movement and of having some one in hiding listening to this conversation.[1] Like all Price's reminiscences, this account has to be accepted with caution. His presence at Blackwood the following Friday (evidence of which was produced at the trial) is inconsistent with his having entirely washed his hands of the affair six days previously. Yet the conversation so accurately illustrates the attitudes of the two men that it is impossible to reject the story altogether. Moreover, Dr. Taylor had heard that it was Price (whom Frost had introduced on one occasion to the Convention) who was to have led the attack in Wales, but that he disappeared a few days before the riots. There is evidence from other witnesses of rumours that something might happen on the Sunday. In any case the approach of Guy Fawkes' Day was causing some apprehension. Every year there had been complaints in the *Merlin* of the rowdiness on this day, and in the disturbed state of the country in 1839, it may have been feared that more than the usual celebrations would take place. If the miners were to hold a demonstration, it would be natural that they should choose a Sunday, their only free day; and as it was only two days before Guy Fawkes' Day, it is not impossible that the night of 3–4 November was chosen on that account.

If little is known of Frost's activities during these days, the movements of the other leaders are less obscure. There were so many of them at Dukestown (Sirhowy) on Monday, 28 October (among them Zephaniah Williams and Jones, but apparently not Frost), that it was later surmised that a secret meeting had been held. It is possible that some plan may have then been determined upon.[2] The various lodges were becoming increasingly active. On the same night the Blackwood lodge held its weekly

[1] *Cardiff Times*, loc. cit.   [2] *Silurian*, 16 Nov. 1839.

meeting, and according to William Davies, the young Chartist who had accompanied Vincent to Stroud, a dispute arose at it both because of the irregular attendance of some of the members and because of a difference of opinion on the use of moral and physical force.[1] It was no doubt becoming evident that this would soon become a question of more than theoretical importance. Most lodges seem to have met every night throughout the week. On the Tuesday, Zephaniah Williams addressed a meeting at his own house, the Royal Oak, and distributed membership cards. He explained the points of the charter, and declared that the policy of the Chartists would be to destroy the workhouses first and then establish free trade and universal suffrage, but he stressed that there was to be no bloodshed. The lodge continued to meet on the following nights, and although he himself was not present, his young son, Llewellyn, read out passages from the *Western Vindicator*.[2] As usual, the meetings in the Pontypool district were more violent in tone. At the Pontnewynydd lodge, on Tuesday night, the chairman explained that he had been sent around the hills to ascertain how the organization of the Chartists was proceeding. In the Merthyr district, he maintained, upwards of 2,000 men were already organized and armed, and he asked his listeners if they were all armed and prepared for the worst. After this the leaders adjourned to another room, no doubt for a secret meeting.[3] At Jones's house, also, on the following night, a delegate visited the lodge and reminded the Chartists of their Whit Monday resolutions to support the Convention in all its measures, and with all their might. He urged them to organize, to procure arms, and to meet every night until Sunday.[4] Zephaniah Williams and

---

[1] Museum MSS., Davies MS. and evidence, 383 and 384.
[2] Ibid., 474, evidence of William Howell.
[3] Ibid., 405, evidence of Emery.   [4] Ibid., 397, evidence of Emery.

Jones were occupied throughout the week in visiting the various lodges 'to stir them up', Williams's duty apparently being to explain matters in Welsh, while Jones spoke in English. The difference between the two men is evident from their speeches. On Wednesday, for example, they visited together the lodge at Crumlin. Williams, in Welsh, explained the points of the Charter. It would soon be the law of the land, he said, and would be obtained without bloodshed, but he recommended the Chartists to 'take some sort of arms to protect themselves'. Evidently, therefore, a demonstration was being contemplated very soon, and at the lodge there was 'some talk of Sunday night'. But Jones valiantly attacked the law, which was intended to protect money, he said, and not persons. He also dwelt upon the hardships of his hearers; the colliers did not know in the morning whether they would return home alive or dead, and they ought to earn more money than any one else. He was evidently rousing up the discontent of the miners to prepare them for action. It was their intention, he said, to liberate Vincent and to put Lord John Russell in his place.[1] From Crumlin the two men went to Blackwood, where they arrived late in the evening. They were met at the Coach and Horses by some of the other leaders. Among them was young William Davies, and they probably deputed him to go to Newport to buy arms. He went there the next day, but, according to his own evidence, although he visited an ironmonger's shop and examined some firearms, he did not buy any. When he returned home at eleven o'clock at night he found a secret meeting in progress at the Coach and Horses.[2] Williams and Jones had again come there together from a meeting they had held at Pengam (Pontaberpengam). There they had warned the people to be prepared, as they

---

[1] Museum MSS., evidence of Richard Williams in Welsh; also MS. 443.
[2] Ibid., Davies as above.

did not know what hour they might be wanted. They even advised them not to attend to their work, but to be ready at any minute to answer the call of their leaders.[1] According to Davies, Frost was present at the secret meeting on the Thursday night, and the wife of the landlord of the Coach and Horses states that he breakfasted there the following morning.[2] But here the evidence is somewhat conflicting, for the landlord of the inn states that Frost did not arrive there until eleven o'clock on Friday morning.[3]

The meeting on Friday had evidently been arranged well beforehand, and the absence of the Chartist leaders from their homes on that day was much commented on.[4] Of what happened on this important occasion we have reliable evidence, for William Davies, who was present, afterwards turned queen's evidence.[5] About thirty delegates arrived at the Coach and Horses sometime before midday, and proceeded to a room upstairs where they held their meeting in secret. Among them were Frost, Williams, and Jones, and among the lodges represented were those of Dowlais, Rhymney, Fleur de Lys, Maesycwmmer, Sirhowy, Argoed, Blackwood, Ebbw Vale, Victoria Ironworks, Llanelly (Breconshire), Blaina, Twyn y Star, Llanhilleth, Crumlin, Croespenmaen, Pontypool, British Ironworks, and Newport. The chair was taken not by Frost but by a delegate named Reynolds, and the proceedings commenced with a prayer offered up by an Englishman, who appeared to Davies to be a native of the Forest of Dean. Thus the conspiracy, such as it was, began

---

[1] Ibid., evidence of John James and William James.

[2] Ibid., 599, evidence of Esther Pugh.

[3] Evidence of Richard Pugh, *Merlin*, 18 Jan. 1840, and Gurney, p. 394. Esther Pugh's evidence is a day out in some other respects, and may possibly be inaccurate on this also, but Davies's evidence is definite enough, and Richard Pugh may have been quibbling; Frost may have returned to the inn at eleven o'clock on Friday. Tovey (MS. 668) states that he saw Frost at the inn on Thursday.   [4] *Silurian*, loc. cit.

[5] Museum MS., Davies evidence as above.

with the invoking of the help of the Almighty. Each delegate was then called upon to state the number of members in his lodge, how many of them could bring guns, how many could bring pikes, and how many could be depended upon. The figures were taken down by Jones, who estimated that they could count upon 5,000 armed men. Arrangements for the rising were then discussed, Sunday night having apparently been decided upon. The organization in groups of ten, each with its leader, which had been used to collect money for the defence of Vincent and others, was adopted, and it was decided that the crowd should march in military order. They were to secure all persons in authority wherever they were met, and hold them as hostages. To begin with it was proposed that the meeting-place should be at Abercarn, but it was thought that this was too far for the men from the Pontypool valley, and eventually Risca was chosen. All were to arrive there at midnight on Sunday night. Davies does not give any indication that there was any difference of opinion expressed at this meeting. Moreover, according to the statement taken from him by the magistrates, Frost 'said a great deal to induce them to rise', though how far this can be entirely relied upon is doubtful, for Davies was then hoping to win the favour of the authorities. A great deal was said about Trowbridge and other places, he added, and about stopping the mails, so that the people in the north would know they had succeeded. Davies does not state whether Dr. Price was among the delegates. Price was seen by the landlord of the Coach and Horses talking to Frost at the door of the inn about midday, but the landlord did not think that he had come inside.[1] The meeting lasted until about four o'clock, when all the delegates had tea. Afterwards Frost saw a workman named Job Tovey, at whose house he had stayed on a previous occasion, and

[1] Museum MSS. 601, evidence of Richard Pugh.

asked him if he could have a bed for the night. Frost, said Tovey, did not mind that the accommodation was rough. Tovey promised to find him a bed, and Frost came to his house about eleven o'clock that night.[1]

The Blackwood lodge had at this time about ten pounds in its funds. It was decided to send a certain person to Cardiff to buy arms, but it was feared he could not be trusted, and so five pounds were given to William Davies to go to Newport again for the same purpose. He called at several ironmongers, but again, according to his statement, he did not buy any, probably because he was afraid that this would implicate him too definitely. While at Newport he called at Mrs. Frost's, and was given two letters and a paper parcel to deliver to her husband. Later in the day, young Henry Hunt Frost brought to him some one whom he said was a friend who wished to see his father, and as the only conveyance which he could have taken was gone, young Frost asked Davies to take him along. Davies's father was reluctant to give him a place in his gig, but was induced by Davies to do so. The stranger was a young workman, under thirty years of age, and came from Bradford. At Blackwood, Davies left his father, and took the stranger to Tovey's house. There he and Frost shook hands, and both left the house so that they could talk together. They returned in about a quarter of an hour. Frost then read his letters and put them in the fire, together with a letter which he received from the stranger. They took tea together, during which Tovey heard Frost tell the stranger that he must return to Newport that night and go to Monmouth, otherwise it would be too late, for the mail would be stopped on Monday, and he would not be able to continue his journey. Frost then, according to Tovey, told him what they were going to do, and the stranger replied that he would go back to

[1] Ibid. 668, evidence of Tovey

his district and tell the people that Frost had taken Newport and that it was time for them to begin. After tea
they left Tovey's house. According to Davies they went
to the Coach and Horses and went upstairs to a bedroom.
There were present Frost, Reynolds, the stranger, the
secretary of the Blackwood lodge, one other person, and,
for part of the time, Davies himself. They spoke of the
north and of the rising, which the stranger thought to be
premature, but Frost said that he could not put it off, as
it had been agreed upon at the meeting of the previous
day. They discussed matters for some time, and then at
about nine o'clock the stranger went away. Davies believed that he was to go through Newport to Monmouth
and on to Birmingham.[1]

Was this stranger the Charles Jones of Lovett's theory?
Unfortunately it is not quite clear whether the Charles
Jones whom Lovett mentions was the person who was in
hiding on account of the Llanidloes rioting or not, although one is fairly safe in assuming that Lovett would
have mentioned the fact if he had any one other than his
fellow delegate to the Convention in mind. Would Davies
therefore speak of a fellow Welshman only as a young
workman from Bradford? Did he perhaps know that it
was Charles Jones, and that he was wanted by the authorities, and did he withhold his knowledge from the magistrates? As will be seen later, Davies's attitude was highly
complex. Nothing appears in the evidence either of
Davies or of Tovey of any discussion with the stranger
about a previous meeting at Heckmondwick or a concerted
plan for an outbreak. Both, however, professed to have
heard that the non-arrival of the mail would be a signal to
the other areas that the Chartists had succeeded at Newport, and Tovey even indicated that a delay of an hour and
a half in its arrival at Birmingham would be sufficient.

[1] Museum MSS., evidence of Davies and Tovey, as above.

Of the authenticity of this it will be seen that there are grave doubts. Yet it is beyond doubt that Frost was in communication with the Midlands and the North, and in the absence of definite evidence, possibly the most reasonable theory is that these areas as well as South Wales were on the verge of an outbreak, although there may not have been a specific plan for the night of 3–4 November. It is worth noting that the news of the riot first reached Newcastle in the form that Frost was in possession of Newport, and this, according to Tovey, was the version of it which the stranger had agreed to give.

On Saturday night the absence of the Chartists from their weekly markets was noticed. The leaders were fully occupied in their own lodges organizing their men. Names were called over, and 'captains' placed over every ten men.[1] Pikes were distributed in some cases. Zephaniah Williams told his men that there were pikes ready for them, but he thought it unwise to distribute them until the following evening, for they might get drunk and foolish.[2] No doubt pressure was brought to bear upon those who were reluctant to come. The secretary of the Blackwood lodge said that now they would find out who was a Chartist and who was not. Any one who did not come would be regarded as a black sheep.[3] Others were more forcible in their expressions. They said that any who were found to have stayed behind would be killed like toads.[4] But as almost every witness who was examined gave for his excuse that he had been forced to come, it is necessary to exercise caution before accepting these statements.

Sunday morning was dull and cloudy, with intermittent rain, and did not promise well for their desperate enterprize. Nevertheless the leaders were early at their work.

[1] Gurney, p. 266.
[2] Museum MS. 343, evidence of Thomas Bowen.
[3] Ibid. 466, evidence of Hodge.
[4] Ibid. 333, evidence of Richard Arnold.

Jones had left his home almost at daybreak, and soon after seven o'clock had arrived on horseback at Abersychan. The men there were already crowding into the beer-houses in the chill half-light of the morning. He told them to go to the Race-course, about a mile below Pontypool, where there were plenty of arms for them, and assured them that Williams had a good supply of guns and pistols. They should be ready to start for Pontypool by about two o'clock in the afternoon, and should force all who refused to come along. Placards had been prepared, he said, which would be posted in Newport the following day, beginning: 'We, the executive government of England', and signed 'John Frost, President'. By Wednesday, he declared, they should either have the Charter and all be pardoned, or the government would be in their own hands.[1]

He was evidently acting a part, as he had so often done on the stage, and, no doubt, felt an elation greater than his most successful impersonations had ever given him. In spite of his bearing and his fine voice he had been a failure as an actor; now his vanity was soothed by what he considered an important role in actual life. Possibly the proclamation of the executive government existed only in his imagination. Much was made of it by the opponents of Chartism, but no trace of it has been found. Jones proceeded up the valley, and across to Nantyglo, where he possibly saw Zephaniah Williams. Then he crossed over to the Sirhowy valley, and about three in the afternoon was seen riding fast through Tredegar in the direction of Blackwood. There the Chartists had met in the morning, and again in the afternoon, in spite of the steady downpour of rain, and had arranged their final meeting for six o'clock.[2]

By this time it must have been obvious to the magistrates

[1] Museum MS. 397, evidence of Emery; *Merlin*, 14 Dec. 1839; 11 Jan. 1840.   [2] Gurney, loc. cit.

in the coal-field that something was afoot. The Lord Lieutenant received information in the morning, and immediately warned the authorities at Newport and Monmouth to be prepared for a sudden attack. He wrote to the Home Office that there was a combined movement from the hills with the intention of plundering and destroying property. Sir John Josiah Guest reported that the Dowlais Chartists, armed with offensive weapons, were being seen going after dark in the direction of Sirhowy. The iron-master at Ebbw Vale fled with his wife to Abergavenny, and the agent stationed at the Abersychan ironworks went into hiding with his wife and children.[1]

Frost had breakfasted and dined at Tovey's house. Men came to see him continually throughout the day, and in the late afternoon he went along with William Davies to the Coach and Horses. According to Davies, Frost then told him to stay at home, as he was not well. Was he perhaps already in love with Frost's daughter, and did Frost, always concerned for the happiness of his family, wish to spare his daughter from further unhappiness? The explanation of Davies's conduct given at the time was, however, less romantic. He was heard to say when he saw the crowd collected in the streets that there were enough men there to eat Newport,[2] but when the signal was given to start, he slunk home and stayed indoors until twelve o'clock the next day. Frost, wrapped in a rough great coat and with a red cravat round his neck, kept pacing backwards and forwards before the inn, no doubt waiting for some appointed signal. The men had now been told that they were to go to Newport, and that they were to meet other contingents below Risca. They were to challenge all they met with the password 'Beans', and if these replied 'Well' all was right

[1] H.O. 40/45, various letters.
[2] Gurney, p. 362. The witness was a very unsatisfactory one. In his deposition he had stated definitely that he could not hear what Davies had said. Ibid. 368.

(Beanswell was a place name in Newport). If they did not know the password they were to be detained. At seven o'clock Jones arrived.[1] Was this perhaps the signal that Frost was expecting? Jones, at any rate, did not get off his horse, but spoke a few words to Frost, and then hurried away. It was at seven o'clock, also, that a man with a glazed hat was said to have brought news from Newport. This episode, which was to be of vital importance in the trial, was based only on the evidence of James Hodge, the most unsatisfactory of all the witnesses against Frost. According to him, he was in a room in the Coach and Horses about seven o'clock, when a man with a glazed hat informed Frost that he had come from Newport, that the soldiers there were all Chartists, that their arms and ammunition were packed up, and that they were ready to join the Chartists as soon as they arrived. It was immediately after this that the men began to move, according to Hodge.[2] Hodge said that he knew William Jones, so that it is hardly possible that Jones was the man in the glazed hat. If such a person did arrive and gave the message, it is difficult not to think that he was an *agent provocateur*, for there was no foundation for his statement. That there was a belief that Frost had arranged matters with the soldiers, and that they would give up their arms is, indeed, shown by other evidence,[3] but no one other than Hodge seems to have seen the man in the glazed hat. It is safest to assume that he never existed.

Whatever may have been the signal for which Frost was waiting, and it was probably the arrival of Jones, he now decided to move. The streets were swarming with Chartists from the neighbouring lodges, and the congestion was

---

[1] *Merlin*, 18 Jan. 1840, Richard Pugh's evidence.
[2] Gurney, pp. 292–311; Museum MS. 466, evidence of Hodge.
[3] Museum MS. 333, evidence of Richard Arnold.

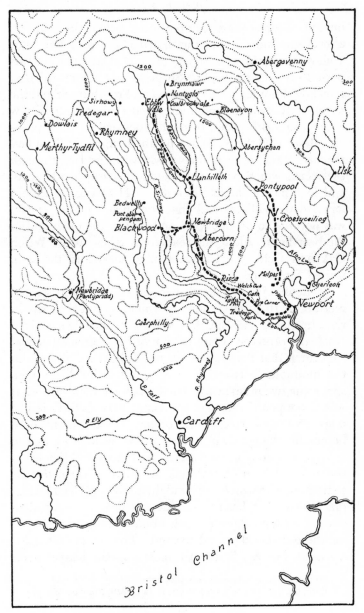

The Advance on Newport, 3–4 November, 1839.

intense. Women and children were crying, the rain was almost continuous, and the disorder was complete. But a shot was fired as a signal to start, and the Chartists passed on into the night. So great was the crowd that they could not all go the same way. Frost himself and the main body took the mountain road over into the Ebbw Valley, and proceeded through Abercarn. Others probably descended the Sirhowy. By about midnight Frost had reached Risca, after toiling slowly with his men through the storm which had arisen, along a badly made road, and in almost complete darkness.[1] How was he to join forces with Williams and Jones on such a night? There was nothing to do but wait, and, out in the open and in the beer-houses along the road from Risca to the Welch Oak and Cefn, the Chartists, now soaked to the skin, waited for hours.

At Zephaniah Williams's beer-house the Chartists had met about 10.30 on Sunday morning, and again early in the afternoon. An English-speaking person then arrived (this was probably Jones or one of his lieutenants), and told them that they should all meet about six o'clock, on the mountain between Nantyglo and Ebbw Vale, at a spot some two miles away. He threatened them with what would happen if they did not come; they should die like dogs. Williams acted as interpreter. He told them to go home and change their clothes, if they wanted to, and to bring bread and cheese with them. He assured them that there would be no bloodshed, but advised them to take something with which to defend themselves.[2] The meeting-place which had been determined upon was a convenient one for all the lodges of north Monmouthshire, and even for those of Dowlais and beyond. Thither the Chartists came 'in droves', frequently molesting the chapel goers

[1] Museum MS. 577; Gurney, pp. 266, 300.
[2] Ibid., pp. 312, 317, 329, 331; *Merlin*, 11 Jan. 1840; Museum MS. 474.

who were attending divine service at the time. One such
incident is well authenticated. (There may have been
several, or perhaps one or two incidents were multiplied,
as was the case with other things on that memorable
night.) At Carmel Chapel, Beaufort, the Reverend John
Ridge was exhorting his flock in a lugubrious manner
which suited the stormy night, the cold candle-lit meeting-
house and the damp clothes of his listeners. They were
all born to die, he was exclaiming, when six or seven
Chartists came through the doorway, one of them saying,
'Yes, some of you sooner than you think.' Outside there
were hundreds more, and the service had to be abandoned,
Ridge himself escaping only by extinguishing all the lights
he could, and hiding under the stairs which led up to his
pulpit.[1]

On the mountain the Chartists stayed for two, or even
three, hours, in the growing darkness and in spite of the
storm which was rising. Apparently they were waiting for
the Sirhowy men,[2] who may, conceivably, have themselves
been waiting for the men from Dowlais and Merthyr.
Zephaniah Williams kept going backwards and forwards
in the dark. He again spoke, both in Welsh and in English, from a 'tump' (Welsh, *twmpath*) on the mountain side.
They were going down to Newport, he said, to show the
people that they were determined to get the Charter made
the law of the land. They would be there by two o'clock
in the morning. But there was to be no shedding of blood.
They need not be frightened; the soldiers would not touch
them. At this there were cries, 'we do not care for them,'
but Williams enjoined them not to break the law, and to
take no one's property.[3] After this the crowd moved down
from the mountain into the Ebbw Fawr valley (Ebbw

---

[1] Ibid. 682.
[2] Ibid. 607, evidence of Richards.
[3] Ibid. 342, 607; Gurney, loc. cit.; *Merlin*, loc. cit.

Vale). In spite of Williams's injunctions, they seem to have been particularly riotous. They put out the blasts in the furnaces, knocked at doors and broke windows and forced the men to come along.

Some of the advance guard had reached Llanhilleth as early as eleven o'clock, and called for drinks at the Coach and Horses of that place. Ten minutes later another band arrived, and about 1.30 a.m. Williams himself came. He was quite wet. He sat down by the fire for about half an hour, drank a pint of beer, and then persuaded the landlord to lend him a horse and tram for which he would pay. The landlord consented to do so, and Williams and some others followed the tramroad as far as Ty'n y Cwm, near the Welch Oak, and only some six miles from Newport.[1] What happened in the meantime, or where he spent his time after leaving Llanhilleth, cannot be ascertained, but Williams was still at Ty'n y Cwm farm when it was already about 6.30 in the morning. The farmer, who was a Welshman, and begged to be allowed to give his evidence in Welsh at the trial, was awakened during the night. He had sought refuge in his barn, but the Chartists had invaded both his house and barn, though without doing any damage. When Williams came he asked the farmer if he might dry himself a little, as he was very wet. He then sat down by the farmer's fire for some time. The farmer asked Williams where they were going and whether they intended to liberate Vincent, to which Williams replied (in the witness' Welsh idiom) that they were not going to attempt it; they were 'going to give a turn as far as Newport'.[2] All the witnesses at the trial spoke of Williams as being peaceably inclined.

Jones had quickly returned from Blackwood to the Pontypool valley, probably taking the road through New-

[1] Gurney, p. 324; Museum MS. 617.
[2] Gurney, p. 347.

bridge and Crumlin, and visiting lodges on his way. At Croespenmaen he told the Chartists to bring their mandrils (the picks used by miners) if they had no arms. 'I will venture this,' said he, drawing his hand across his neck, 'that we shall Lave a flag on top of Newport Church Tower before 10 o clock in the morning,' and then theatrically produced a pistol without making any comment on it.[1] In the meantime his lieutenants Britan and Shellard had been rounding up the men and instructing them to meet at the Race-course. Jones arrived there about ten o'clock, and after much shouting they moved off towards Croesyceiliog, marching five abreast, the men with pikes first, those with guns afterwards, and then those who only had whatever they could get.[2] As they went along they visited the public-houses at Croesyceiliog and elsewhere, and their martial array does not seem to have lasted long.

On their way some of Jones's men fell in with a brewer of Pontypool, one Barnabas Brough, who was returning home late at night. He has related his adventures in a pamphlet entitled *A Night with the Chartists*, and this admirably describes the confusion which prevailed. In spite of the wet day he had gone with a neighbour to visit his sister at Cardiff. On their way home in the evening the mayor of Newport warned them that the Chartists were on the march, and advised them not to proceed any farther. Brough had, however, so often heard the cry 'The Chartists are coming', like the cry of 'Wolf, wolf', that he paid no attention to it. But their horse's galled shoulder, which had caused them trouble earlier in the day, now became so bad that when they reached Croesyceiliog they decided to leave the horse and gig at the Cock Inn, whose landlord was one of Brough's customers, and

---

[1] Museum MS. 370, evidence of Herbert Davies.
[2] Ibid. 397, 432; Gurney, p. 378.

walk the remaining four miles home. They had only gone about half a mile when they suddenly heard a crowd coming and found themselves surrounded by a large number of armed men. They were forced to turn back with the Chartists and were placed under a guard of four pikemen. Brough made some attempt to escape, but only fell into a ditch by the side of the road. Miserably wet and covered with mud he was forced to march as far as the turnpike-gate at Malpas, scarcely more than a mile from Newport. The Chartists took possession of the gate house, and Brough was there allowed to warm himself by the fire. All his captors were equally wet, and the gunpowder in their pockets was 'in a state of semi-liquidity'. Yet so fatigued was Brough that in spite of his condition he fell asleep. Within an hour he was awakened and given orders to march. But he had removed his boots, and now found that his feet were so swollen that he could not put them on again, and it was in his stockinged feet that he continued his way. He found that they were going not towards Newport, but through country roads and lanes in the direction of Risca. After stopping at one or two places they reached the Welch Oak. It was now about 6.30 in the morning. Brough, who knew Frost, was told that the latter was there, and bribed one of the Chartists to fetch him. Frost consented to come. According to Brough he looked unusually pale, haggard, and much fatigued, and was evidently dispirited. But he ordered that the two men should be released, telling Brough that he respected him as a friend and a gentleman though he hated his politics. The two men took to the fields as quickly as they could, and eventually reached home. Frost's action in releasing Brough was one of humanity, but it proved disastrous to him, for at the trial it was used as evidence that he was in supreme command of the mob.

Part of Jones's contingent had thus joined forces with

Frost at the Welch Oak. But where was Jones himself and the rest of his men? His movements are as obscure and confused as those of the other leaders. He seems to have accompanied the first group even as far as the Malpas turnpike (although he kept out of the sight of Barnabas Brough, who was an old acquaintance of his), for he was seen at the turnpike gate about one o'clock.[1] Then he probably returned to fetch up the remainder of his men. In the complete darkness and the drenching rain this was not an easy task, and it may be that this accounts for the delay. Or was his courage beginning to fail? At any rate he kept telling his men that unless they stood together the leaders would be hanged; and he even surrendered his arms before returning. About five o'clock he was at the Cock Inn, Croesyceiliog, where he remained for some time until another party came up.[2] He then placed himself at its head, and seems to have proceeded as far as Malpas. On the way he encouraged his men by repeatedly assuring them that he expected to meet Dr. Price with seven pieces of cannon.[3] But his company does not seem to have reached Malpas until nearly nine o'clock. Here some of his followers broke into the stable yard of Malpas Court, now the residence of Thomas Prothero, Esquire, formerly of the Friars (Lapstone Hall). They did not encounter the redoubtable 'prize fighter' himself, but they compelled his gardener and his coachman to come along.[4] From Malpas the company turned up a lane which would lead them to the turnpike road between Risca and Newport, but before they had gone very far they saw a miner coming towards them across the fields. He told them of what had happened at Newport, and Jones exclaimed, 'Damn me, then we are done.' Yet

[1] Gurney, loc. cit.
[2] Museum MS., deposition of D. Jones, commercial agent, in letter to T. Phillips.　　　　　[3] Ibid. 388, evidence of Dovey; cf. 485.
[4] Gurney, p. 392.

he commanded his men to follow him. They took the road away from Newport,[1] and then probably made for their homes as best they could.

Meanwhile the Chartists were waiting endlessly along the road and in the public-houses from Risca to Cefn. The congestion was intense, and no one seemed to know what to do. The original plan of arriving at Newport at two o'clock had been abandoned hours before. Soon daylight would come, and the authorities would be prepared for them. Eventually, according to James Hodge (the witness against Frost whose evidence was very much shaken at the trial), a man on horseback bearing a lantern with a candle in it came towards Risca, and ordered the men to proceed to Cefn where Frost was waiting for them. He told them that half the soldiers had gone to Pontypool or Abergavenny.[2] Hodge thought that he was a deserter, and it is worth noting that one of the killed was believed to be a deserter from the 29th regiment, which had been drafted to Newport before the arrest of Vincent. Was he, perhaps, the person referred to by Jones in the only letter of his of which there is a copy. In protesting his innocence Jones says: 'Persons employed by them as spys knew well our intentions were not treasonable, that the attack on the Westgate was never contemplated, and was only put in practice by the Emiseries of the magistrates, some of whom unfortunately fell a sacrifice to their perfidy'.[3] Whether this deserter had played a part in organizing the advance on Newport, and whether he was a spy or *agent provocateur* can scarcely now be determined. However this may be, both Frost and

[1] Gurney, p. 389.
[2] *Merlin*, 7 Dec. 1839; Museum MS. 466, evidence of Hodge.
[3] *Merlin*, 25 July 1840. O'Connor believed it was a deserter from the 29th who fired the first shot. Others maintained that one of the killed was an *agent provocateur* who had claimed that he was a deserter. *Birmingham Journal*, 14 Dec. 1839.

Zephaniah Williams kept going backwards and forwards between the Welch Oak and Cefn until as late as seven o'clock.[1] They then moved on to a place called Pye Corner. Here, according to Hodge, Frost ordered the men with guns to go to the front, and the men with pikes to come next. Such was Hodge's deposition to the magistrates, and such was the statement that he made during the trial, but in cross-examination he was forced to admit that he did not know who had given these orders.[2] But according to Hodge's deposition, when Frost had given the orders he ran up to him and said: 'In the name of God, what are you going to do?' to which Frost replied that they would attack Newport and take it, would blow down the bridge to stop the Welsh mail from proceeding to Birmingham, so that its non-arrival there for an hour and a half would give the signal for an attack on Birmingham and an outbreak in the North. From Pye Corner the mob proceeded into Tredegar Park and along the tramroad (Sir Charles's 'golden mile'). Frost and his crowd were apparently in front, and Williams's men brought up the rear. The day had now dawned, a bright and glorious morning more like July than November, but this only served to show up the misery of the straggling crowd of mud-bespattered Chartists. In the Park they stayed for a while so that they could assume some sort of order, and Williams was heard to give the not-too-military-sounding command to 'rank themselves tidy'.[3] Eventually they moved on. Just outside the Park was a weighing-machine, at a place called Courtybella, where, according to their evidence, two boys were standing. They saw the Chartists come along, hurrahing as they went. Frost had with him a man called Jack the Fifer.

---

[1] Museum MS. 607, evidence of Edward Richards; Gurney, p. 363.

[2] Museum MS. 466; deposition in Gurney, p. 308; see ibid., pp. 299 and 310. [3] Museum MS. 372.

When they reached the machine they stopped and asked one of the boys where the soldiers were. According to his evidence, he said that about ten or a dozen had gone to the Westgate Hotel, upon which a Chartist said that it wasn't the Westgate he wanted but a waistcoat, for his was damned wet. One boy maintained that both Frost and Jack the Fifer then gave the order 'march', but the other said that it was only Jack the Fifer who did so. Then, according to one of the boys, the Chartists split into two parties, one going up the road past the Friars to Stow Hill, and the other continuing straight on through Commercial Street.[1] But a very reliable witness, Joshua Thomas, contended that not one individual came along Commercial Street.[2] This disconcerted the examining magistrates so much that they seriously considered prosecuting Thomas for perjury, for the evidence of the two boys was of the utmost importance, and if their testimony could be proved inaccurate on one point, doubt would be cast on the remainder of it.[3] They did not prosecute Thomas, but apparently did not inform the law officers of the Crown, for the Attorney-General used the boys' evidence with regard to the division of forces in his opening speech,[4] and the defence was able to call Thomas with the most telling effect. Yet it is the party which was said to have gone along Commercial Street which is traditionally thought to have been led by young Henry Hunt Frost. Serious contemporary accounts and modern fiction have both accepted the episode of Henry Hunt's leadership,[5] probably because of its dramatic and sentimental

[1] Gurney, pp. 204–12.

[2] Ibid., p. 513. Daniel Evans, witness for the Crown, also did not see any one come along Commercial Street. Ibid., p. 227.

[3] Museum MS., letter from prosecuting solicitor to Maule, 8 Jan. 1840.

[4] Gurney, p. 68.

[5] *Annual Register* (*Chronicle*), 1839, p. 221; *Particulars of the Trial of John Frost*, London, n. d. [1840]; John Watkins, *John Frost, a Play*, 1841; Haydn, *Dictionary of Dates*, 1868; Geoffrey Trease, *Comrades for the Charter*, 1924.

value. But it is quite safe to assume that there was no division in the Chartist forces, that they all went up the lane past the Friars to the turnpike on Stow Hill, and there it was that they stopped for the last time.[1]

Active preparations had been made at Newport throughout the previous day and night. The Lord Lieutenant, Capel Hanbury Leigh, had communicated with the mayor early on Sunday, and four men and a corporal had been sent to guard his own house. His selfishness in withdrawing these men at this critical time gained him much opprobium, and involved him in some correspondence with the Home Office, already sufficiently annoyed at the publication of his request for troops six months previously.[2] These were possibly the soldiers who, according to the man with the lantern, had gone to Pontypool. By the evening the mayor and two other magistrates had sworn in 500 special constables, and stationed them in the three principal inns of the town. These special constables were sent from time to time to patrol the town, and they arrested many of the most prominent Newport Chartists, bringing them to the Westgate Inn, where some were detained, the others being sent to the workhouse. This is probably the reason why there were so few Newport men in the riot. That there was an attempt to call them out is shown by the case of Patrick Hickey, the only Irishman involved. He and three other Irishmen and a boy were all sleeping in one small room when a messenger called him. He refused to administer an oath to the three men, who were drunk, anyway, but he himself went out to join the Chartists.[3] About six o'clock in the evening the mayor sent two men on horseback to reconnoitre. At Rogerstone, on the Risca road, they passed a number of

[1] Gurney, p. 177.

[2] H.O. 40/45; *Dublin Review*, Feb. 1840.

[3] Museum MS. 590, evidence of John Pollock; for the refusal of the Irish to join the Chartist movement, see *Merlin*, 23 Nov. 1839.

men, who did not molest them, but at Risca they realized
that a large crowd had gathered, and so they returned to
report. Their purpose may have been suspected, for the
Rogerstone men now tried to prevent their return. One
of the scouts received a wound in his leg caused by some
sharp instrument, but both succeeded in getting by. They
returned to the Westgate at about eleven o'clock.[1] The
mayor then immediately sent a messenger for troops to
Bristol by way of Beachley Ferry. The magistrates of
Bristol, however, told him, as well as a second messenger
who came later, that they had none to spare. The
messengers informed the superintendent of the ferry of
this when they returned the following afternoon, and he
sent his steam packet to its moorings. To his astonishment
troops did arrive on the opposite bank about ten o'clock,
but he could not now get his boat floated, and it was nine
o'clock on Tuesday morning before the troops ordered at
eleven on Sunday night reached Monmouthshire. This
bungling might have had very serious consequences, and
it led to a bitter exchange of letters in the *Merlin*.[2] About
daybreak Henry Williams, who was later wounded at the
hotel and was to be an important witness for the defence,
again went out to reconnoitre, and saw the huge crowd
making its way towards Tredegar Park.[3] The mayor
thereupon ordered two handbills to be issued, one calling
upon all special constables to assemble at the Westgate,
and the other charging all persons who might be assembled
immediately to disperse and peaceably to depart to their
habitations, the Riot Act having been read.[4] He also sent
a messenger to Captain Stack, the officer commanding
the company of the 45th then stationed at the workhouse.
In response Captain Stack ordered Lieutenant Gray
together with two sergeants and twenty-eight privates to

[1] Gurney, pp. 235, 257.   *Merlin*, 9 Nov. 1839.
[3] Gurney, p. 529.   [4] *Merlin*, loc. cit.

proceed to the Westgate. They arrived there at 8.15 a.m. After a little delay they went into the courtyard where they stayed about ten minutes, and then were ordered to go into a public room at the front of the hotel. They had

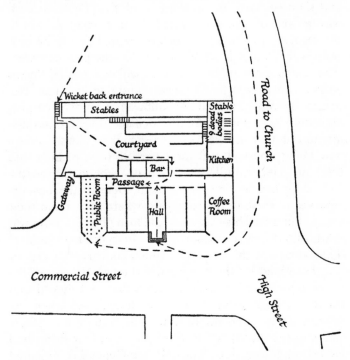

been there for scarcely more than five minutes before the Chartists appeared.[1]

At the turnpike on Stow Hill Frost was heard to say: 'Let us go towards the town and show ourselves to the town.'[2] Down the hill they came, with considerable uproar, although apparently not causing much fear to the spectators. Some attempted to enter at the back of the Westgate Hotel, but the main body gathered before it,

[1] Gurney, pp. 247–52.   [2] Ibid., p. 169.

and Frost gave the command: 'Turn round and show your appearance to the front.' What happened afterwards is none too clear. The crowd pressed on to the main doorway where a number of special constables were standing, and shouted 'Give us up the prisoners'. (That, at least, was the version which appeared in the general account in the *Merlin* for 9 November, before the matter had become controversial, and it was assumed that the prisoners were those taken in the night. Later, as will be seen, a different version was given.) A special constable shouted 'No, never', in reply, and there followed a scuffle, caused, according to a witness for the defence, by a constable's attempting to take away a Chartist's pike. Windows were now being smashed and the Chartists were rushing into the hall. Henry Williams was badly wounded, and the constables fled as best they could, some to the upstairs rooms, and some to the courtyard where they found their retreat cut off. This was when the firing began. Who was it who fired first, the Chartists or the special constables? This, also, was the subject of much controversy. A witness examined by the magistrates (he was the son of the superintendent of the police) stated that he believed that the firing had begun inside the hotel, but when re-examined later (no doubt when the importance of the point was realized) he declared that the first firing had come from the outside. The Solicitor-General commented on this contradiction in a marginal note on his depositions, and, needless to say, the witness was not called at the trial.[1] Probably the question can no longer be solved. The weight of the evidence seems to prove that the firing began inside the hall, but whether it came from the Chartists who had forced their way inside or from the special constables it is impossible to say.

The shutters of the room in which the soldiers were

[1] Museum MS., depositions of Thomas Hopkins.

stationed were still closed. Shots came in through the glass above the shutters, and hit the ceiling, though it is doubtful if any pierced the shutters themselves; in any case no one was hit. The mayor and Lieutenant Gray then consulted with each other (there was a slight difference of opinion as to whether the mayor had given and the officer taken orders), and as a result Gray told his men to load with ball cartridge. Then the mayor and the officer went to the window to remove the shutters. (Here again there was some rivalry as to which had taken the post of greatest danger, the side of the window nearest the main door of the hotel.) At that moment the mayor was seriously wounded in the arm and slightly in the hip. Immediately afterwards Gray gave the order to fire, and the soldiers sent a volley right into the crowd— they were not in the habit of firing into the air, he said. Then they fired into the passage which led to the hall, and as soon as the smoke in the room had cleared, they fired again. The firing through the window had occupied scarcely half a minute, but inside the hotel it continued for almost ten minutes. The noise was deafening, and the smoke was so intense that the mayor narrowly escaped being shot by a soldier. It is possible that those who had entered from the courtyard and into the hall did not know exactly what was happening on account of the smoke. They tried to rush the room in which the soldiers were, but faltered when they encountered their own dead, according to Lieutenant Gray, and then received the fire of the soldiers. On an average the latter had fired only three shots each.[1] The damage done to the hotel both by the Chartists and by the firing of the soldiers does not seem to have been very much, for in spite of an inclination

[1] Gurney, pp. 233 ff. and 247 ff., evidence of Sir Thomas Phillips and Captain Basil Gray, also Museum MS. 586, deposition of Sir Thomas Phillips.

on the part of everybody to make a little profit out of the affair, the landlord put in a claim for only £90. 19*s*. 9*d*., as compared with the £105. 7*s*. which he charged for refreshments for the special constables during the night.[1]

At the first shot fired by the soldiers, the crowd had dropped whatever arms they had, guns, pikes, and mandrils, and fled in wild disorder—except apparently one wooden-legged man, who was seen to fire three times at the hotel. The description given of him was not too clear, even on such an important point as to which of his legs was wooden, and in consequence the lives of all wooden-legged men in the neighbourhood of Newport were for a time placed in jeopardy.[2] According to the *Merlin*, twenty-two dead bodies were discovered.[3] Among them was that of a youth, aged nineteen, who was said to have written the following letter on the eve of the riot:

Pontypool, Sunday Night. November 4th. 1839.
Dear Parents,—I hope this will find you well, as I am myself at present. I shall this night be engaged in a struggle for freedom, and should it please God to spare my life, I shall see you soon; but if not, grieve not for me. I shall fall in a noble cause. My tools are at Mr. Cecil's, and likewise my clothes. Yours truly, George Shell.[4]

It was a courageous letter, and won for Shell a place of honour in the memory of his comrades, but it did them a

[1] Usk MSS., Treasurer's vouchers.
[2] Museum MS. 376, evidence of Margaret Davies and others.
[3] *Merlin*, 16 Nov. 1839. *Annual Register*, 1839, p. 249, however, gives ten as the number on which an inquest was held. They were said to have died 'by an act of justifiable homicide by some persons unknown'.
[4] *Merlin*, 23 Nov. 1839. The authenticity of this letter was accepted both by the Chartists and their opponents. It is not, however, entirely beyond question. Its expression is unexpectedly good for a working lad (Shell was a cabinet-maker) and 'yours truly' is an unusual way for a youth to address his parents. The letter is also wrongly dated. Shell's father had been a Chartist at Pontypool before leaving for Bristol sixteen months previously. See ante, p. 110. He had recently written his son a letter advising him to abandon Chartism and this letter was found in the boy's box. He came to claim his son's body. Museum MSS. 379, 626.

disservice, for it was used as proof that there had been a premeditated attack on Newport. Another of the dead was a member of the Merthyr W.M.A. This seems to prove that some of the Merthyr Chartists whom the magistrates had reported to have left home had joined the rioters. But what became of the others? There were, undoubtedly, more Chartists in Merthyr and its neighbourhood than in any other area in the coal-field. When Vincent had facetiously suggested that the Home Office should supply arms to the Chartists as well as to the Christchurch Yeomanry, he had given the following figures: Newport, 5,000; Pontypool and its vicinity, 8,000; Blackwood and Tredegar, 10,000; Nantyglo and its vicinity, 10,000; Merthyr and its neighbourhood, 20,000,[1] and although too much should not be made of these figures, they, nevertheless, probably represent the relative strength of Chartism in the various areas, a fact borne out both by the contributions to Chartist funds and by the signatures to the Petition. It would be unsafe to assume that the Merthyr Chartists were all moral-force men, for Merthyr had a reputation for violence since the Merthyr riots of 1831 and the days of the 'Scotch Cattle'. Were the Merthyr Chartists misled by the egregious Dr. Price? It will be remembered that he had been seen at Blackwood on the previous Friday, and that Jones fully expected him to join the Chartists with seven pieces of 'cannon'. Even the authorities took this seriously, for among the papers of the solicitor for the prosecution the following memorandum is twice entered: 'Obtain evidence that Price was possessed of cannon and that they were sold and melted up a day or two after the riots',[2] and many witnesses were questioned as to his movements. Price's own explanation is perhaps the most surprising part of all his reminiscences about the Chartist period.

---

[1] *Western Vindicator*, 8 June 1839.   [2] Museum MS. 485, 601.

He declares that he had been warned not to come to Newport, because the soldiers had orders 'to shoot the man
with the long hair', and that the person who warned him
was the Reverend James Coles of Michaelston-y-fedw.
But the Reverend James Coles, although Price makes no
mention of the fact, was the chairman of the magistrates
who examined the Chartists.[1] Whatever may have been
the part he played, Price thought it wise to disappear. He
declares that a reward of £100 was offered for his capture,
and although this is probably not true, contemporary newspapers do state that such a reward was offered.[2] He escaped,
according to his own account, by putting on a woman's
clothes and boarding at Cardiff a ship bound for Liverpool, whence he made his way to London and to Paris.

Others had adventures scarcely less remarkable, and
many were the tales which were later told of men who
had been out that night and were afraid to return home.
Some had hidden for days in the woods of Wentwood;
others were lost sight of entirely for years, having made
their way to Liverpool and reached the New World.
The leaders were not so fortunate. Bills were immediately
posted, offering rewards of £100 each for the capture of
John Frost, Zephaniah Williams, and William Jones, as
well as of Jack the Fifer and David the Tinker, both from
the Tredegar Ironworks.[3] Frost had been seen soon after
the firing walking sharply through Tredegar Park. He
was holding a handkerchief to his face as if he were
crying, and scarcely replied when he was spoken to.[4] He
then took to the woods, in the direction of Cardiff, and
near Castleton he hid himself in a coal 'tram'. There he
stayed for eight hours, in greater agony of mind than
he had ever been in before in his life. When dusk came he

[1] *Cardiff Times*, loc. cit. and 23 Jan. 1893. It may be worth noting that
Price was the son of a clergyman who had lived all his life at Rudry, which
is near Michaelston-y-fedw. [2] *Cambrian*, 16 Nov.
[3] *Merlin*, 9 Nov., 16 Nov. [4] Gurney, p. 232.

crept out of the 'tram', and the first thing which he saw was the bill offering £100 reward for his capture. He went stealthily towards Newport in order to take leave of his family,[1] but before seeing them he turned into the house of Partridge, the printer, whose premises communicated through a garden with his own. He was miserably wet and exhausted and borrowed some clothing from Partridge. While he was having some food, there was a loud knocking at the door. As Partridge did not open it, the door was eventually forced in, and Thomas Jones Phillips, the clerk to the magistrates and Frost's opponent over many years, appeared. He had already searched Frost's own house and seized his papers, and now wished to obtain what papers there might be at Partridge's. He was immensely surprised to see Frost, but he arrested him immediately, and took from him three loaded pistols, a powder flask, and some ball. He then took him to the Westgate Hotel. Frost begged to be allowed to go into his own house as he passed it, and, after he had been brought before the magistrates, implored that he should be placed in custody in his home, but this was not permitted, and it was seventeen years before he was able to enter this house in Newport again.[2]

It was nearly a week before Jones was taken. This happened in a wood near Crumlin. He threatened his pursuers with a pistol, but then gave himself up. He had on him a copy of Hugh Williams's *Horn of Liberty*, the address and song celebrating the Llanidloes riots.[3] Zephaniah Williams almost succeeded in escaping, and was at large for nearly three weeks. He had apparently reached home and obtained some money, and then had made for Cardiff. He was remotely related by marriage to the

[1] *Western Mail*, 17 Mar. 1877.
[2] Gurney, pp. 417 ff.; *Merlin*, 9 Nov.; Museum MS., evidence of Capt. Gray.　　　　　　　　　　　　　　　　　[3] *Merlin*, 9 Nov.

Portuguese consul at Cardiff, Richard Todd.[1] Todd's wife seems to have begged her husband to save him, and he approached his sister's husband, Captain Head of the *Comet*, but the captain would have nothing to do with the affair. Todd was more successful with a Captain Williams of the *Vintage*, but the Cardiff police had now got wind of Zephaniah Williams's movements, and at three o'clock on the morning of 23 November, the day on which the *Vintage* was due to sail for Oporto, they boarded the ship. They found there asleep a man who gave his name as Thomas Jones of Bridgend, but who eventually admitted that he was Zephaniah Williams. He had on him £102 in gold, together with some smaller money, including eleven Spanish dollars. He was immediately taken to Newport, and so great was the fear that he might escape again that he was kept handcuffed to an officer night and day until he was placed safely in Monmouth gaol. Todd also found himself arrested, but was released on bail.[2] Of the two other 'commanders' for whose capture a £100 reward was offered, David the Tinker disappeared—unless he was the person of that name who was a well-known character in Tredegar in the sixties (after the Chartists had been pardoned).[3] Jack the Fifer made his way to Virginia, and four years later wrote to his home asking for information of his friend, the Tinker. He had just been offered a commission as an officer in an army destined for Texas, and with that he, too, disappears.[4] Both friends were committed for treason, *in absentia*.

[1] The exact relationship was this: Williams's wife was the sister of Dr. John Llewellyn of Caerphilly, whose wife was the sister of Mrs. Todd.

[2] H.O. 40/46, letters from mayor of Cardiff; Museum MS. D. 4. 36 and 15. 11; *Merlin*, 23 Nov. and 14 Dec. 1839.

[3] Powell, *History of Tredegar* (Cardiff, 1885), states that this person was the Chartist.

[4] *The Times*, 27 Feb. 1844. There was a John Rees among those sentenced to transportation for their part in the riot, but this was not the Fifer, although his name also was Rees. The tinker's name was David Jones.

The Attack on Newport

The feeling produced in Newport was one of stupe-
faction, which increased, if anything, after the riot was
over. The spectators do not seem to have been terrified
at the Chartists' approach, but the riot had unexpectedly
ended in bloodshed, and all wondered uneasily what they
had escaped. Thomas Prothero declared that he had
never read of anything like it in the history of civilized
nations. The Chartists had invaded Newport like a horde
of American savages, intending to massacre all who
opposed them, and to spread rapine, plunder, and
devastation. It was only Providence which had saved the
town by means of the torrential rain, and he felt convinced that there was no one who had lived through that
night in Newport who had not bent his knees in gratitude
to Divine Providence.[1] For weeks this was the theme of
sermon and of pamphlet—that the Almighty was in that
tempest, that the Lord had fought against the enemies
of Israel and desecrators of the Sabbath.[2] But neither this
confidence in the support of the Almighty nor the arrival
within a few days of 600 soldiers together with a battery
of artillery, which made Newport appear like a garrison
town,[3] entirely calmed the nerves of the burgesses, and
even as late as 20 December they were thrown into a
state of great alarm. In the late evening of that day loud
firing was heard in the direction of the hills. People who
had gone to bed dressed themselves in terror, and many
fled from the town. Several mothers gave birth to premature children, and even the wife of Colonel Considine,
the officer commanding the forces at Newport, was
thrown into hysterics which lasted all night, an experience
the gallant soldier dreaded more than a Chartist attack.
Infantry, cavalry, and artillery were ordered out. But

[1] *Merlin*, 23 Nov.
[2] *Ymddiddan rhwng Mr. Bowen and William Thomas*, 1839; E. Jenkins,
Chartism Unmasked, 1840; *The Two Colliers*, 1840; T. Morris, *Cynghor da
mewn amserau drwg*, 1839.　　　　　　　　　　　　[3] *Merlin*, 16 Nov.

the alarm was false; the firing came only from Ruperra,
the seat of Sir Charles Morgan's heir, who had fired off
some old cannon in honour of his own son's birthday.
Colonel Considine wrote to the Home Office, with an
asperity which reflected his personal experience, to complain of this 'inexcusable thoughtlessness'.[1]

But as the nerves of the townspeople became steadier,
fear gave way to pride. It was, indeed, a night which in
their flowing cups would long be remembered. Many
marvellous tales now came to be told. Even the *Annual
Register* described how the mayor with much coolness and
intrepidity read the Riot Act amidst showers of bullets
before he ordered the military to fire.[2] Then there was
the story of how the soldiers had run short of ammunition,
how no one was prepared to obtain more for them until a
youth volunteered, dashed to the barracks, and valour-
ously returned with his pockets loaded with cartridges.
The story was believed for fifty years and more[3] and was
in no way shaken by the evidence that the soldiers had
twenty rounds of ammunition each, and that on an
average they had fired only three shots. Several special
constables, although their cowardice as a body was
severely criticized by the magistrates, put forward a claim
to being the anonymous person who had shouted 'No,
never' at the door of the hotel. Even in higher places there
was some rivalry. The mayor and the lieutenant strove
for the honour of having incurred the greatest danger.
Dowling, the proprietor of the *Merlin*, wrote an account
which described in glowing colours the activities of his
uncle, the member for the boroughs, who was not even in
Newport on that night.[4] Blewitt had taken charge of the

[1] H.O. 40/45; *Merthyr Guardian*, 28 Dec.; *Charter*, 29 Dec.
[2] *Annual Register*, 1839, p. 221.
[3] W. N. Johns, *The Chartist Riots at Newport* (Newport, 1889), p. 42.
[4] Anonymous [Dowling], *The Rise and Fall of Chartism in Monmouthshire*, 1840.

situation on the following day, in view of the mayor's wounds, but that this was not altogether appreciated is shown by a remark pencilled in the margin of the mayor's statement on his action: 'Contemptible trickery to deprive a brave man of his meed of praise'.[1] Then there was the question of numbers. The *Merthyr Guardian*, which had consistently ridiculed and decried the strength of the Chartists, now placed the number of the rioters at 20,000. A witness at the trial placed it at between 400 and 500.[2] The latter estimate is certainly too small; in any case the witness was not in a position to see the whole crowd, and the figure of 5,000 given by the *Merlin*, and based on the distance for which the crowd stretched up Stow Hill, seems to be a reasonable one.

With pride and relief came jollification and the reward of virtue. A dinner was given in honour of the 45th regiment. Lieutenant Gray (a gallant Irishman commanding Irishmen as the *Dublin Review* and the *Limerick Chronicle* proudly claimed)[3] was promoted to the rank of captain, and Captain Stack to the rank of major. A few days later came a more important meeting 'to give public thanks to God and consider means of honouring the mayor'. The honour took the form of a service of plate valued at 800 guineas, and subscribed to by over 600 persons.[4] Addresses of thanks had poured in on the mayor, especially from the neighbouring towns. He had sent a warning to Cardiff on the Sunday, and that town had quickly prepared itself for a Chartist attack. Its council now presented the town's grateful thanks to him.[5] Usk, also, whose bridge would have been a point of strategic

---

[1] Museum MS.   [2] Gurney, p. 227.
[3] *Dublin Review*, loc. cit.; *Merlin*, 16 Nov.
[4] *Merthyr Guardian*, 26 Sept. 1840.
[5] *Cardiff Records*, iv. 425–6; *Cardiff Naturalist Society Transactions*, xv (1883), p. 83; H.O. 40/46, letter of William Bird to Lieut.-Col. Moberly, 6 Nov.; *Merlin*, 23 Nov. 1839.

237

importance had the Chartists advanced to rescue Vincent, and for whose defence 180 special constables had been enrolled, presented an address of congratulation.[1] In Newport an address was drawn up asking him to continue in office as mayor for another year, but this he declined.[2] A greater honour had now befallen him. The queen had been pleased to show her appreciation of his conduct by conferring on him the honour of knighthood, and, further, had allowed him to dine with her. The latter had been at the suggestion of Charles Greville, in whose *Memoirs* the incident is described. The Home Secretary had thought that 'etiquette would not permit one of his rank in life to be invited to the Royal table'—although the Prime Minister's father had been a country attorney in his day. But Greville had persuaded him that 'it would be a wise and popular thing to keep him there and load him with civilities—do good to the Queen and encourage others to do their duty—and send him back rejoicing to his province'. 'Everybody approved of it,' continues Greville, 'and the man behaved as if his whole life had been spent in Courts, perfectly at his ease, without rudeness or forwardness, quite unobtrusive, but with complete self-possession, and a *nil admirari* manner which had some-thing distinguished in it. The Queen was very civil to him and he was delighted. The next morning he went to Normanby and expressed his apprehension that he might not have conducted himself as he ought, together with his grateful sense of his reception; but the apology was quite needless.'[3] A few weeks later he received the freedom of the City of London.[4] What, one wonders, did old Thomas Prothero think of all this honour conferred upon his junior partner? He himself would certainly have dealt

[1] *Merlin*, 14 Dec., 21 Dec.   [2] Ibid., 9 Nov.
[3] Lytton Strachey and Roger Fulford (ed.), *The Greville Memoirs* (London, 1938), iv. 221.
[4] *Dictionary of National Biography*, art. T. Phillips.

quite as 'energetically' with the Chartists had he been given the opportunity. But, although he had now founded a 'county family' and was soon to be chosen High Sheriff for Monmouthshire, his family had to wait eighty years before it obtained its first title in the person of his grandson, Rowland Prothero, Baron Ernle. Yet if the 'prize fighter' gained little out of the affair except the satisfaction of seeing his opponent given the knock-out blow in the last round of their lifelong contest, his daughter was more fortunate, for she secured a husband in one of the officers of the 45th.[1]

[1] *Merlin,* 28 Nov. 1840.

VIII

THE TRIAL

No sooner was the riot over than the authorities were busy hunting out suspects and collecting information. They received the willing assistance of numberless individuals, for the class feeling roused against the Chartists was wellnigh incredible. Letters, anonymous and otherwise, poured in, revealing the whereabouts of fugitives. Iron-masters made use of their position to do their utmost to procure evidence. Samuel Homfray of Tredegar, for example, had 'companies out in every direction to obtain information', and took particular note of any new workers who might sign on at his ironworks, as they might be using false names, and be wanted by the authorities elsewhere. Others supplied information which might be useful in cross-examining witnesses, especially any who were likely to be called by the defence. Suspects were arrested as far afield as Waterford, where a ship bound for New York was forced into harbour by gales. From Cork, also, came offers of assistance. The police of that city wrote voluntarily offering their service in South Wales. That they would do their duty was significantly underlined, and the authorities would soon see, they claimed, that their short guns would be just as effective as the long muskets of the regiments of the line. Daniel O'Connell, who had so often boasted that he could call upon 500,000 fighting Irishmen, condemned the Chartists as traitors, and took pride in the fact that 100 of the special constables enrolled at Cardiff were Irishmen. The antipathy between the Irish and the Welsh workers of the coal-field, which had shown itself in free fights on many a Saturday night, had, indeed, now assumed a greater importance, and the Irish had taken sides with the opponents of the working class.[1]

[1] Museum MSS., several letters, including those of Samuel Homfray,

The Trial

The magistrates began their inquiry on the morning after the riot. Their chairman at first was Reginald James Blewitt, the member for the Monmouth boroughs, and so keen was the interest taken in the results of the inquiry that even Sir Charles Morgan performed his magisterial duties, possibly for the first time. But the work was too arduous to be undertaken merely because of interest, and after a few days the bench was occupied by three or four magistrates only, presided over by the Reverend James Coles, the friend of Dr. William Price. W. T. Harford Phelps was appointed solicitor for the prosecution, and Maule, now solicitor to the Treasury, was sent down from London to give his assistance. Much of the cross-examination of witnesses was done by Thomas Prothero, who found it an occupation particularly to his taste. The 'talent and acumen' which he showed in his 'rigid and searching' examination was much commented upon in the local press. This work occupied no less than twenty-four days, for over 200 witnesses were examined. It had not been completed when the magistrates left Newport for Monmouth to be present at the sitting of the special commission, so that some witnesses had to be transferred with them, and the examination continued there. The magistrates had thrown their net wide. Not only those who had taken part in the riot were suspect, but also any who had been prominent Chartists. For example, John Frost's uncle, Edward, a member of the Newport town council, was arrested, because he was the treasurer of the local W.M.A. He was committed for trial, but was released on bail, and the law officers decided eventually that there was not sufficient evidence to proceed against him.[1] Old Samuel Etheridge, the veteran radical of Newport, was committed on the

1 and 24 Dec.; H.O. 40/45, letter of Cork police; *Merlin*, 14 Dec., O'Connell's speech; *Charter*, 16 Feb. 1840, for arrest at Waterford.

[1] *Merlin*, 16 Nov. 1839; Museum MS., letter Phelps to Maule, 2 Jan. 1840.

supreme charge of high treason. His house had been searched, and among his papers was found the plan for the organization in groups of ten. But Maule intervened in his case, also, and the charge was changed to one of conspiracy.[1] 'Circumstances of suspicion' were stated upon oath which tended to implicate the Reverend Benjamin Byron, at whose chapel Frost's family worshipped. A warrant was therefore issued to have his house searched also, and this was done by special constables, but nothing was found to justify his apprehension. He still continued to support the Chartists' cause, however, and a correspondent later informed the magistrates 'that ever since Frost's confinement he has at every service performed, prayed for the liberation of Frost and the destruction of his enemies'.[2] Very many of the prisoners were discharged (usually with advice from the Reverend James Coles, to change the tenor of their ways), but nevertheless the examination was conducted with great bitterness, in strange contrast with the trial which followed. In all, twenty-nine prisoners were committed to prison, twenty-one of them indicted for high treason, and the capacity of Monmouth gaol was taxed to the utmost, so that the Chartists had to be placed three in a cell.[3]

As the examinations dragged on for over a month, they grew wearisome, although occasionally they were enlivened by humorous incidents. The magistrates received a letter, typical of times of upheaval, which informed them that the outbreak had been foretold in the Book of Daniel (chapter xi). It was signed by the Prophet-Emperor of Wales, but the prophecy did not offer them much guidance

[1] Museum MS., letter Phelps to Maule, and *Merlin*, 23 Nov.; Etheridge's trial was stopped by Mr. Justice Williams, who directed the jury to return a verdict of not guilty. *Merlin*, 18 Jan. 1840.

[2] Ibid., 16 Nov.; Letter to Phelps, 6 Jan. 1840; T. Rees and J. Thomas, *Hanes Eglwysi Annibynol Cymru* (Liverpool, 1871), i. 117–19.

[3] H.O. 40/45; Museum MS., letter of Charles Ford, Keeper, 23 Nov. 1839.

in the work which remained to be done.[1] The case of an Irishman, Thomas Walsh, also caused some diversion. He was chasing his pig through the street when he collided with Captain Stack and upset him. The streets of Newport were dirty at all times, and in mid-November were covered with mud, and the gallant captain was so infuriated at the injury to his dignity and his uniform that he had Walsh arrested for assault. Walsh remained in custody for two days, in great fear lest his case should be confused with that of the Chartists, and when he was brought before the magistrates the following dialogue ensued:

Rev. J. Coles: Prisoner, this is the most outrageous assault I ever heard of, to knock down an officer of Her Majesty's service.

Walsh: I could not help it, yer Honour.

Coles: Not help it, Sir! Could not help knocking people down in the street when you meet them!

Walsh: No, yer Honour; it was a big fat woman, Sir,——

Coles: Silence, Sir! Captain Stack, with the manly forbearance which distinguishes him, declines to press the charge against you; and you are bound to thank him for his kindness. But if he had drawn his sword on you that night——

Walsh: Oh Lord! night, yer Honour! why it was in the middle of the broad daylight!

Coles: Listen to me, Sir!—so much the worse; but if Captain Stack had drawn his sword on you, I would not answer for the consequences. You are now discharged, and go immediately and thank Captain Stack for his forbearance.

Walsh: I thank yer Honour and Captain Stack too.[2]

Tremendous local interest was roused by the presence in court of the 'sorcerer', Israel Firman, a quack doctor and scissors grinder then living in the neighbourhood. He was ninety-one years of age, and had served his apprenticeship as a herbalist in Philadelphia, but at the age of forty-four he had been pressed into the British navy at Antigua in the Leeward Islands, and since his release had lived in

---

[1] Museum MS.　　　　　　　　　　[2] *Merlin*, 23 Nov.

England. His gaunt, cadaverous appearance, together with the mystery of his life, caused a sensation which his evidence tended to increase. He had been associated with the Chartists, and had been arrested for participating in the riot, but he claimed that he had been roused in the middle of the night and compelled to go along. Whether this was true or not he now turned queen's evidence. His experiences may perhaps have increased his usual irascibility, for he proved far too much, implicating persons whom he could not possibly have seen, and the authorities wisely did not call him at the trial.[1]

The press made it impossible for the prisoners to receive a fair trial, for it declared them guilty of the supreme offence of high treason before they were tried. The *Manchester Guardian* was particularly violent. It argued immediately after the occurrence that the charge should be not one of riot, but of levying war against the queen's troops and the queen's authority, and declared that the Chartists must be taught that they could not embark on such schemes with impunity.[2] The *Merthyr Guardian* even regretted that the bodies of traitors were no longer quartered, otherwise one of Frost's limbs could have been placed over Pontypool Park, another over Llanover, a third over the door of the council chamber at Newport, and a fourth over the Home Office—a tilt at the Whig Lord Lieutenant, the former member for the boroughs, and the government department which had made Frost a magistrate.[3]

It is little wonder, therefore, that when Frost appeared before the magistrates on the first day of the examination (Tuesday), they did not hesitate to charge him with high treason. He was asked if he required professional assistance, and replied that he would defend himself. The

[1] Museum MS. 417, 442; *Merlin*, 7 Dec., &c.
[2] Quoted in full in *Cambrian*, 16 Nov.
[3] *Merthyr Guardian*, 16 Nov.

authorities evidently feared that an attempt might be
made to rescue him, for he was removed at daybreak the
following morning, escorted by a company of the 10th
Hussars as far as Usk bridge, and from there to Monmouth
by a company of the 12th Lancers. The next two days
were largely taken up with the case of Partridge, who was
also indicted with high treason for having harboured Frost,
although this charge was later reduced to one of sedition
and conspiracy. On Friday William Jones was examined,
and committed on the same charge. He kept up the part
he was playing by ostentatiously cross-examining the witnesses, and taking copious notes. On the ninth day young
Henry Hunt Frost was brought up for examination.
Apparently no warrant had been issued for his apprehension, but the authorities evidently intended to bring a
charge against him, for a dossier marked *Regina* v. *Henry
Frost* had been prepared. In this they probably overreached themselves, for the boy's youth (he was now seventeen years of age), and his modest yet dignified demeanour
produced a revulsion of feeling in the court, which was
unusually crowded in anticipation of his examination, and
won much sympathy for his father. Chartist papers, such
as the *Northern Star*, expressed intense indignation at the
action of the magistrates. The evidence against him was
curious. A witness had seen him on Sunday evening, and
had become suspicious of him, apparently because he had
on a 'foraging cap'. He had followed the boy, who had
disappeared into a courtyard by Hope Chapel. The witness suspected that he was bearing messages to his father,
but he had to admit that if this was so, the boy was taking
a most peculiar way to get to Risca, and that he had not
run away from him. A second witness deposed that the
boy, in company with two other men, had sheltered for
a while in his house near the Welch Oak, about three
o'clock in the morning, though he stated that he had had

no conversation with him. That was all the evidence. Yet several witnesses were called to prove 'the state of the town' and the 'parties along the road', although these matters were not connected with the boy, and can only have been brought in to prejudice him. Phelps had to admit that a 'material witness' whom he had intended to call could not be found, so the boy was discharged, Coles taking the opportunity of warning him to abandon the evil habits to which he had become accustomed. Nevertheless, Phelps does not seem to have given up the case, and later on there were persistent rumours in the newspapers that a warrant had been issued for the boy's arrest and that he had absconded. Geach wrote to Phelps indignantly denying this, and undertaking to produce the boy whenever a charge was preferred against him.[1]

On the day after Henry Frost's examination (that is, on Friday, 15 November) interest centred around a very mysterious stranger who had arrived on the previous evening by the coach from Worcester, and had put up at the Westgate Hotel, the very inn where the magistrates were sitting. He had entered into conversation with the landlord in the morning, and had explained to him that his purpose was inquire into the origin of the riot, and the landlord had very naturally informed the magistrates. They ordered him to be detained and brought before them. His appearance—he was well over six feet in height —and his blustering manner drew much attention. He expressed annoyance at his detention, and explained that he believed the riot to have been due to Russian agency, which was at work in various parts of the country. He refused, however, to give the magistrates the facts on which he based his belief, and they ordered him to leave the

[1] Museum MS. 409, 416, 577, 616; also letter Geach to Phelps, 2 Dec.; *Merlin*, 16 Nov.; *Bristol Mercury*, 16 Nov.; *Scots Times*, 4 Dec.; *Merthyr Guardian*, 1 Feb.; *Cambrian*, 1 Feb.

town. But no sooner was he outside the court-room than a letter from the mayor of Birmingham was handed to Coles, and was found to contain a description of one William Cardo, who two nights previously had addressed a Chartist meeting there, and had stated that he was going to Newport to find out the truth about the riots. The description exactly fitted the stranger whom the magistrates had just examined, and he was immediately brought back. He admitted that he was Cardo, and that he had been the delegate from Marylebone to the Convention. On him were found a memorandum book which contained a list of places in South Wales, and a sheet of paper indicating a plan for the organization of the country, which apparently was to be split up into divisions, districts, subdistricts, and sections, though no geographical areas were named. Cardo seems to have explained to the magistrates in private that the Russian agent was Major Beniowski (the Pole who had contributed articles on military science to the *London Democrat*). Next day the new mayor of Newport, Thomas Hawkins, sent a full account of his evidence to the Home Office, stating incidentally that he could get no information of Major Beniowski. He informed the Home Secretary that Cardo had been discharged and ordered out of the town. He was seen off with the mail, and while this was being waited for another suspicious character had been seen, whom an army officer had thought to be Dr. Taylor. This, however, is inaccurate, for, according to his own account, Dr. Taylor had left London for Newcastle a few days before the riot, and had afterwards proceeded to Carlisle, where he was arrested.[1] But on the following day (17 November) the mayor wrote again to the Home Office asking that some one should be sent to Newport who could recognize Beniowski, for he had just received an anonymous letter from Bristol, stating

[1] *Lovett Collection*, ii. 211, letter from Taylor to Lovett, 10 June 1841.

that Beniowski had been sent to South Wales, and was taking with him 138 lb. of ball cartridge in readiness for the march on Monmouth which was to take place when Beniowski gave the orders.[1]

This anonymous letter is the only independent evidence of any connexion between Beniowski and the Newport rising. Yet this connexion is the basis of the most sensational theory of the origin of the riot, a theory which undoubtedly came into existence in the unstable brain of David Urquhart. He was a former diplomatic agent at Constantinople, and a great admirer of Turkey, which he considered an ideal state, and so Russia had become for him, as it was for his friend, Karl Marx, the arch-enemy of Europe. Moreover, he maintained that when the Polish revolution of 1830 had caused the Archduke Constantine to flee from Warsaw, he had left behind documents which had fallen into his own hands, and which showed that Russia was intriguing throughout Europe in preparation for a general upheaval, and he was convinced, as well, that Palmerston had betrayed his country to the Russians. In 1838 he had conducted a campaign throughout the country to warn the workers of the Russian danger, but apparently without much success. He now became convinced that Russia was behind the Chartist movement, and to explain the connexion between them he later published a series of letters in his periodical, *The Free Press*, in 1855, and in its successor, *The Diplomatic Review*, in 1872. The most important of these letters was one dated 22 September 1839, which stated that a plan of a general insurrection had been drawn up by a Polish immigrant who was to take command in the mountains of Wales, and that the Russian fleet was in the North Sea ready to assist. This letter Urquhart claimed to have communicated to the Prime Minister, but as is usual in such matters, it had

[1] *Merlin*, 16 Nov., 30 Nov.; *Bristol Mercury*, 23 Nov.; H.O. 40/45.

met with no response. In any case, both the author and the recipient of the letter are anonymous, and there is no evidence of its having existed apart from Urquhart's statement. Urquhart himself had come into contact with the Chartists through being a Tory candidate for Marylebone, which was also Cardo's 'constituency'. The Chartists had interrupted his meetings, but he had induced them to listen to him, and in a private talk with their leaders he had elicited from them (at about three o'clock in the morning) the plans which had been drawn up for a general insurrection. 'They had not gone far into their narrative when we came upon a Russian agent as a mover and director of the whole plan', says Urquhart. Beniowski's name had perhaps been mentioned, and Urquhart started on his obsession. He convinced them that they were all tools in the hands of Russia. 'Not an instant was lost' afterwards in breaking up the nefarious plan, but 'Frost was missed by half an hour'—which is patently absurd if Urquhart had received the letter of 22 September in time to communicate it to the Prime Minister well before the outbreak, as he himself claimed. One of the leaders whom he convinced was Cardo, and when he wrote in 1872, he brought forward the plan found on Cardo at Newport as proof that the organization for the rising was identical with that of the Greek-Russian Hetairia, the secret society which had played a part in the War of Greek Independence. But this plan is such an elementary one, merely indicating a division into districts and sub-districts, that it is absurd to see in it the influence of any society, secret or otherwise, and it was, in any case, probably drawn up by Cardo himself, after his conversation with Urquhart. Urquhart's sensational theory of Russian intrigue can, therefore, safely be dismissed. So, also, can the belief that Beniowski took part in the Newport rising. It will be noted that the anonymous letter received on 17 November from Bristol by the mayor of Newport claimed that he was on his way to South Wales after, and not before, the riot, and then presumably for the purpose of liberating Frost from Monmouth gaol. It is certainly true that he had spoken at a meeting in Bethnal Green on 15 November, when 'animated speeches' were made with regard to averting the possible fate of Frost, and the anonymous letter may refer to remarks made on that occasion, but there is not one scrap of evidence to show that he was in Monmouthshire either before or after the riot. Cardo, however, had become a complete convert to Urquhart's gospel, and after his return from Newport he addressed large meetings in Manchester and Bolton, expounding to them the Russian theory of the riot, as well as the Russian danger to British commerce in the Near East and the treacherous intrigues of Palmerston.[1]

When the court resumed its sitting on Monday, 18 November, Frost's friend, W. P. Roberts, the Bath solicitor and future 'Miners' Attorney-General', was brought before it. He had been released on bail after Frost's fruitless efforts on his behalf, and had evidently come to South Wales to do what he could for Frost. He had been arrested at Blackwood on the previous day, where he had been found accompanied by two of Frost's daughters 'disguised as servants'. The clerk to the magistrates, Thomas Jones Phillips, informed the Home Office that his object was 'no doubt to ascertain the feelings of the people towards Mr. Frost and whether they were disposed to attempt another outbreak'. It is far more likely that he was collecting evidence for Frost's defence, and the magistrates were

[1] *Free Press*, xiii (1855); *Diplomatic Review* (1872–3), pp. 20–36, 202–31; *Birmingham Journal*, 14 Dec. 1839; *Northern Star*, 14 Dec. 1839; J. H. Harley, 'David Urquhart', *Contemporary Review* (Dec. 1920), pp. 400–4. Cardo was dishonest and was not in much favour with the Chartists. There had been trouble in the Convention about his travelling expenses, *Northern Star*, 7 Sept. 1839. For Bethnal Green meeting, *Lovett Collection*, ii. 122.

certainly not above doing what they could to hinder him. They kept him in custody, even after his examination, but no charge could be brought against him, and the following day he was dismissed. His application for the payment of his expenses during his detention was refused.[1]

In the course of twelve days' examination, no less than twelve people had been indicted with high treason, and yet the legal advisers of the magistrates must have been aware that no evidence had been produced which could justify such a serious charge. It was not until the thirteenth day that such evidence was obtained. The case before the magistrates was that of Jenkin Morgan, a milk vendor of Newport, and, as it happened, a tenant of Thomas Prothero's. While it was proceeding, a witness named James Hodge was called, and was examined by Thomas Prothero, by whom he was employed as a miner at Blackwood. The evidence which he gave did not concern Jenkin Morgan in the least, but was evidently directed against Frost. Geach strongly objected to it on this ground, but Prothero maintained that it was in order, as Frost was charged not only with treason but with conspiracy, and the evidence was material in proving the existence of conspiracy. (If there was this additional charge against Frost, it had not been made public.) There followed an extremely acrimonious passage of arms between Geach and Prothero, who claimed that Geach had no standing in the court, as Frost had declared that he would defend himself. The magistrates supported Prothero, and allowed him to continue his examination, and Prothero justified himself with the curious remark that he wished all the evidence against Frost to be produced at the examination, so that he should not be taken by surprise at the trial—in itself an indication that Frost would be surprised at the nature of the evidence.

[1] H.O. 40/45 and *Merlin*, 23 Nov.

Hodge claimed that he had been forced unwillingly to accompany the Chartists. It was he who had heard the man in the glazed hat assure Frost that all the soldiers at Newport were Chartists. He, also, had heard the man with the lantern tell Frost that half the soldiers had gone to Pontypool. But, in particular, he had heard Frost arrange his men at Pye Corner, had asked him what, in God's name, he intended to do, and had been told that his purpose was to blow down the bridge and stop the Welsh mail from proceeding to Birmingham, so that its non-arrival there would be the signal for an outbreak in the Midlands and the North. This was obviously evidence of the utmost importance, for it proved the existence of a plan for a widespread insurrection; in short, it was evidence of treason. No doubt in view of their importance, a copy of Hodge's depositions was immediately sent to the Home Office. But even at this preliminary examination Hodge contradicted himself. He was asked whether he had previously been examined, and declared that he had not, but then confessed that he had been 'examined' by Thomas Prothero.[1]

After Hodge had given this evidence, corroboration was obtained from three other witnesses. Of these the most important was William Davies of Blackwood. Whatever part he may have played on the Sunday night, Davies had thought it wise to disappear, and on the Monday, at midday, he had ridden away, with the women of Blackwood shouting after him, 'You turncoat, you do stop at home and send down people to Newport to the slaughter.'[2] Police officers had immediately begun a search for him, at Merthyr, at Neath, and elsewhere,[3] and one had surmised that he might have gone to Canterbury where his

[1] *Merlin*, 30 Nov.; H.O. 40/45; Museum MS. 466, depositions of Hodge.
[2] Museum MS. 423, evidence of Mary George.
[3] Usk MS., Treasurer's Accounts. They claimed 17s. 6d. a day expenses, apart from hotel charges.

father's brother was a Baptist minister. The conjecture was accurate. Davies arrived there on 20 November, (more than two weeks after the riot), and made enquiries at the inn where he stayed the night concerning the times when the packets left Dover for Calais. But he did not leave immediately, going instead to see his uncle. The police officer was hard on his heels, and arrested not only Davies himself, but also his uncle, on a charge of harbouring him. The sequel was extraordinary. Davies's father induced the under-sheriff for Monmouthshire to undertake his defence, and there ensued an acrimonious interchange of letters between the under-sheriff and the magistrates. They objected to his appearing in this capacity, and he retorted that he was convinced of Davies's innocence, adding that it was as important for the innocent to be acquitted as for the guilty to be condemned.[1] But he seems to have changed his mind, for he abandoned his client, who had to seek another adviser. The chief witness against Davies was a William Harris, who had heard him say at Blackwood that there were enough men there to eat Newport. Harris, also, had heard a man on horseback near Risca say that half the soldiers had gone to Abergavenny, and this man had in addition, he claimed, used Davies's phrase about eating Newport. Harris did not mention the lantern, and Hodge, on the other hand, could not have confused his neighbour, Davies, with a deserter, unless he was deliberately lying for some purpose to protect Davies, and was using the dead man to cover his statement. Israel Firman had, indeed, said that he had seen Davies on horseback near Risca, but when re-examined had declared that it was not Davies whom he had seen. But on the day after his examination Harris made a second statement to the effect that he had been drunk when he had made the first, and that it was false. He was,

[1] Museum MS., several letters of Henry Mostyn.

no doubt, severely questioned in private about this, for he returned to court and made a third statement. He now declared that the first was true, but that he had become frightened when he left the court, as several people had looked at him, and Davies's father had beckoned to him, and although no one had threatened him, he feared what might happen if he gave evidence against Davies. Davies was then charged with conspiracy and riot only, for the evidence was not clear enough to bring the charge of treason. He was released on bail, himself in £200 and two others in £100 each.[1] But there was a further development. Davies was now induced to turn queen's evidence, probably through pressure brought to bear on him by his father. His evidence was of vital importance, for he knew what had taken place at the meeting on the Friday before the riot, and had brought the delegate from Bradford to see Frost. At the Friday meeting, he said, it was agreed to 'seize all authorities, wherever they could be found, and stop the mails, so that the people in the north would know they had succeeded'. He did not, however, state specifically that there was to be an insurrection in the north, and it is not possible to say how definite his statement was or whether it was made in reply to a leading question. Three copies of a statement exist in his own hand, in addition to his depositions to the magistrates, but vital as his evidence was, the prosecution was unable to use it at the trial, for he absconded again, and this time eluded the police.[2]

The second of the witnesses about the mail was Job Tovey, at whose house Frost had slept before the riot. He, also, had absconded, and was not caught until 23 December, well after the Grand Jury had returned a

[1] *Merlin*, 7 Dec.; Gurney, pp. 361–72.
[2] Museum MS. 383, evidence of William Davies; three MSS. in Davies's handwriting; *Merthyr Guardian*, 1 Feb. 1840.

The Trial

True Bill. His depositions on two important points bear a striking resemblance to those of his neighbour, Hodge. He had heard Frost say that the non-arrival of the mail at Birmingham for an hour and a half would be the signal for an outbreak, and, also like Hodge, he had heard Frost, beyond Risca, give orders that the men with guns should go in front and the pikemen come afterwards. At the trial, it will be remembered, Hodge had to admit that he did not know who had given these orders. Is it possible that Hodge and Tovey had agreed upon what they should say? That there is some mystery about Tovey's evidence is shown by the fact that he was not prosecuted for complicity in the riot, although on his own admission he accompanied the mob; but neither was he called as a witness, although he, also, could have given evidence of the presence of the Bradford delegate. Unless he had again absconded, which is unlikely, the magistrates must have thought it unwise to call him.[1]

The third witness was John Harford. He had been arrested a fortnight after the riots, and had been taken to the Union workhouse at Newport where he was detained for twelve days. He had then had a conversation with some one whose name he professed not to know, and had given evidence, being afterwards set at liberty. According to him the non-arrival of the mail in the north 'would be the tidings that they would commence there on Monday night'. He added the sinister detail that Frost had said he expected 'to see two or three of his friends or enemies in Newport'. It was evident at the trial that the witness was prepared to say anything to secure his own liberty, and his evidence was all the more unsatisfactory as the magistrates were unable to produce his depositions, which had, apparently, been lost.[2]

[1] Museum MS. 668, evidence of Tovey; 773, letter from Maule notifying his capture.   [2] Gurney, pp. 354–61.

Meanwhile Zephaniah Williams had been brought before the magistrates in a state of almost complete collapse, and had been committed for treason, and at length the arduous duties of the examining magistrates had come to an end. Sir Thomas Phillips probably expressed their opinion when he stated that the 'evidence against the delinquents is so strong that it is hardly possible to anticipate that they will escape, although everything that can be done by intimidation, bribery, fraud, and perjury will be brought to bear on the occasion'. He had a 'firm reliance that justice would overtake them, even in this world'.[1]

That there was much threatening and intimidation is beyond doubt. Witnesses, either from fear or from sympathy with the rioters, were extremely reluctant to give evidence. One person, the brother-in-law of Edwards the baker, was prosecuted for stating that the jurymen at Monmouth would be marked and would have 'their guts cut out', and for adding, that 'if £100 would liberate Frost or any one of them' he could find the money.[2] There were rumours that it was intended to kidnap the most important witnesses, or even to waylay them on their way to Monmouth, and it was thought wise to send them in a group under escort.[3] Colonel Considine thought it necessary to take precautions even against an attempt to rescue Frost, and the magistrates of the neighbouring towns asked for armed forces.[4] There were persistent rumours of correspondence between Merthyr and the north, and of inquiries being made whether Merthyr

[1] Letter dated 17 Dec. 1839 from T. Phillips to Rev. T. Prothero, son of Phillips's senior partner (property of Mrs. Wiseman Clarke, great grand-daughter of Thomas Prothero, and kindly lent to the author through the good offices of her sister, Lady Bradney).

[2] Museum MS., deposition of Jeremiah Morley.

[3] Ibid., letters of Phelps to Maule, 23 and 24 Dec.

[4] H.O. 40/45, Col. Considine's letters, 25 Nov. 23 Dec.; Merthyr Magistrates report to H.O., 23 Dec., Marquis of Bute's report, 31 Dec.

would be ready to rise at a few hours notice. One small act of revenge the Newport Chartists did commit. Jenkin Morgan, the milk vendor, was indicted with high treason. His wife, to obtain a little money, then proceeded to sell small portions of a rick of hay which she had on her farm. But as she owed some rent, her landlord, Thomas Prothero, stopped the sale, and arranged to take the rick 'at a certain sum'. Two nights later the rick was in flames. Prothero was infuriated, and offered a reward of as much as £100 for information, but with no result.[1] The *Western Vindicator*, also, called upon the authorities to 'beware how they treated the People's men now in their power',[2] but its career was coming to an end. The issue of 2 November appears to have been seized, for no copy of it seems to have survived. The government was determined to suppress seditious newspapers, and informed the local magistrates to that effect. The mayor of Cardiff thereupon seized a packet of *Vindicators* destined for Newbridge (Pontypridd), and Thomas Jones Phillips with some special constables carried out a midnight raid on the shop of Edwards the baker's wife, who was attempting to gain her livelihood during her husband's imprisonment by selling papers. They seized all her stock, including copies of the *Northern Star* and other newspapers, as well as the *Western Vindicator*, in order, they said, to check 'the evil of which the country, and this district in particular, have so long and so justly complained'. The Home Office immediately informed Thomas Jones Phillips that his action was illegal unless done under a magistrate's warrant. He admitted, in reply, that it was not, but stated that he had been prepared to 'risk the consequences'. His victim was in any case not in a position to sue for justice. So Vincent's newspaper ceased to exist,

---

[1] *Merthyr Guardian*, 1 Feb. 1840.
[2] *Western Vindicator*, 23 Nov. 1839.

although an unsuccessful attempt was made to revive it in another form.[1]

In the meantime Blewitt, the member for the Monmouth boroughs, was clamouring for a special commission to try the prisoners, to avoid the delay which waiting for the next assizes would involve. Even Tory newspapers thought this inadvisable. Its only recommendation, said the *Dublin Monitor* was that the punishment of crime following close upon its perpetration was well calculated to inspire the public mind with terror. The moral force of justice, however, depended upon its coolness and absence of passion, and this was annihilated when men were tried for their lives in hot blood. A special commission should not be issued merely to 'satisfy the cravings of Mr. Blewitt'. Chartist papers pointed out that to allow the prisoners to be tried by a middle-class Monmouthshire jury was to allow them to be murdered. As well might a lamb expect to escape from a den of hungry wolves, said the *Northern Star*, as Frost from a jury composed of persons animated with a rancorous feeling against him. The *Edinburgh Review* agreed that a trial in Monmouthshire was a farce, for the prisoners would be tried not by their peers but by a jury of the class they had alarmed.[2] Nevertheless the government acceded to the demands of Mr. Blewitt, and within two weeks of the riot a special commission of Oyer and Terminer was issued under the Great Seal to inquire into high treasons committed within the county of Monmouth, and a special commission of gaol delivery as to all persons in custody for such offences.[3]

Whatever may have been the attitude of the more

[1] *Sun*, 13 Dec.; *Merlin*, 14 Dec.; *Charter*, 15 Dec.; Museum MS. 769; H.O. 40/45, correspondence T. J. Phillips; H.O. 40/46, correspondence of R. Reece, Mayor of Cardiff.

[2] *Dublin Monitor*, 16 Nov.; *Northern Star*, 30 Nov.; *Tait's Edinburgh Review*, Dec. 1839, pp. 823-4.   [3] Gurney, p. 3.

extreme Chartists towards the riot, the general body had heard of it with amazement. The *Scottish Vindicator* expressed the opinion of the majority when it wondered how the 'honest, sincere, intelligent, generous and virtuous Frost' could have become involved in it. The editor attributed it to a government plot, for he thought that the idea of secrecy was foolish, as government spies must have known of it.[1] But in spite of the misgivings felt by so many, the energies of all were now directed towards Frost's defence. The organization of this was undertaken by Frost's step-son, William Foster Geach. He himself had fallen on evil days. The suspicion of forgery which Prothero and Phillips had roused by their action against him in July 1838 had ruined his practice in Pontypool, and he had become bankrupt.[2] He had then tried, without much success, to start a practice again in Bristol, for bankruptcy did not then prevent a solicitor from practising.[3] In spite of his own misfortunes and the knowledge that there were overwhelming difficulties ahead of him, he devoted all his time to the defence of his step-father, and conducted it with a skill which must arouse admiration. On 22 November he wrote to the Home Office expressing a hope that the rumours of a special commission were unfounded. Such a commission, he claimed, would not allow time to collect evidence for the defence, and moreover delay was essential to allow the prejudice against Frost to subside. He also asked permission to see Frost's papers, which the magistrates had seized on 4 November, but to which they refused to grant him access. The reply which he received took no notice whatsoever of his request to postpone the

[1] *Scottish Vindicator*, 30 Nov. 1839.
[2] *The Times*, 1 June 1839; *Merlin*, 13 July 1839.
[3] Information kindly supplied by T. G. Lund, Esq., assistant secretary, Law Society. Geach practised at Bristol from 1828 to 1830 and 1839 to 1840, and at Pontypool from 1830 to 1839. At Pontypool he also carried on business as a corn and timber merchant.

trial, and refused him permission to see Frost's papers. He then went up to London to put the case to the Home Office in person, and on 4 December he obtained the permission he desired. But Frost's papers, characteristically enough, had nothing in them which could be considered treasonable, and the prosecution made no use whatsoever of them. Geach again wrote to the Home Office urging delay in the interests of justice, as the excited state of the public mind, together with the feelings of anger and revenge which were being roused against Frost, must influence the class from which the jury would be impannelled, and from which Frost could expect no sympathy. He now asked, in addition, for a grant towards the defence, especially as the special commission would involve greater expenses, for, as the regular assizes were not sitting, counsel would have to be taken down specially from London, but the only reply which he received was that the Home Office had no power to recommend a grant.[1] The Chartists, therefore, had to find the money themselves, and numerous collections were made. Geach had appealed to O'Connor, and he announced that he would allot a whole week's profits of the *Northern Star* for this purpose. He also raised a levy of one penny on all readers by putting the price up by that amount. The largest sum raised by any one district was £45 from the male and female Chartists of Merthyr and Aberdare.[2]

The dismay of the Chartists at the appointment of a special commission turned to consternation at the announcement that it was to be conducted by Mr. Justice John Williams.[3] This fellow-countryman of Judge Jeffreys (he was born at Bunbury in Cheshire), had made his name as Junior Counsel in Queen Caroline's case, but he was

---

[1] H.O. 40/45, letters dated 22 Nov. and 6 Dec.; *Merlin,* 7 Dec.
[2] *Northern Star,* 30 Nov., 7 Dec., 14 Dec., 21 Dec.; *Sun,* 15 Dec.; *Charter,* 22 Dec., 29 Dec.   [3] *Western Vindicator* (new series), 7 Dec.

notorious on account of the savage sentence he had passed on the Dorchester labourers in 1834, and his unreasonably severe strictures on their conduct. Fortunately the Lord Chief Justice decided to participate. He was Sir Nicholas Tindal, one of the greatest judges of the century, a man renowned for his learning and skill in the analysis of evidence, and also for his impartiality and good sense, and invariable kindness. To these two judges was added a third, Sir James Parke, also a man of great learning and of almost superstitious reverence for the technicalities of the law.

The judges arrived in Monmouth on the morning of 10 December. They had stayed the night at Ross, and were met at the border by the Lord Lieutenant and the High Sheriff, and escorted to the county town. At ten o'clock the commission was declared open, and the court was then adjourned so that the judges could attend divine service. This was conducted by the High Sheriff's chaplain, the Reverend George Irving of Llantrissent. His text was tendentious enough—'while they promise them liberty, they themselves are the servants of corruption' (2 Peter ii. 19)—and he made the most of the occasion. Throughout the whole of history, said the reverend gentleman, there had been the struggle of the will of man against God for what was falsely called liberty. False prophets had arisen from time to time and set themselves and their victims against all that was holy. In recent times there had arisen an idolatry of reason, which was a fiercer, fouler, and more bloody heathenism than any that had ever laid waste the East. It was this infidelity which was the source of the present evil. The preacher ended by proving 'in the most eloquent manner' that without the establishment of a *national* Christianity (for he evidently saw the cloven hoof of Nonconformity in Chartism) there never had been and never could be peace on earth.¹ At two o'clock the grand jurors were called. The panel contained no less than 180 names,² for all the free-holders of the shire were anxious to serve. The selection of the jury out of this large body was no easy matter, and caused a little heart-burning, but eventually the maximum of twenty-three jurors were chosen. Among their num-ber was Lord Granville Somerset, brother to the Duke of Beaufort, who acted as foreman; Sir Charles Morgan's son, Octavius Morgan; his grandson, the Honourable William Rodney; his brother-in-law, Samuel Homfray; Joseph Bailey, M.P.; William Addams Williams, M.P.; Reginald James Blewitt, M.P., and Sir Benjamin Hall, M.P. To them, the Lord Chief Justice delivered a charge which fully justifies his great reputation for learning, clarity, and fairmindedness.

He disclaimed, at the commencement, any intention to deal with the disturbances which had taken place, but it was a matter of notoriety that they had occurred, and it was highly probable that indictments for high treason would be preferred against some who were supposed to have taken a part in them. He confined himself to an exposition of the law relating to high treason. This he maintained to be the crime which was calculated to pro-duce the most malignant effect on the community at large, for it was subversive of all law and order. Its punishment, therefore, was the most severe in law. But on account of this severity, the law of treason had been confined within certain definite limits which he proceeded to indicate. By the Statute of 25 Edward III (1352) treason was declared to be compassing or imagining the death of the king or levying war against the king in his realm. By 36 George III (1796) it was enacted that com-

¹ *The Times*, 11 Dec. 1839 (as the sermon was delivered on 10 Dec. he must have supplied it beforehand to *The Times*). The sermon is given *verbatim* in *Morning Herald*, 18 Dec.

² *Rise and Fall*, p. 61. Johns, op. cit., p. 50, gives the figure 260.

passing, imagining, or devising to deprive the king of his sovereign power, or to levy war against him in order to force him to change his measures or counsels should be included under the crime of treason. The offence, therefore, under this Act, consisted in the compassing and imagining of certain acts and not in the commission of the acts themselves. But since the thoughts of men were known to the Supreme Being only, treason required the commission of overt acts, such acts being the proof of treason and not the treason itself. The acts would differ in each particular case. Where the object of the treason had not actually been perpetrated, meetings to propose it, or the procuring of arms and ammunition, or money or other necessaries for this purpose, or the administration of any illegal oaths to bind men together to accomplish it, would be considered treasonable acts. But further the specific acts must be included in the indictment, and none other used to prove the prisoner guilty of treason, and still further, by a statute of William III's reign two witnesses were necessary, either both of them to the same overt act, or one of them to one and the other to another overt act of the same treason. In the present case, said the Lord Chief Justice, there was no reason to suppose any intention to injure the person of the queen. He therefore confined himself to the treason involved in levying war against the queen. Here he quoted high authority to show that if a large number of persons, whether armed or otherwise, collected together to effect any object of a private nature, or revenge a private injury, such acts of violence might be high misdemeanours, but they did not constitute treason. In order to prove treason it must be shown that the persons concerned had a general object in view, such as to compel the queen to alter her measures or government. For example, if there were an insurrection to remove a particular enclosure, that would not be treason; but if the insurrection were for the purpose of removing all enclosures it would lay the perpetrators open to this charge. Moreover, in treason there was no distinction between the man who instigated the treasonable design and the one by whose hand the act of treason was committed; both were equally guilty in the eye of the law. And finally, while assembling together with a treasonable purpose was a levying of war although no blow was struck, actual conflict with the queen's troops must, beyond all doubt, amount to the levying of war under the Act of 1352 and to the offence of devising to levy war under the Act of 1796. In particular he therefore directed the attention of the jury firstly to the motive of the prisoners, whether it was private or general, and secondly to whether there were two witnesses to prove the overt acts. He ended by expressing his sorrow at the occurrence, which was fortunately a very rare one, and suggesting the diffusion of religious instruction as the only remedy. Calling upon the Grand Jury to dismiss from their minds all they had heard upon the subject before entering the court, he enjoined upon them to do their duty, whether this would lead them to dismiss the accused to their homes or otherwise, regardless of all consequences.[1]

The Grand Jury did not take long to make up their minds, for in spite of the number of the prisoners and the fact that witnesses must be called for each, they had reached a decision by three o'clock on the following afternoon. The judges were then sent for, and in solemn silence, a True Bill for high treason was declared found against John Frost, Charles Walters, John Lovell, Richard Benfield, John Rees, George Turner (a wooden-legged man), Zephaniah Williams, Edmund Edmunds, Jenkin Morgan, Solomon Britan, William Jones, James Aust, another John Rees (the Fifer), and David Jones (the Tinker). A True

[1] Gurney, pp. 4–12.

Bill for burglary was found against four others, while in the case of one person only no bill was found. (It will be remembered that of the twenty-one indictments of high treason, those against Etheridge and Partridge had been changed to conspiracy.) The twelve who were in custody out of the fourteen indicted with treason were placed at the bar, and informed that a True Bill had been found against them. The court was then adjourned until 31 December. On the day following the verdict of the Grand Jury, that is on 12 December, Maule handed to each of the prisoners a copy of the indictment and a list of jurors; five days later he supplied them with the list of witnesses.

The Lord Chief Justice's charge met with a mixed reception in the country. The opponents of Chartism in Newport thought it worth reprinting as a cheap pamphlet, as it would have a salutary effect in the hills. The Chartists thought otherwise. Treason, said the *Charter* newspaper, was not a crime palpable enough for the ordinary man to understand, as he could theft or murder. Besides, treason by statute could be everything, anything, or nothing. For how could the succession of Victoria be explained but by treason—the invitation to William of Orange, the levying of war with Dutch soldiers, all that was meant by the Glorious Revolution, was treason against a king *de jure* and *de facto*. Magna Carta itself was the consequence of treason. Who then were traitors and not traitors, it asked.[1] Whatever may have been the answer to this question Frost must be defended, and on the day after the session of the Grand Jury, a number of his friends, among them O'Connor and O'Brien, met at Bolt Court. Both O'Connor and O'Brien wished to hold large public meetings to present to the country the true facts about the riot. Some even wished to threaten the government with an insurrection of 2,000,000 men, if the

[1] *Charter*, 29 Dec.

prisoners were punished. Others protested against the use of violent language—there had been far too much of it in the last six months—and thought it inadvisable to call public meetings, as paid agents of the government might speak at them and prejudice Frost's case. Eventually it was decided that meetings should be held and subscriptions invited. It was also announced that counsel had been retained.[1]

Frost's friends had briefed two very remarkable men. The first to accept a brief was Fitzroy Kelly, 'one of the most acute and powerful advocates at the bar' in the opinion of his opponent at the trial, the Attorney-General. He was generally reputed to be the most eloquent barrister in England. Later he was to serve as Solicitor-General and he was the last to hold the office and title of Chief Baron of the Exchequer. But a far greater lawyer was retained in Sir Frederick Pollock, Frost's junior counsel in his trial for libel. Like Kelly he was a conservative member of Parliament, and therefore could have little sympathy with his client's political views. But his position was still more strange. He had been Attorney-General in the hundred days administration of Sir Robert Peel in 1834, and as Melbourne's ministry might fall any day, he would almost certainly be Attorney-General again within a few months. Thus while defending the Chartists in December, he ran the risk of having to prosecute them soon afterwards if there were any further outbreaks. Why then did he accept the brief? Possibly he welcomed the chance of crossing swords with his Whig counterpart; he was, in any case, a man of generous disposition and had more sympathy with the working class than did the Whigs (he was the son of a saddler), and quite possibly he had in mind the great example of Erskine in the treason trials of 1794. He was, in fact, a great lawyer worthy to

[1] *Charter*, 15 Dec.

be placed beside Erskine, and was probably the most learned advocate of his day. He became Attorney-General again in 1841, and was Kelly's predecessor as Chief Baron of the Exchequer.

Geach, in the meantime, had been active on behalf of his stepfather. Frost's property, the Royal Oak, was transferred to his mother, Sarah Roberts, so that it would not be confiscated if he were condemned,[1] and it was, now, perhaps fortunate that William Foster's will had declared Frost's wife's property to be in no way 'subject to the control, forfeiture, debts or engagements' of her husband. Geach also sent a petition to the queen from all the prisoners denying that they had had any feeling of hostility against her, and asking for pecuniary assistance,[2] but again without response. His chief work, however, was to collect information about the long list of 317 jurors and 236 witnesses with which the prisoners had been supplied,[3] and it was the skill and thoroughness with which he did this that made possible Pollock and Kelly's remarkable cross-examination at the trial. He had advised Frost's friends that public meetings would be dangerous and inadvisable, and they had decided to abandon them, issuing instead a public address to expose the malignity of the prosecution and the condemnation of Frost in the newspapers before his trial.[4] A new Convention had now met, and it also offered its assistance in Frost's cause. But its delegates numbered only eight (among them was Beniowski, delegate from the Tower Hamlets) and it proved to be stillborn.[5] Yet Geach's greatest difficulty was to find any witnesses to appear for Frost. This is made

[1] *Life of John Frost* (1840), p. 2. Hovell, the best historian of Chartism, is wrong in thinking that Frost had started innkeeping (*op. cit.*, p. 186), as in many details concerning Chartism in South and Mid-Wales.

[2] H.O. 40/45, 21 Dec.

[3] *Cambrian*, 28 Dec.; Gurney, pp. 183, 581.

[4] *Charter*, 22 Dec., 29 Dec.   [5] Ibid., 29 Dec.

strikingly clear by the fact that even Daniel O'Connell was approached. He could give no assistance, however. He would withhold from no man in peril of his life any fact of which he was cognisant, he said, but he did not believe that he had any evidence to give.[1]

Great interest was aroused throughout the country as the day of the trial drew near. The Attorney-General declared himself to be 'deep in the law of treason',[2] and this was no doubt true of the counsel for the defence as well, if not even of the judges. The charge of treason, which had been common enough in the previous century, had now become infrequent, and there had been no treason trial since that of Thistlewood in 1820, so that few were familiar with the law. The leading Chartists who were still at liberty, and were able to do so, arrived in Monmouth, among them Feargus O'Connor, who remained there throughout the trial. The innkeepers of Monmouth, hoping to reap a good harvest, overreached themselves in the prices which they asked for rooms, for the crowd was not quite as huge as they expected.[3] Nevertheless the town was full enough, what with sightseers and soldiers, and the London police who were specially brought down to keep order in court (at a cost to the ratepayers of £112. 8s.).[4] Witnesses also were brought along in shoals, in every description of vehicle, from coaches and four to humble chaise-carts (at a cost of £297). They were a motley crowd composed of opponents of Chartism and friends now turned queen's evidence, and the list of their names must have given the prisoners sad food for thought in their cells. As the courtroom was small there was great competition among the public for seats, but admission was granted by ticket only,

[1] Newport Library MS., letter from O'Connell, dated 30 Dec.
[2] Mrs. Hardcastle (ed.), *Autobiography of John, Lord Campbell* (London, 1881), ii. 126. [3] *Merlin*, 4 Jan. 1840.
[4] Usk MS., Treasurer's vouchers, 6 April 1840.

and the firmness of the London police was largely instru-
mental in preserving order.

Tuesday, 31 December, at last arrived, a bleak winter's
day, and found Monmouth alive with activity. Shortly
after nine a bugle call rang out, and the Lancers and
infantry assembled and proceeded to the prison. Soon
afterwards they escorted two vans to the court-house, and
out of these came the twelve men indicted with treason,
in two separate parties of six, all handcuffed and chained
to each other. Frost's appearance must have surprised
those who now saw him for the first time, and who had
been led by the newspapers to expect a brutal villain.
He had been ill in prison, no doubt on account of his
exposure on the night of the march to Newport and
throughout the following day (the prison doctor dia-
gnosed 'biliary derangement' and prescribed arrowroot),
and he was pale and somewhat weak, but his manner and
expression were those of a mild and thoughtful man of
fifty-four. His 'calm and chastened demeanour' throughout the trial won for him the admiration even of his
opponents.[1] Zephaniah Williams also had regained his
composure, while Jones assumed an air of careless
bravado. At ten o'clock the judges arrived at the court
house, preceded by ten London policemen, and accompanied by six javelin men and six trumpeters. They
robed themselves in their scarlet and ermine vestments
and entered the court-room followed by their train-bearers,
gentlemen ushers, and the metropolitan police. Beneath
them in court was a phalanx of counsel; at the bar the
twelve prisoners stood in silence, and the rest of the room
was completely filled with spectators. The lists were thus
prepared for a forensic battle on a grand scale. On the
one side were two lawyers, one reputed to be the most
learned and the other the most eloquent of the time. On

[1] *Decline and Fall*, pp. 8 ff.; *Charter*, 5 Jan., 12 Jan.

the other side were the Attorney-General, Sir John Campbell, later Lord Chief Justice, and the Solicitor-General, Sir Thomas Wilde, later Lord Chancellor. The odds, from the outset, were enormously against the former pair, but the stake was one of life or death, and all that skill, industry, and cunning could do was accomplished.

The trial started with the reading of the indictment, an enormously long document, couched in terms which were almost impossible for the layman to understand. There were four charges, and divested of their legal phraseology they amounted to this. The first charge indicted the fourteen men, together with other false traitors, whose names were unknown, to the number of two thousand and more, with levying war against the queen, and indicated the ways and means by which war was levied, that is by marching in battle array, seizing arms, forcing subjects of the queen to join them, attacking the Westgate and firing upon the magistrates and the queen's troops. The second charge was of precisely the same nature, that is of levying war against the queen, but it did not indicate the ways and means. Both of these charges evidently came under the statute of 1352. The third charge was one of intending and imagining to depose the queen, and indicated the overt acts by which the charge was to be supported, that is attempting to get possession of Newport and to cut off communications by seizing the mails, conspiring to attack the queen's troops, and to compel her to change the law by force, as well as the acts listed under the first count, which were both treason in themselves and the proof of treason. The fourth count greatly resembled the third; it was of conspiring to levy war against the queen, and once more the same overt acts were recited in proof of this. These two counts evidently related to the Act of 1796. Thus, in short, the prisoners were charged with levying war against the queen, and with conspiring to

levy war against the queen with the intention of compelling
her to change her measures. To these charges, whether
they understood them or not, the prisoners pleaded not
guilty, without raising any objection on any score.[1] Frost's
counsel thereupon declared that they appeared for him
alone, and so the other prisoners were removed from the bar.

Then came the swearing of the jury. Over 300 had been
called, and seventy-six did not answer their names. Many
were found to be dead or excused on various grounds,
but the remaining fifteen were fined £10 each.[2] From
the beginning it became obvious that Pollock and Kelly
were going to fight the case *à l'outrance*. They objected to
the jury being called alphabetically as the number which
the prisoner could challenge was limited to thirty-five,
and the lists at the end of the alphabet might be packed.
This point was conceded by the prosecution and the jury
were picked from the ballot box. They challenged several
jurymen, but when one was challenged by the Crown,
they objected that the Crown had no right peremptorily
to challenge a juryman, without indicating the reason, and
argued the matter at great length. This the judges overruled. They then argued that in the case in question the
Crown was too late, as the juror had actually got the New
Testament in his hand before the Crown challenged, but
it turned out that he had taken the book without being
directed to do so, so the Crown's challenge was accepted.
A whole day was spent in skirmishing of this kind, presided
over with complete urbanity and patience by the Lord
Chief Justice, and it was late in the evening when the
full jury were sworn. They were then 'charged' with the
prisoner, and as it was difficult to continue in the dimly
lit court-room (the charge for candles throughout the trial
was £22. 15s.) the court was adjourned.

[1] Gurney, pp. 13–26. There is a brief analysis on pp. 628–9.
[2] *Trial of John Frost*, by a Barrister (1840).

John Frost

On New Year's morning, just as the Attorney-General was about to state the case for the Crown, Pollock intimated that he had an objection to raise with regard to the witnesses. He took by surprise both the Lord Chief Justice and the Attorney-General, who were completely nonplussed when he went on to declare that the defence had not been supplied with the list of witnesses according to statute. The Attorney-General was evidently rattled; he even declared that the solemnity of a court of justice must be observed, and insisted upon proceeding with his address to the jury. But the sting was taken out of his eloquence, for he could not divest his mind of a wonder as to what Pollock was now up to. His statement of the case was temperate. He elaborated the difference between a public and a private motive. He then detailed the facts of the riot, insisting upon the command assumed by Frost, the non-arrival of the Welsh mail as a signal for general insurrection, the knowledge Frost had obtained that the troops were in the Westgate, the demand made to the special constables to surrender, and the firing on the soldiers of the queen. It was obvious that the plan which he had adopted was to prove three things, that Frost was in command of the mob, that the object which the mob had in mind was not a private one, such as releasing Vincent, but the general one of starting an insurrection throughout the country, and that the mob had deliberately fired at the queen's soldiers, knowing them to be in the Westgate. His interpretation of the facts was a reasonably fair one from the point of view of the opponents of Chartism, and he was scrupulously fair in indicating circumstances when even an attack on the queen's soldiers might not be treason. In one instance only was he guilty of gross unfairness. In his account of the meeting on the Friday before the riot, he made use of information which could only have been derived from William Davies's evidence. Unless he was unaware that Davies had absconded, and therefore unaware that he could call no evidence to substantiate his statements, he was guilty of prejudicing the minds of the jury by suggesting to them facts relating to a conspiracy which were certainly true, but which he could not prove.[1]

When he had concluded and the first witness was called, Pollock renewed his objection that no list containing the witness's name had been supplied to the defence in accordance with the statute. Maule was then called and examined about the delivery of the list. Pollock evidently enjoyed the excitement which he had caused in court, especially among the opposing counsel, who were still mystified, and it was only after a long time and in the most elaborate language that he came to the point, that the indictment and the jury list had been presented on 12 December, and the list of witnesses on 17 December, whereas the statute declared that they should be delivered simultaneously, ten days before the trial. There then ensued an argument on almost a titanic scale, occupying the whole of the remainder of the day, and filling no less than a hundred pages in the printed account of the trial. There was no question of Maule's benevolent intentions in supplying the prisoners with the jury list at the earliest possible moment, and it was argued for the Crown that the statute had been substantially complied with. But Pollock strongly objected to distinguishing between a 'liberal construction' and a 'strict construction' of the statute; he insisted that the only construction possible was the 'true construction'. It was a most astute move on his part, for the jury could only convict or acquit Frost on the evidence produced, and if no witnesses could be called he must be acquitted. The Attorney-General argued with some asperity that Pollock and Kelly were trying

[1] Gurney, p. 65.

to 'fritter away an act of Parliament', for even if the objection were valid, it was made too late, as it should have been made before the prisoner had pleaded to the indictment. To this Pollock, followed by Kelly, replied that it could not have been made at any other time, although Pollock admitted, incidentally, that the objection had not been thought of beforehand.[1] At the end of the day the judges declared that they had decided to allow the trial to proceed, but that there was sufficient doubt for the matter to be submitted to further consideration by the judges at Westminster, should the verdict of the jury make this necessary. When the court reassembled next morning Pollock endeavoured to get a ruling from the judges that should the technical point be decided in his favour, Frost would be entitled to acquittal, but the court ruled cautiously that he would be entitled to the same benefit as if the point had been decided at the trial, without declaring what that would have been.

Such was the great question of legal procedure raised by Frost's trial. A certain amount of mystery remains attached to it. Why, for example, did Pollock not raise the objection earlier? The answer possibly is that had he done so, the only result would have been the postponement of the trial for ten days, so that the lists could have been presented simultaneously in accordance with the statute. This would have been some advantage to Frost, for it would have provided much needed time for the collection of information, and might have allowed the passions of the jury to cool. But it is hardly likely that the verdict would have been altered. Was it, then, consummate strategy on the part of Pollock to delay raising the objection until it was too late for the trial to be postponed, and risk all on getting a complete acquittal for Frost on the grounds of a technical miscarriage of justice? Such

[1] Gurney, p. 87.

an eventuality would not be unthinkable in trials for treason, and the pride of craft involved in the technicality would appeal strongly to lawyers, especially those of the mentality of Baron Parke. This was the interpretation generally accepted at the time, but it does not agree well with the facts, for the possibility of an objection arose not in the mind of the great lawyer, Pollock, but in that of the future convict, William Foster Geach. In all probability Geach was not able to draw Pollock's attention to it until after the court had adjourned on Tuesday night, and Pollock raised the objection at the first available opportunity, that is, when the court reassembled on Wednesday morning, both he and Kelly having spent nearly the whole of the previous night in an examination of precedents.[1]

The tremendous odds against Frost, with which the trial started, had thus been changed, for even if the verdict of guilty were arrived at, there was now always the possibility that it might be set aside by the judges. This seems to have inspired Pollock and Kelly to even greater efforts on behalf of their client. They waived their professional dignity so far as to visit Frost in gaol in the company of O'Connor—a rare occurrence on the part of barristers of their standing. They were greatly impressed by his bearing, and assured him that they would wait upon him whenever he thought it necessary.[2] They excelled themselves in the handling of witnesses. The plan of the prosecution was to call witnesses first to show what had happened at the Westgate and then trace the riot back to its origin. But several of these witnesses the defence succeeded in

---

[1] The *Newport Herald* and the *Newport Gazette* both attribute the discovery to Geach (quoted *Cornwall Chronicle* (Tasmania), 2 Sept. 1846). The version adopted in the text agrees with Pollock's admission (Gurney, p. 87) that he had not thought of the objection beforehand. Pollock's search for precedents might partly account for the belief current at the time locally that he did not sleep more than three hours out of twenty-four throughout the trial (*Rise and Fall*, p. 71). [2] *Charter*, 12 Jan. 1840.

having disallowed, and others they discredited. They minutely scrutinized the description of the witnesses, a matter of obvious importance, since 550 witnesses and jurymen had had to be sought out in a little over ten days. No doubt with the help of Geach, they struck upon the fact that the parish of St. Woollos extended beyond the borough of Newport, so they argued with great ingenuity that 'in the parish of St. Woollos in the borough of Newport' was a misdirection. This the judges overruled, but on the grounds of misdescription the most vital witness with regard to the organization in groups of ten was excluded. That this success of the defence caused their opponents some consternation is shown by an anonymous note among Phelps's papers suggesting ways by which the difficulty in description could be overcome. 'This is a most material witness in Jenkin Morgan's case', continues the note, 'and without his evidence there is a doubt of conviction, and as Jenkin Morgan is the only case we have been able to bring home to anyone living in Newport, it is highly important to make an example of him, one half of the inhabitants of Newport being Chartists and badly disposed persons.'[1] But Jenkin Morgan, poor man, did not know of the weakness of the case against him, and was one of the five persuaded to withdraw the plea of not guilty on the understanding that their lives would be spared.[2] Even more vital was the attempt of the defence to get excluded the evidence of acts or declarations not done in Frost's presence, but the judges held that if Frost did what others said it was proposed to do, then this was evidence of conspiracy. Witnesses whom they could not get disallowed, Pollock and Kelly did their utmost to discredit. One of the boys who had heard the order given to march at the

[1] Museum MS. 486.

[2] He was not transported, however, and was released from prison in 1844 together with Lovell and Waters. He was then in bad health and in extreme poverty. *Merlin*, 29 June 1844.

Courtybella Machine was shown to be in Phelps's employment. A former partner of Thomas Prothero's was forced to admit that he could not swear to not having said that the lords who had voted against the Reform Bill deserved to be guillotined. A person who had turned queen's evidence and gave important information about the meetings of the lodges before the riot was shown to have served six months' imprisonment for theft. James Hodge's 'examination' by his employer, Thomas Prothero, before he gave evidence was brought out. Hodge also had to admit that he did not know who had given the orders at Pye Corner, although he had stated in his depositions that it was Frost. Much was made of an inconsistency in the times when he declared that he was at Pye Corner and at Blackwood, to the mystification of the Attorney-General, who did not know that he had put back the clock two hours as soon as he had got home, and had asked his wife to call in a neighbour in order to draw her attention to the time, and to the fact that he was in bed.[1] John Harford, the other important witness with regard to the Welsh mail (for Davies had absconded and Tovey was not called), was led to contradict himself as to whether he was arrested for complicity in the riot or not, and was badly shaken on the question whether he had made his declaration against Frost to secure his own liberty. And finally the drunkenness and changes in the evidence of William Harris were stressed, so that the Solicitor-General, who was completely taken by surprise, decided to abandon him as a witness.

The case for the Crown was thus badly shaken. Out of the 236 witnesses, only 38 had been called, and several of these had not proved very satisfactory. It was permissible to suppose that the 200 not called would have been even less so. Pollock's line of defence had also become clear through the way in which he questioned witnesses with

[1] Museum MS. 659.

regard to Vincent's imprisonment and the presence of the soldiers at the Westgate Hotel. He commenced his address as soon as the court reassembled on Monday morning, and spoke for over five hours. It was a consummately clever speech, intended to conciliate the jury and flatter their intelligence while he destroyed the evidence of the prosecution step by step. He began by admitting that criminal actions were committed, but contended that they were not treasonable, and appealed to the jury not to allow their feelings with regard to the consequences of these actions to colour their interpretation of the intentions of the prisoner. He showed that it was one witness only (and he the son of one of Frost's bitterest enemies) who had been called to prove that the mob had cried, 'Surrender yourselves our prisoners', at the Westgate, in spite of the overwhelming importance of this point. Pollock, on the other hand, would call a witness of the greatest reliability—Henry Williams, the special constable who had acted as the mayor's aide-de-camp and had himself been wounded—to show that they had cried, 'Surrender our prisoners,' referring to those taken in the night. Why, he asked, had not the man who replied 'Never' to this demand been called? Was it because he might contradict the other witness with regard to the exact words of the mob? Pollock then proceeded to examine the question of the Welsh mail. If it was the intention of the Chartists to destroy the bridge, why had they not attempted to do so, instead of attacking the Westgate? But, apart from this, Pollock showed that the non-arrival of the Welsh mail at Birmingham as a signal was absurd, for the mail did not go direct to Birmingham, as it went first to Bristol. Moreover, the coach which took it went no farther than the ferry; the mail bag was taken by a different coach to Bristol, where the letters were re-sorted, and, again, the mail-coach from Bristol to Birmingham did not wait for the South Wales bag if it had not arrived in time, so that the coach would arrive in Birmingham irrespective of what had happened in Newport. The whole story was merely an invention of Hodge's. Was it, in any case, likely that Frost would have explained his intentions to Hodge? As for Harford's elaboration that the outbreak in Birmingham would commence on Monday night, it was sufficient to show that the mail did not leave Bristol before Tuesday morning. Pollock's exposure of Hodge's contradictions, of the tampering with Harford before he gave evidence, and of Harris's drunken depositions was devastating, so that the theory of a general insurrection was destroyed. What, then, of the attack on the troops at the Westgate? Pollock had elicited from Captain Gray a fact which had surprised him (and no doubt the prosecution)—that the troops were in the Westgate barely half an hour before the riot. How then could Phelps's boy, who had admittedly come from the opposite direction, know they were there? His statement was only 'one of the inventions with which the case abounded'. Moreover, Pollock had forced Captain Gray to admit that he had no evidence that the crowd had fired after the troops had been seen, and he maintained that as soon as it was obvious that a continuation of the attack on the Westgate meant resistance to the forces of the Crown, the crowd dispersed. That Frost had no intention to throw the country into confusion was shown by his having made provision on the Friday for the payment of a bill of exchange and actually paying it on the Monday on which the riot occurred. What, then, had the Chartists had in mind? Pollock dwelt upon the concern which the workers felt with regard to Vincent's imprisonment, and their unavailing attempts to get his conditions improved. Their purpose, therefore, was to carry out a great demonstration before making another appeal to the magistrates. Some individuals may have wanted to release Vincent (the relative positions of Monmouth and Newport

to the coal-field made an attack on Newport as a preliminary to one on Monmouth an absurdity), but on the
evidence called by the Crown itself Pollock showed that
Zephaniah Williams had said that this was not their intention. That the demonstration had ended in a riot was
true, but the experience of the Reform agitation some
years previously had made it necessary to adopt a more
lenient interpretation of the legality of public assemblies.
Pollock concluded by declaring that a verdict of not guilty
would pacify the country more than 10,000 troops en-
forcing obedience at the point of the sword.

Witnesses for the defence were few; it was, in any case,
the duty of the Crown to prove guilt rather than the duty
of the prisoner to prove his innocence. Evidence was,
however, called to show the concern for Vincent, to prove
that the crowd had cried, 'Surrender our prisoners,'
to prove that the Welsh mail went via Bristol, and to prove
the payment of the bill of exchange. Lord Granville
Somerset was also called to show how Frost had saved his
brother from violence during the election of 1831—a subtle
reminder to the Whigs of a time when they were less severe
upon rioting. Kelly then availed himself of the privilege
allowed only to a prisoner tried on a charge of treason,
that of having the jury addressed by his second counsel.
Kelly's speech occupied five and a half hours. It followed
the line of Pollock's argument very closely, and introduced
scarcely anything new, but in tone it was very different
from that of Pollock. In print it does not read as well as
Pollock's, and yet contemporaries regarded it as immensely
superior,[1] the truth being that Kelly's rhetoric depended
entirely on the spoken word. He tried by an overwhelming
spate of words to shake the confidence of the jury in any
decision they had arrived at, and then argued for the
benefit of the doubt for his client. Where Pollock had

[1] *Life of John Frost* (1840); *Merlin,* 4 Jan. 1840.

shaken the credibility of the Crown's witnesses, Kelly poured his scathing sarcasm upon them, and ridiculed a case which was so meagre that wretches like Harris, self-condemned perjurers, had to be called in support of it. And it was not only the witnesses but the examining magistrates who came in for a share of his vituperation. 'Creatures getting up evidence to shed the blood of their fellow men', he called them, because they had kept back Henry Williams's evidence which went far to disprove a charge of treason. The Attorney-General had 'made a parade of wounds and of afflictions' which had nothing to do with treason, in one case cross-examining a witness for three-quarters of an hour with regard to his sufferings, in order to aggravate the feelings of the jury against Frost, but Henry Williams's wounds were not mentioned, although he was a friend of the mayor's, for his evidence was contrary to the case for the Crown. Kelly ended with an impassioned appeal to the emotions of the jury. When he had finished the Lord Chief Justice asked Frost whether he wished to add anything to what his counsel had said, but he declared himself fully satisfied with their statement of his case.

While the great orator was speaking, Pollock wrote in a letter to a friend: 'We are certainly not without hopes that Frost may be acquitted, and that the magnificent point of law reserved by the Judges may never be decided, for I will venture to say that the mistake will never be made again.'[1] The case for the Crown had, indeed, taken on a different complexion when the Solicitor-General rose to reply, and his task was far more formidable than that of the Attorney-General. In one matter only did he score a triumph—he successfully pricked the bubble of Kelly's eloquence, for in this, getting in the last word was of supreme importance. 'If strong expressions could get

[1] Lord Hanworth, *Lord Chief Baron Pollock* (London, 1929), p. 115.

acquittals for prisoners', he said, 'my learned friend would be a safe and admirable counsel; no man can utter them stronger; no man can utter them upon less foundation,' and he insinuated that Kelly's emotional appeal was an indication of the weakness of his case. His tone towards Pollock was respectful, but during his reply he engaged in several passages of arms with Kelly. Yet he was forced to yield one point after another. He struck out Harris's evidence; he abandoned the argument based on the demand 'Surrender yourselves prisoners'; he admitted that there was no evidence to prove the intention of the rioters to make the Charter the law of the land, as the Attorney-General had maintained, and thus virtually abandoned the mail theory; he admitted that no treasonable papers had been found in Frost's house (though he suggested that Frost might have taken care of this). His attempts to rehabilitate Hodge and Harford were not very successful, yet he cleverly countered Pollock's 'demonstration' theory by showing that none of the witnesses for the defence had heard of a forthcoming demonstration, or had heard of a demonstration having previously been held at night. He ended by arguing that even if no shot had been fired and no life lost, the marching of the prisoner and his fellows, seizing men and guns in their progress, was an act of treason, of levying war against the queen. The attack on the Westgate, whether they knew the soldiers were there or not, was an overt act which could be cited in support of this charge.

The Lord Chief Justice's summing up, which followed, proved the chief sensation of the trial, for it was evident from the start that he was labouring for an acquittal. It was a careful résumé of all the evidence, taken witness by witness, and it is somewhat tiresome to read. But he once more stressed the need of a general purpose to prove the charge of treason, and pointed out that the Crown had abandoned its contention that the object of the rioters was to establish the Charter as the law of the land. More than once he reminded the jury that it was for the Crown to prove the guilt of the prisoner and not for Frost to prove his innocence, and concluded by insisting in the strongest terms on the need for complete certainty before a verdict of guilty could be found. The embarrassment which he caused the law officers of the Crown can best be shown by quoting a letter written by the Attorney-General on the same day:

'I have passed a very anxious day, as if I myself had been on trial. To my utter astonishment and dismay Tindal summed up for an acquittal. What he meant, the Lord only knows. No human being doubted the guilt of the accused, and we had proved it by the clearest evidence. It was of the last importance to the public tranquillity that there should be a verdict of guilty. Chief Justice Tindal is a very honourable man, and had no assignable reason for deviating from the right course. Yet from the beginning to the end of his charge he laboured for an acquittal. Before he concluded I had not the faintest notion that the jury could act otherwise than according to the view he gave them. When they retired I called a consultation of all the Crown counsel at my lodgings to consider what was to be done upon the acquittal, and we agreed that there was no use in prosecuting the others for treason. Whilst we were still in deliberation, a messenger announced the verdict of guilty.'[1]

The Attorney-General could thus explain the judge's attitude only as 'deviating from the right course'. It is not necessary to seek an 'assignable reason' for this deviation, for he undoubtedly thought Frost innocent, but possibly an 'assignable reason' why he was not as prejudiced as the others against Frost, and was therefore able to view his case with greater impartiality, may be found in the fact that he was the cousin of W. P. Roberts, the Bath

[1] Mrs. Hardcastle, op. cit., p. 127.

solicitor, and Frost's personal friend.[1] But neither Pollock, Kelly, nor the Lord Chief Justice could shake a Monmouthshire jury. They announced before retiring that they did not think it would take them long to reach a verdict, and within half an hour they had returned and announced their verdict of guilty, adding that they wished 'to recommend the prisoner to the merciful consideration of the court'. Frost's manner throughout the trial had not shown any symptom of excitement. He had followed every step of the proceedings so carefully that he was able to correct the Lord Chief Justice on one point in the evidence —a correction which the judge accepted—but when the verdict was pronounced his face became convulsed, and he sank back into the dock overwhelmed with agony.[2]

After Frost's case had ended there was an evident loss of interest, for the verdicts in the remaining cases could not be in much doubt. Nevertheless Zephaniah Williams's case occupied four days. Even the most hostile witnesses against him admitted that he was peaceably inclined, but Shell's letter was now produced to prove that the Chartists had expected a struggle in which lives might be risked. His counsel spoke for eight hours. He dealt at length with the rioting during the Reform agitation and quoted Lord John Russell's violent speeches. But with this Baron Parke dealt very severely in his summing up. Opinions expressed by other persons, he said, even if they amounted to sedition or treason, were no concern of the jury, who should dismiss them completely from their minds. He accepted Frost's guilt as proved (and also, apparently, that of Jones), so that association with Frost in his enterprise was sufficient to prove Williams guilty of treason. The jury took much the same time as those who had given their verdict in the

[1] R. G. Gammage, *The Chartist Movement* (London, 1894), p. 79.

[2] *Charter*, 12 Jan.; *Cambrian*, 18 Jan. Frost himself stoutly denied that he had been affected in this way.—Letter to his wife, 22 Sept. 1840, in *Udgorn*, Nov. 1840.

case of Frost and with the same result. Jones's trial occupied only two days. He, differing from his associates, spoke at length in his own defence. He admitted that he had warned the Chartists to provide themselves with arms, but this was only to defend themselves, he said, in case the soldiers fired on their demonstration as they had done on the Chartists at Birmingham. Mr. Justice Williams summed up in great detail, once more defining treason and quoting previous trials for treason. The jury returned the same verdict with the same recommendation. The prosecution then indicated that it withdrew its charge against four of the other defendants (two, including the wooden-legged man, because of a doubt as to identity, and two since there was a doubt whether they had acted voluntarily) and they were declared acquitted, being thus considerably more fortunate than others who were to appear on a lesser charge. The remaining five appeared at the Bar and pleaded guilty, having been informed that the sentence of death would be commuted in their case.[1]

And so, on Thursday, 16 January, the eight men were brought to the Bar to receive sentence. The court was crowded as soon as the doors were opened, and at nine o'clock the judges took their seats and put on their black caps. It fell to the Lord Chief Justice to pronounce the barbarous sentence imposed for the crime of treason. Disembowelling while alive, which had been practised on a member of the Tredegar family a hundred years previously because of his participation in the Jacobite Rebellion, had been abolished by an Act of 1814, but the sentence still involved a revolting outrage on the bodies of the dead. The Chief Justice, scarcely able to control his voice through emotion, condemned the prisoners to be drawn on a hurdle to the place of execution, to be hanged until they were dead, to have their heads severed from their bodies, and

[1] *Merlin*, 11 Jan.; *Charter*, 19 Jan.

the body of each to be divided into four quarters which were to be at the disposal of Her Majesty. After the sentence the prisoners were removed, but as they stepped into the van, Jones called to the watching crowd for three cheers for the Charter.[1] But there still remained a chance that the sentence would be set aside on the technical objection to the presentation of the lists, and for twelve days the prisoners remained in their condemned cells awaiting the decision. Great interest was shown in the matter, especially by members of the Bar, and the court of the Exchequer was crowded when the question was argued for three days before the fifteen judges. Pollock, Kelly, and Sir William Follett appeared for the prisoners, and the Attorney-General for the Crown. Eventually it was decided by nine judges to six that the objection was valid, but three from the majority ruled with the minority that it had not been taken in time, so by a vote of nine judges to six Frost and his associates remained condemned. The result was ironical, for the Lord Chief Justice, who had believed Frost innocent, now, as always, stood for a liberal interpretation of the law, and considered the objection invalid, whereas Parke and Williams, sticklers for a rigid interpretation, ruled that the objection was both valid and taken in time. Had the question been decided at Monmouth, therefore, a majority of two judges to one (and those the two who considered Frost guilty) would have stopped the trial and secured his acquittal. On such vagaries of the law did his life depend.

In view of the evidence produced at the trial which had now come to an end, what, then, can be said of the motive of Frost and his associates in embarking on the enterprise which had led to their condemnation to death? It is a question which greatly puzzled contemporaries, and its answer at the present day is made more difficult by the

[1] *Bristol Mercury*, 18 Jan.

fact that nearly all accounts of the event were written by persons hostile to Chartism. The motive of personal revenge on the part of Frost against his enemies in Newport, especially Thomas Prothero and Thomas Phillips, in which the latter professed to believe, can safely be dismissed.[1] So, also, can the theory of a general insurrection based on the signal of the non-arrival of the Welsh mail, a theory elaborated on account of the exigencies of the prosecution. There were undoubtedly rumours among the crowd about 'stopping the mail' as there were about 'taking possession of Newport', and Thomas Phillips reported this to the Home Office two days after the riot, but the use of the non-arrival of the mail as a signal for insurrection is another matter, and cannot have been seriously entertained by any one as familiar as Frost was with the course of the Welsh mail-coaches. The release of Vincent, again, is not a very probable motive, at least not an immediate one. The Lord Lieutenant warned the mayor of Monmouth on the Sunday morning that it might be the intention of the Chartists,[2] but this was before their line of march had become known. The descent of the Chartists from Pontypool to Newport before virtually retracing their steps to proceed towards Monmouth which this theory would involve, makes it patently absurd.

The matter is complicated by the existence of one manuscript copy of a supposed confession by Zephaniah Williams.[3] It is in the form of a letter to Dr. McKechnie, the surgeon commander of the convict ship which took the prisoners to Van Diemen's Land, a man whose kindness was commented on by Frost, Williams, and Jones. Williams elaborates a detailed plan by which, he says, it was

[1] H.O. 40/45, letter of Phillips dated 6 Nov.; *Trial of John Frost by a Barrister*, pp. xiii and xiv; *Rise and Fall*, loc. cit.

[2] National Library of Wales, MS. letter; Llangibby MS. C. 835.

[3] In Lord Tredegar's Library. Kindly placed at my disposal by his Lordship.

intended to start an insurrection in order to establish a republican government in Britain. Five thousand men were to march from Merthyr to seize Brecon, an equal number to seize Abergavenny, others were to attack Cardiff, in addition to the main attack on Newport, Sunday night being decided upon as the soldiers would be in the public-houses. But the plan, he says, was not adopted, as Frost thought it unnecessary. He claims, however, that as soon as a day was fixed for an attack on Newport messengers were sent to various parts of England, and the Chartists in these places were to take for granted that a rising in Wales had been successful if the mail did not arrive in time. Williams did not know what preparations had been made in England, apart from what he had been told by Frost and one messenger who had returned from England. There is no reason to doubt that Williams was the author of this document. His object in writing it, however, was probably to curry favour with the authorities by supplying them with a reasonable version of the purpose which the Chartists had had in mind. But little reliance can be placed upon it, for, according to hostile witnesses produced against Williams himself at his trial, he had repeatedly said there was to be no outbreak—that they were only going to 'give a turn as far as Newport', and in a letter written to his wife at the same time as he wrote this 'confession', he claimed that there had been no intention to harm any one, in person or in property.[1]

Undoubtedly the vast majority of the Chartists did not know what their purpose was, and undoubtedly also, many of the leaders had different objects in mind. Vague rumours circulated among them as to what was intended, and these came out in the evidence of those who turned Crown witnesses. It is safest to assume that the only common purpose they had was a great demonstration of strength in

[1] Letter in *Udgorn*, Sept. 1840.

Newport. Had they intended to attack Newport they could easily have entered it by three different routes and effectively cut off its communications, but they were at pains to join forces before approaching the town. The only contemporary biographer of Frost who was favourably disposed towards him says:

'Those who have said that Mr. Frost was long engaged in organizing the people for the Newport outbreak, must hereafter hold their peace, or be content to have attached to them the imputation of uttering against a man who has it not in his power to defend himself, an injurious allegation which there exists no evidence to establish. . . . The gathering on the eve of the riots had no direct object laid down.'[1]

Frost fully realized the dangers involved in a demonstration, but his hand was forced by the extremists.

'I was not the man for such an undertaking,' he is reported to have said in prison, 'for the moment I saw blood flow I became terrified and fled, but what was I to do? I went up to the mountains a few months ago; on that occasion the men surrounded me and said, "Mr. Frost. if you will not lead us, neither you nor your family shall live at Newport; we are beginning to suspect you".'[2]

He had therefore been reduced to the desperate policy of allowing events to take their course and decide the issue themselves. But the storm, the absence of any unity of purpose, the complete lack of discipline, the delusion of the workers as to their own solidarity, and particularly the fatal delusion (based on the experience of the French Revolution, when officers as well as men had been disaffected) that the soldiers would not fire on them, all combined to make the enterprise pathetically futile.

[1] *Life of John Frost* (1840), pp. 6–7.
[2] *Shrewsbury News*, quoted by Miss Myfanwy Williams.

IX

THE AFTERMATH

THE great legal issue, discovered by Geach and seized upon by Pollock, had thus been argued before the fifteen judges and had been lost. Nevertheless it was the fortnight's delay between the verdict and the decision of the judges which saved the lives of the prisoners. Had it not been for this the Cabinet would have had them executed immediately. The matter was discussed at a cabinet meeting on 9 January, the day on which the verdict became known in London, and among the ministers present was the diarist, John Cam Hobhouse, the friend and literary executor of the arch-rebel, Byron. Time was when he had been an uncompromising radical. For two weeks, in 1819, he had kicked his heels in Newgate, having made the remark that it was the Horse Guards alone which prevented people from pulling members of Parliament out of the House of Commons by the ears, and locking up the doors and throwing the key into the Thames. But he had since become a resting and thankful Whig, and was a bitter opponent of Chartism, as his *Recollections* show.[1] Melbourne was of the opinion that the recommendation of the jury for mercy need not be considered; the jury had been frightened, and so had the judge. He felt that decided measures were necessary to prevent anarchy, and he was prepared to take them. Hobhouse remarked that as the object of the Chartists was to knock them all on the head and rob them of their property, they might as well arrive at the catastrophe after a struggle as without it; they could do no worse than fail, and they might succeed—to which the Prime Minister

[1] Lord Broughton (J. C. Hobhouse), *Recollections of a Long Life* (London, 1911), v. 240 ff.

replied, 'Exactly so.' By the time sentence was passed, opinion had hardened. The Home Secretary complained to the Cabinet that the Attorney-General had had no authorization to promise their lives to the five Chartists who pleaded guilty. 'All however agreed', adds Hobhouse, 'that Chief Justice Tindal pleaded like an advocate for Frost, so much so that when the jury went out, all the Crown counsel retired to consider what they should do when Frost was acquitted, which they considered certain.' This reaction of the Cabinet was shared in the country. Sir Thomas Phillips wrote to the Home Office saying that every one was astonished at the Lord Chief Justice's summing up, and that it was only the firmness of the jury which had saved the country. The mayor of Cardiff wished to pacify the county of Monmouth by hanging Frost at Newport, Williams at Blackwood, and Jones at Pontypool.[1] Irate generals regretted that the soldiers had not killed 200 instead of 20; it might have saved bloodshed in the end, they thought. 'Such is the effect of the reform act', added one of them, 'and more especially the municipal reform.'[2] In Court circles the elegant reprobate, Charles Greville, noted that the judges were much censured for not having themselves decided the point raised, and for not having asked the jury their reasons for recommending the criminals to mercy.[3]

At the same time the Chartists redoubled their efforts to save Frost. Public meetings were held in all parts of London, in the midlands, and in the north; articles appeared in Chartist newspapers entitled 'Shall Frost be sacrificed', while petitions were submitted to the queen and to Parliament from so many places that it would be pointless to specify them. Brougham, who presented

[1] H.O. 40/57, letter dated 14 Feb.
[2] R. W. Jeffery (ed.), *Dyott's Diary, 1781–1845. A Selection from the Journal of William Dyott, sometime General in the British Army* (London, 1907), ii. 304.
[3] Charles Greville, op. cit. iv. 229.

some of these petitions to the House of Lords, declared that he had never known a subject which had caused so much public interest. South Wales naturally shared in this activity, and among its petitions was a very remarkable one from the Reverend Micah Thomas, for thirty years the principal of the Baptist Academy at Abergavenny. It was couched in humble terms, yet it glowed with conviction in the justice of his plea. He had been a keen advocate of reform, but had always abhorred violence, he said. His personal acquaintance with Frost was slight, but he knew of him as a man of inflexible resolution and indomitable courage, which had never forsaken him until the unlooked-for attack of his deluded associates on the Westgate Hotel. The failure of his courage then implied something favourable on the score of intention. He had a fair and honourable reputation in private life and was justly reputed for his humanity. Personal and local prejudice against him raged and predominated, said the petitioner, and the Tories, in their hatred of the government, would gladly sacrifice him on the gibbet in order to drive the people to desperation. A pardon alone would pacify the country, and would be in the interests of the government itself.[1] Other protestors were not so moderate in their language. Some made much of the queen's forthcoming marriage: were the ministers ambitious to lay three bloody heads between their mistress and her wedded lover? Heads were dangerous bowls to play with, they said—and much more to the same effect.[2]

But the government was adamant. The Home Secretary had written to Monmouth granting a respite for a few days pending a discussion of the subject by the whole

---

[1] Museum MS., copy of petition, 20 Jan. 1840, in petitioner's own hand.
[2] Add. MSS. 35151, p. 197; H.O. 40/57, several documents; Placard printed by Denyer and Gabell [*sic*], Corn Market, Newport.

Cabinet. His letter reached Monmouth on 29 January, and it was on that day that the Cabinet met for the express purpose of disposing of the matter. It was, says Hobhouse, a painful deliberation. Melbourne gave it as his opinion that Frost had been convicted of the highest crime known to British law, and that the welfare of society and the demands of justice required that he should suffer the extreme penalty. Each minister then gave his opinion in turn, and after some hesitation on the part of Palmerston and Macaulay it was decided unanimously that Frost should die. It was considered by some that it would not be necessary to execute Williams and Jones, but the Lord Chancellor, who insisted upon the death penalty, declared that, if anything, they were more criminal than Frost. Normanby, therefore, wrote to Monmouth fixing the execution for the following Thursday.

Pollock was taken aback by this development. In the letter which he had written at Monmouth while Kelly was speaking, he assumed that, whatever the verdict, Frost's life was safe, for the government would not settle the practice in trials for treason by hanging a man, and throughout his life Pollock assumed that as two of the judges who had tried the case had upheld his objection, execution was an impossibility.[1] But the three judges gave it as their opinion (in a letter to the Home Secretary, dated 31 January) that this consideration was entirely overruled by the decision of the majority of the fifteen judges.[2] A reasoned petition presented by a number of members of Parliament on the same day was, therefore, disregarded, and Pollock, who had interviewed the Prime Minister no less than six times, was despondent. Brougham, however, advised him to try once again, and at his seventh interview he was told that the

---

[1] Hanworth, op. cit., pp. 115–16.
[2] Letter given in full in Barrister, op. cit., pp. xvi and xvii.

sentence was changed to one of transportation for life. He believed, and it has been assumed ever since, that this was due to his intervention,[1] but Hobhouse's diary shows that this was not so. On the day on which he had concurred in the above opinion, the Lord Chief Justice had seen the Home Secretary, and had told him that the prisoners' lives ought to be spared. The Cabinet could not disregard his advice, and the Prime Minister confessed that it would now be difficult to execute the prisoners. The other ministers, who had expressed their opinions so strongly in favour of execution, accepted the situation in silence. It was therefore decided to ask the Lord Chief Justice to state his views in writing, and to commute the sentences to transportation for life 'as an act of grace, unconnected with any objections which the lawyers had made in the course of the trials'. Thus Frost owed his life to the intervention of the Lord Chief Justice, who had vainly tried to save him at Monmouth. Possibly the Home Secretary was not uninfluenced also by Micah Thomas, for he took the unusual course of informing him personally of the change.[2]

For three weeks Frost and his companions had suffered the agony of the condemned cell. They shared one room at their own request. A turnkey attended on them to cut their food, for they were refused the use of knives and forks, to prevent the possibility of suicide.[3] Yet Frost maintained throughout his life that the prison governor had repeatedly asked them how they wished their bodies to be disposed of, and he could explain this in no other way than as an attempt to induce them to commit suicide.[4] The High Sheriff had given orders 'as to the making of the necessary arrangements for the intended executions should

[1] *Rise and Fall*, p. 85; *Merthyr Guardian*, 8 Feb.
[2] Museum MS., Normanby to Micah Thomas.
[3] *Merthyr Guardian*, 1 Feb. 1840.
[4] Letter to O'Connor, 4 May 1840 (copy in Lord Tredegar's Library); *Udgorn*, Nov. 1840; *Two Lectures*, p. 6.

they unfortunately take place' the day after the verdict, without even waiting for the judges' decision,[1] and Chartists long remembered the gruesome detail that the condemned men could hear in their cells the noise of the carpenters erecting the gallows.[2] They knew nothing of the agitation which was going on for a reprieve. Yet, once the government had finally made up its mind, it acted with great speed. Instructions were sent the next day to Colonel Considine and to the prison authorities, and at midnight, on Sunday night, the prisoners were roused from their sleep and were taken, trembling and not knowing what was going to happen to them, to the gaoler's room. It was there that they were told of the change in their sentence. Then they were bundled into a van, handcuffed and chained and guarded by six policemen, and, with an escort of twenty-four soldiers of the 12th Lancers, they drove away into the tempestuous night. They showed great anxiety to know where they were being taken, but were not told, and Williams and Frost discussed the matter in Welsh. Little did they think when they started on their enterprise that they would now be where they were, Frost said in English, casting a reproachful look at Jones. But at four o'clock in the morning they found that they were in Chepstow, where they were immediately put on board the steamer *Usk*, together with their gaoler and soldiers of the 19th regiment. The weather was extremely rough, and it took them fifteen days to make the journey around Land's End to Portsmouth, for they had to put into harbour at several places, where their presence caused much interest. (It was even rumoured that the Cornish miners contemplated rescuing them.) At Portsmouth they were transferred to the *York* hulk, and within a week they were

[1] Usk MSS., Monmouth Gaol, entry 17 Jan., by Colthurst Bateman, High Sheriff.
[2] W. E. Adams, *Memoirs of a Social Atom* (London, 1903), i. 197.

removed to the *Mandarin* convict ship and had started on their long journey to Van Diemen's Land. The authorities themselves were surprised at their sudden removal, for the convicts were not even allowed to see their families or friends, although Geach, after an interview with the Home Secretary, obtained permission to see Frost at Portsmouth in the presence of an officer.[1]

Terrible as was the fate to which Frost, Williams, and Jones were now condemned, they could not complain of their new sentence, for however innocent they were of the crime of treason they were certainly guilty of riot, and would undoubtedly have been sentenced to transportation on this charge. Only three years previously a Blaenavon workman had been sentenced to transportation for life for stealing a Bible and a Prayer Book from the local church, while the following year three men had received the same sentence at the Monmouthshire Assizes for stealing a colt.[2] Transportation was therefore a matter of common occurrence for much less serious crimes than the three Chartists had committed. Nevertheless their friends were encouraged by their partial success to work for a complete reprieve, and once more a flood of petitions reached the queen and the government from England, Wales, and Scotland. Among them were two from Merthyr Tydfil (the first having 15,786 signatures, and other being signed by nearly 11,000 women). One came from the Dorchester labourers, and one from Frost's mother, wife, and six children.[3] Lord Teynham presented a petition signed by 1,500 inhabitants of Newport to the House of Lords, and engaged in a sharp altercation with the Home Secretary on the matter, while J. T. Leader moved in the House of Commons for a free pardon. His motion had to be postponed, and Leader

[1] *Merlin*, 8 Feb., 15 Feb.; *Charter*, 9 Feb., 23 Feb. The cost of their transference (apart from the steamer *Usk*) was £14. 16s. Usk MSS.

[2] *Merlin*, 6 Aug. 1836, 1 April 1837, 5 Aug. 1837.

[3] *Merlin*, 15 Feb., 14 March; *Merthyr Guardian*, 7 March.

tried to get an assurance that the prisoners would not be transported before it was debated. However the debate did not take place until 10 March when the convicts had been at sea for nearly two weeks. Leader argued that the trial was invalid, and that the prisoners were punished for political reasons. He was supported by Hume and by Duncombe who believed that if Frost could not be legally executed he could not be legally transported either. Fox Maule, who replied for the government, merely repeated the decision of the fifteen judges. But there was little interest in the debate. Neither Pollock nor Kelly was present, and the motion was defeated by the meagre vote of 70 to 7. Yet among the 'Ayes' was the name of B. D'Israeli.[1]

Petition now was futile, and both Francis Place and the *Charter* newspaper severely warned the Chartists not to divert their movement from its true purpose in a fruitless endeavour to obtain the recall of the convicts, who had richly deserved their fate through their wanton appeal to force.[2] Nevertheless agitation continued; meetings were held and resolutions passed. At Merthyr Tydfil both Llewellyn Williams and Henry Hunt Frost represented their fathers at a meeting to petition the queen for a free pardon, and a few days later Henry Hunt read one of his father's letters to a large audience at Bristol.[3] A Frost committee was formed to give pecuniary assistance to the families of the convicts.[4] In 1841 a play, entitled *John Frost*, was produced to support the cause. The author admitted in a foreword that he had had difficulty in getting a publisher, and his work has neither literary merit nor historical accuracy. For dramatic effect he had had

---

[1] *Parliamentary Debates*, lii. 391, 1049, 1109, 1133–50.
[2] *Charter*, 15 March; Add. MSS. 35151, p. 359, Francis Place's Correspondence.
[3] *Cambrian*, 2 Jan. 1841; *The Times*, 13 Jan. 1841.
[4] Add. MSS. 37774, Minutes London W.M.A. (reconstituted 12 Oct. 1841) dated 2 Nov. 1841.

to make Mrs. Frost oppose Chartism, while carefully explaining in a footnote that she had not done so in actual
life. A sentimental interest also was introduced by arbi-
trarily making Vincent fall in love with one of the five
Frost daughters. The sentiments of the play are best expressed in the words of the Prologue:

> All foes are conquered when we conquer fear,
> As did bold Shell, who braved a bloody bier.
> To gain his rights he took the manliest course—
> The plain straightforward argument of force!
> Vengeance is now our cry. Remember Shell!
> We'll live like him—at least we'll die as well.
> Silurian Frosts again shall lead us on,
> And freedom's baffled battle yet be won.[1]

For a time interest died down, but once more there was a
revival of agitation in 1846, possibly because Pollock was
now Chief Baron of the Exchequer, and Kelly Solicitor-
General. Duncombe again introduced a motion for a free
pardon. He said he had been charged with the presentation of no less than 249 petitions, signed by 1,400,000 persons, including one from six of the jurymen who had tried
Frost. (Three of the other jurymen were now dead; two
could not be found, and one could not sign his name.)
The debate was chiefly remarkable because of Macaulay's
speech. He had himself been asked to present a petition
from Edinburgh, but had refused, on the grounds that the
convicts were 'great criminals . . . who would, if their
attempt had not been stopped in the outset, have caused
such a destruction of life and property as had not been
known in England for ages'. He deplored the morbid
feeling of sympathy which made people petition for mercy
for criminals. In strange contrast was the speech of Mr.
D'Israeli deploring the 'inexorable severity' with which

---

[1] *John Frost, a Play*, by John Watkins, Chartist (London, 1841). It was
acted at Nottingham. *The Times*, 17 Feb. 1844.

Frost and his associates were treated. Yet Macaulay's oratory prevailed, and the motion was defeated by 196 votes to 31.[1] Two years later, when the 1848 disturbances had broken out, the great historian was writing his panegyric of the Glorious Revolution. As this had taken place a century and a half earlier, he bestowed upon it unrestrained adulation; even a revolution which had taken place fifty years earlier he could understand, although he did not altogether approve of it. But the mild leaders of 1848 were 'barbarians, compared with whom the barbarians who marched under Attila and Albion were enlightened and humane', and their doctrines were such that 'if carried into effect, would, in thirty years, undo all that thirty centuries have done for mankind . . . doctrines hostile to all arts, to all industry, to all domestic charities.'[2] Such has always been 'the Whig view' of disturbances which have the misfortune to be contemporaneous.

Monmouthshire had now got rid of its Chartists; all that remained to be done was to pay the expense of the riots. Every one wished to make something out of it, and accounts kept coming in, so that by April 1840 the total had reached £1,744. 13s. 9d. The clerk of the peace tried to recover this sum from the Treasury, but with no success. He had some difficulty also with the Mayor of Newport (Thomas Hawkins), who disregarded repeated requests to produce an account of the money spent by him, so that eventually he had to be threatened with legal proceedings, unless he did so within ten days.[3] Into the paean of thanksgiving and mutual congratulation which had followed the riots, a discordant note had thus been introduced. The Crown witnesses also found life none too pleasant. James Hodge returned to his home in Blackwood, but every one there

[1] *Merthyr Guardian*, 7 March, 14 March 1846; *Cornwall Chronicle*, 2 Sept. 1846 (quoting *Newport Herald*), and 30 Sept. (quoting *Sunday Times*).
[2] T. B. Macaulay, *History of England*, chapter x.
[3] Usk MSS., Quarter Sessions Accounts; *Merthyr Guardian*, 16 Jan. 1841.

believed that he had acted as a government spy. No one would speak to him; men continually told each other in his hearing that every witness ought to be shot, and when his windows were stoned and a bloodstained note threatening his life was thrust under his door, he fled in terror. The 'sorcerer' Israel Firman dared not return to his home, and the magistrates had to pay the expense of removing him and his family by boat from Newport to London. Other witnesses appealed for assistance, and were promised immediate and constant work by grateful mine owners, and were even supplied with arms with which to defend themselves. But as soon as they began work all the other men instantly left the coal 'level' where they were occupied, and nothing would induce them to work with them, so that the proprietors, who had to keep their collieries going, were forced to dismiss the witnesses. Even Barnabas Brough found that no one would now drink his beer, and he attributed his bankruptcy to the evidence which he had given.[1]

What, in the meantime, had become of the convicts? Frost's period in the *York* hulk was one of the worst in his life. Alternate hope and despair had told upon his vitality, already lowered by his illness in prison, and the fifteen days' tempestuous voyage around Land's End had made him seriously ill. In this state he found conditions on board the hulk unbearable, and the food was so bad that for four days he could take nothing but bread and water. In addition to this the brutality which he personally experienced was worse than at any other time. When Geach saw him at Portsmouth he thought that he was 'evidently fast dropping into eternity' through mental and bodily suffering, and when he was being transferred to the convict ship, he was so very weak that he himself hardly expected to live. A piece of tarpaulin was thrown over

[1] *Merlin*, 1 Feb.; *Silurian*, 8 Feb.; *Merthyr Guardian*, 15 Feb.; Brough, op. cit. (His brewery was sold on 2 July 1840).

The Aftermath

him where he lay on the barge, to keep out the bitter cold, and once on the *Mandarin* he was placed immediately in the ship's hospital. At Falmouth the ship had to put in to refit, because of the bad weather, and there a young man boarded her to distribute tracts to the convicts, and promised, at his request, to send Frost a copy of the *Pilgrim's Progress*. There also Frost took the opportunity to write to his wife. It was a letter full of Christian resignation, of deep affection for his wife and concern for his daughters. He implored his wife not to follow him into exile, but to devote herself to the care of their children. He still had some hope that he might return to his home.[1] But at sea the weather proved remarkably fine; in fact, within a month the ship was almost becalmed and could only proceed at about twenty miles a day.[2] Frost's spirits, therefore, rose, and the surgeon-commander of the ship, Dr. McKechnie, proved unexpectedly kind. Not only Frost, but Williams and Jones, also, speak of him as their friend. He had 214 convicts in his charge, among them Francis Roberts, John Jones, and Jeremiah Howell, the three Birmingham Chartists who had been sentenced to death for their part in the riots of 15 July.[3] Yet, before reaching the Cape, a strange incident occurred. A convict handed Frost a letter suggesting that the ship should be seized and taken to South America. Williams was in favour of an attempt, but Frost wisely refused. The governor of Portsmouth had warned him that if there were any commotion on board, the troops would act with great

[1] *Lovett Collection*, ii. 180; *Merlin*, 21 March 1840; Gammage, p. 171; Letter to Morgan Williams, 4 May 1840, MS. copy in Lord Tredegar's Library.

[2] Newport Mercantile Presentment, ii (May 1840), no. 84. Captain Shaw of the *Kilbain* went on board the *Mandarin* and saw Frost, who declared that he would far sooner have been executed than transported.

[3] H.O. 11/12, Transportation, under *Mandarin*, 24 Feb. 1840. The five who had pleaded guilty at Monmouth had their sentence changed to three years' imprisonment, *Charter*, 9 Feb. 1840.

promptitude, and Frost believed that this was a trap set for him. He did not think that the convict could have had access to the necessary paper for the letter to be genuine, and some remarks of the surgeon later confirmed him in his belief.[1] Nevertheless, a sailor and a prisoner were flogged for a supposed design to mutiny, and Frost witnessed for the first time a spectacle which he was to see with sickening frequency in the next four years.[2] But whether there was a mutiny or not, there was scurvy, and so the ship had to put in at the Cape to get fresh water and provisions. They left here on 12 May, and for a time the sea was still calm, but in June tremendous gales arose, and on Whit-Monday (did Frost, one wonders, think of the great Blackwood demonstration of the previous year) it was feared that the ship might be lost. Yet it survived, and in spite of recurrent storms throughout the month, it anchored before Hobart Town on 30 June, four calendar months after leaving England.[3]

The reception of the Chartists in the penal colony was unexpected. An opposition newspaper, the *Launceston Advertiser*, declared roundly that 'no person attentively reading the trial can form the conclusion that Frost ever contemplated "levying war against Her Majesty" which is the treason complained of', and hoped that the three men would soon be set at liberty.[4] The authorities also behaved in an extraordinary manner. The three Chartists were not treated in the same way as the other prisoners—they did not, for example, have to put on the yellow prison dress but kept their own clothes—and yet they were sent immediately to the terrible settlement at Port Arthur on

[1] *Two Lectures*, p. 6; *The Times*, 17 Sept. 1864, reproducing letter from Frost to *Star of Gwent*.
[2] *Merlin*, 25 July. *Two Lectures*, p. 10.
[3] Frost letter to his wife, 21 July 1840, reprinted *The Times*, 13 Jan. 1841, and as a separate pamphlet (published Manchester).
[4] *Launceston Advertiser*, 23 July, 6 Aug.

Van Diemen's Peninsula, where generally only convicts who committed crimes on the island were sent, a settlement guarded by soldiers and police dogs, and in which convicts were known to commit murder merely in order that death might remove them from its horrors. And yet again the governor, Sir John Franklin, insisted that the Chartists were not placed here as extra punishment, and in fact Frost was made a clerk in the commandant's office, while Williams became a superintendent in the coal-mines, and Jones was given a post in the boys' prison at Point Puer. The transference to Port Arthur caused strong feeling in the colony, and lest his family should fear that they were in the chain gangs, Frost wrote a lengthy account to his wife on 21 July. It was a courageous letter, minimizing the horror of his position and putting a brave face on things, but unfortunately it was printed in *The Times* and as a separate pamphlet, and the Tories immediately seized upon it to show that the convicts were not being punished at all, but were in paid positions under the government, even having in their charge 'the important and sacred duty of education', another example, it was claimed, of the vile duplicity of the Whigs.[1]

If this letter gave Mrs. Frost any consolation, she was sadly in need of it, for long before she had received it her son had been sent to join his step-father. Geach's troubles had now overwhelmed him. On the day on which Frost was declared guilty, a true bill was found against Geach at the Central Criminal Court for obtaining a large sum by means of false pretences, the person on whose behalf application was made not being named. He was liberated on bail, but in July was arrested, apparently on two other charges of forging promissory notes supposed to have been drawn by Miss Rachel Herbert, of Hill House,

[1] *Morning Post*, quoted *Merthyr Guardian*, 23 Jan. 1841; *Courier*, quoted *Launceston Advertiser*, 3 June 1841.

Abergavenny, one of his wife's relatives, and by another person. He was brought before his enemies Sir Thomas Phillips and Thomas Hawkins, the mayor of Newport, and they committed him to the Monmouth Assizes, bail being refused. The case came before Baron Parke in August. Miss Herbert gave her evidence with great reluctance, and was evidently brought into the matter against her will. Geach cross-examined the banker who was the chief witness for the prosecution for no less than five hours, and drew even from the severe judge a high commendation of his ability. Apparently his transactions with this banker (whose banking house he owned) had amounted to £165,400 over eight years, and apparently also no one had been defrauded. The jury found great difficulty in reaching a verdict. They returned to court to ask the judge if they could find a verdict of guilty with no intent to defraud, but he declared they could not. After some time they returned again with the verdict of guilty, but with a strong recommendation to mercy. Parke immediately challenged them to state their grounds, and they declared that they did not believe the prisoner had had any intent to defraud. The second charge was dealt with the next day, and in defending himself Geach indiscreetly admitted himself guilty of the first. The jury returned the same verdict with the same recommendation. Parke commented on this in passing judgement, and on Geach's ability, but seldom, he said, had so extensive a fraud been practised, for Geach had obtained false credit to the extent of no less than £20,000, and he passed sentence of twenty years' transportation. Geach, who had maintained his neat habits in dress and his business-like manner until the end, broke down when the effect of his sentence on his step-father was mentioned. Fairly soon he was removed to the hulks and sent to Van Diemen's Land. His wife joined him, and under the name of Mrs. Foster opened a school in a cottage in Hobart.

The Aftermath

Her relatives seem to have taken some offence at this, and wished to offer advice and help, but in spite of his ill health Geach's pride led him to refuse. He was, however, recommended by the Governor for a conditional pardon as early as December 1846, but owing to the time taken by communications to London, and, no doubt, to official delay, notice of this did not reach the colony until June 1848.[1] His sentence had overwhelmed his mother with anguish, and soon after it had been passed she gave up her home in Newport and went to live at Stapleton, near Bristol. Yet her tale of grief was not complete, for within two years her young son, Henry Hunt, had died after a long illness.[2]

In the office of the commandant (an Irishman, Charles O'Hara Booth) Frost had an opportunity to witness the operation of the convict system at its worst. Only the previous year, Sir William Molesworth had, in the House of Commons, described the convict code as 'not equalled in severity in any part of the civilized world'. It could not bear comparison with the treatment of Russian prisoners in Siberia, and Lord Stanley, when as Colonial Secretary he reorganized the system two years later, declared it his intention to make the punishment of transportation worse feared than death. The harrowing sentences inflicted may be found described not only in Frost's accounts, which might be thought biased, but in *The Horrors of Transportation* (1841) by the young Catholic priest William Ulla-thorne, then vicar-general of Van Diemen's Land and later one of the greatest bishops of the Catholic Church in nineteenth-century England. Flogging could be imposed without a trial by the authority of one magistrate, and

[1] *Merlin*, 18 Jan., 11 July, 25 July, 22 Aug., 6 Sept.; *Merthyr Guardian*, 25 July, 22 Aug., 20 Sept.; *Cambrian*, 1 Aug. 1840; *Merthyr Guardian*, 17 Sept. 1842; *Cornwall Chronicle*, 2 Jan. 1841, 2 Sept. 1846, 5 Dec. 1846, 8 July 1848.
[2] She lived at 14 Montpellier. Letters dated 26 Aug. 1842 and 12 Sept. 1845 in Newport Library. Henry Hunt died 22 March 1842, *Merlin*, 2 April 1842, see also *Star of Gwent*, 1 Dec. 1860 (Frost's letter).

Frost frequently saw one convict after another flogged until the ground beneath the triangle was soaked in human blood. Insolence of manner was a sufficient crime to merit flogging. Frost even saw a youth who had withstood his punishment without screaming summarily sentenced to a further thirty-six lashes for insolence, because he had a smile on his face when he was released from the triangle. The influence of this on the character of the convicts can easily be imagined. Frost noted that a youth, who was one of the best behaved men on the station, was given thirty-six lashes for having his hand in his pocket, and afterwards became one of the worst offenders, returning to the triangle time and again. In addition, the terrible 'silent system' of the cells broke the spirits and minds of the most obstinate criminals, and many committed murder to get out. Living conditions were deplorable, and unnatural vice was prevalent. Molesworth justly characterized the system as 'inefficient, cruel and demoralizing, full of absurdity and wickedness'.[1]

But Frost's period in the commandant's office came to a sudden end. In his letter of 21 July he had expressed the hope that if Lord John Russell (then Colonial Secretary) 'should break the seal of my letters he will have so much of the gentleman about him as to send them according to their address'. This letter, which the commandant had passed, was intended for his family only, but one of his daughters allowed it to be published. The time had gone when Frost could indulge in pleasantries about 'his old correspondent', and the little, squeaky-voiced minister now took his revenge for the attack on his dignity in the previous year. Instructions were immediately sent to Van Diemen's Land, and Frost, who had long ago forgotten

[1] W. D. Forsyth, *Governor Arthur's Convict System* (London, 1935); W. Ullathorne, *The Horrors of Transportation briefly described* (Birmingham, 1841); Frost, *Two Lectures*, p. 10; *A Letter to the People of the U.S.*, pp. 8, 12.

what he had written, was brought to Hobart for 'trial' by Sir John Franklin, and for the above remark he was sentenced to two years' hard labour. So, at the age of fifty-seven, he found himself back on Tasman's Peninsula working with a gang in a stone quarry, and sleeping at nights with twenty to thirty others in a vermin-infested hut. He was apparently removed from his first station for impertinence to the superintendent (was this perhaps the time when, according to Zephaniah Williams, he was threatened with the triangle for not touching his cap with sufficient respect?), and put to carrying logs at a new station which was then being made (Impression Bay). Here a writer in *Fraser's Magazine* visited him, and found him dressed in a leather cap and grey prison clothes. His appearance was careworn, according to the writer, yet he still continued to hope for a release. Frost himself declared that he was actually stronger than he had ever been before in his life.[1]

Zephaniah Williams had had still more unfortunate experiences, which he described graphically in one of a series of most remarkable letters to his wife, Joan. According to his story, four of the men under his supervision attempted to escape and forced him to accompany them. They had stolen a canoe, and after getting away from the station they made their way through the bush for four days. Eventually Williams escaped from them, struck a road, and gave himself up. Whether this story is entirely true may, perhaps, be doubted; Frost says that Williams had favoured mutiny on board the *Mandarin*, and later he undoubtedly tried to escape, while another writer states that it was only lack of provisions which now robbed him of

[1] Frost, op. cit.; *Cambrian*, 15 July 1842, quoting letter from Port Arthur, 14 Dec. 1841; *Silurian*, 17 Sept. 1842, giving article in *Fraser's Magazine* in full; *Merthyr Guardian*, 3 June 1843. It should be added that the *Merlin*, 16 Jan. 1841, has a number of dots after the offending remark, implying that Frost had indulged in further sarcasms at the expense of Lord John Russell, but it is unique in this.

success. However this may be, and although the other convicts corroborated his story that he had been forced to go with them, he was now sentenced to two years' hard labour in chains. He was set to work at stone breaking, and was chained between two murderers; the remainder of his time he spent in silence in a dark cell measuring six feet by four. This 'silent punishment' he endured for sixteen weeks. After that he was removed to the huts, but here the vermin were even worse than in the cells, and his blankets were almost alive with lice. A report was published in British newspapers that he had killed a man in desperation and had been hanged. His wife and two children wrote in great anxiety to the Home Office to ask for information, and were told that it was another convict with the same surname who had been executed. He was kept at this settlement even after his two years in chains were at an end, and he claimed that that was because he had proved so useful to the authorities. He was, in fact, a very remarkable man, as events were soon to show, and he had proved his usefulness in finding water for the settlement and in giving advice on how to make iron castings. In January 1844 he was removed from the peninsula and sworn into the police at New Norfolk, at a salary of 12*s.* a week. Here again he rendered an extraordinary service, which is well-authenticated as it was the subject of a recommendation to the Governor of Van Diemen's Land (now Sir Eardley Wilmot) sent, on his behalf, both by his police super-intendent and by several members of the public. Some seventy lunatics had run amok, and it was feared that the soldiers would have to shoot to prevent them from setting their building on fire and escaping to the town. But Williams, who had been in a position to render them little kindnesses, risked going among them, and managed to pacify them. The Governor forwarded this memorial to London with a recommendation that Williams should be granted a ticket of leave, but the Whigs had now returned to office (1846), and the new Home Secretary, Mr. Gladstone, stubbornly refused even this small concession. At the same time Williams himself petitioned the Colonial Secretary for a free pardon, on the ground of his exceptional services, and this was naturally refused.[1]

The refusal of a ticket of leave is the more surprising as Jones had been granted one some months previously. When he arrived at the colony Jones had adopted an air of bravado, and had been inclined to talk too freely. But a hint had sufficed, and he had learnt his place, and when the writer in *Fraser's Magazine* visited Port Arthur, he found Jones saying grace before meat for his refractory pupils in a circumspect and orderly fashion. He had managed to please the authorities better than his two companions, and in 1844 had acted as a common informer.[2] He had then served as constable in Hobart, before being given the ticket of leave which allowed him to earn his living as he chose. Williams also was granted a lesser concession in September 1846, when he was allowed to leave the police, and was indentured as a servant at an hotel in Launceston. Here he found the work heavy—the coach for Hobart for which he had to prepare left at 4 a.m., and he was frequently serving in the bar until 10 p.m.—but he was treated as one of the family by the landlord and his wife. Jones frequented the house, but Williams seldom spoke to him, for his 'ambition and arrogance' were unbearable. Jones had for some time been driving a stage-coach, but he now returned to his old occupation and entered into partnership with a French watchmaker in

[1] *Merthyr Guardian*, 8 May 1841 (quoting *Hobart Advertiser*, 24 Nov. 18.) ; 12 Aug. 1843, 2 Sept. 1843; Frost, op. cit.; Zephaniah Williams, Letters in *South Wales Daily News*, April 1877, letters dated 3 Jan, 27 Jan. 1846; Gladstone's letter to Governor, 2 Sept. 1846; Sir James Graham's refusal of free pardon, 12 Nov. 1846; *Cornwall Chronicle*, 13 Nov. 1847.
[2] *Launceston Advertiser*, 19 July 1844.

Launceston. His new prosperity found expression in extravagant clothes, and he sent for his wife to come out and join him. The antipathy between him and Williams developed into a quarrel, and the latter had occasion to tell Jones that his 'pride, assumption and arrogance' revolted him, also that 'he knew his origin and course of life' and could not associate with him. Apparently there was something in Jones's 'course of life' which delicacy prevented Williams from mentioning in his letter to his wife. But his quarrel with Jones cost him dear. Together with another convict he had made a plan to escape, and arranged with the proprietor of a vessel trading between Launceston and New Zealand to pick them up from a small boat outside the harbour. He was forced by his position to take the landlord and his wife into his confidence, but begged them not to inform Jones. Jones, however, noticed his absence, and suspected from the answers of the landlord what had happened. He therefore immediately told the police and took a coach to Hobart to inform the authorities. Owing to difficulties in navigation the two runaways failed to get past the police at the river's mouth. They then returned at once to Launceston, and no one would have been any the wiser but for Jones's action. Williams found himself once more brought up for trial, and once more sentenced to twelve months' hard labour in chains in 'that worse than hell on earth', Tasman's Peninsula. Yet this time his sentence was greatly mitigated, and he declares that he 'suffered little'. On 14 November 1848 he was released. But Jones's prosperity also was short lived. When his action became known, the Frenchman separated from him and 'left the great man to his own resources'. He tried to set up in business on his own, but before his wife had arrived, he had become penniless. He then tried to earn his living as he had done in the old days, as a strolling player, sometimes appearing in the character of William

Tell, and sometimes as Sir Watkin Williams Wynn, but this, as Williams said, did not 'look well to support his great pride and pomposity', and he was reduced to great poverty.[1]

Immediately after his release Williams made his first remarkable discovery—he found coal in the immediate neighbourhood of Hobart. Four men who were interested in mining had indentured him as a servant, and he persuaded them to buy 500 acres of land. They supplied the capital, but were ignorant of actual mining operations, and so Williams was to receive a fifth share of the proceeds. Within two weeks Williams was writing to his wife in great elation that he believed his income would be £1,000 a year, and stating that he should soon be sending for her. Three months later the purchase was complete; they were ready to start sinking, and Williams wrote that he believed the property would be worth half a million pounds, for coal was now sold in Hobart at 14s. to 18s. a ton, and he estimated that he could put it on the market at a total cost of 3s. a ton. But now he had full cause to realize the enormity of his position. As soon as the venture seemed likely to prove successful, he found that his partners were going to get rid of him. As an indentured servant, no contract entered into with him was binding. He therefore begged the governor for a ticket of leave, and won his support, but communication with England was slow, and six days before the ticket arrived the four scoundrels had 'returned him to the service of the Crown'. He now wrote to his wife (27 December 1849) in greater despair than he had ever felt before, both because of the dashing of his hopes and because he had allowed himself to express in his previous letters to her his dreams of wealth. He did not now know whether to advise his family to come out to him or not, for

---

[1] *Merthyr Guardian*, 26 Sept. 1846; *Merlin*, 27 Aug. 1847, 29 April 1848, 17 June 1848; *The Times*, 6 Aug. 1847; *Cornwall Chronicle*, 20 Nov. 1847; Williams's letter dated 28 Nov. 1848, in *South Wales News*, loc. cit.

the colony was not as flourishing as it had been—all were leaving for the gold rush in California as fast as they could get ships to take them. He bitterly complained that the Irish rebels of 1848 had been given their ticket of leave as soon as they landed, whereas he had had to wait nine years. But even in the postscript of this despairing letter he stated that since writing he had entered into agreement for coal land, and was going to commence on his own. It proved a desperate struggle for nearly two years, and he was forced to take a Canadian rebel into partnership in order to have the advantage of his capital—the sum of £30—in return for which he was to have an equal share. Yet they succeeded, and in March 1851 the Tasmanian papers were reporting that they had sunk a shaft eighty feet in depth, and had struck a six-foot seam.[1] By August they were able to produce between thirty and forty tons a day, and Williams wrote to his wife in great joy. He had justified himself, and had broken the monopoly of his enemies who had hoped to put the price of coal that winter up to 30s. a ton, and he now looked forward to the society of his wife and their two children, Rhoda and Llewellyn. At last the boy would have an opportunity to develop his talent as a harpist—the opportunity of which his father's misfortunes had robbed him.

Once on the road to prosperity his fortune does not seem to have changed. For some reason he sold his share in the Hobart mine (for £800, according to Frost), probably because he had already discovered better coal elsewhere. This was in the north of the island, about sixty miles from Launceston. Here he was when he received his conditional pardon, which allowed him to live wherever he liked outside the British Isles.[2] He had fully expected

[1] *Cornwall Chronicle*, 29 March 1851, 2 April 1851.
[2] In a letter to his wife, 17 July 1853 (*Merthyr Guardian*, 19 Nov. 1853), and to his son, 25 July 1853 (*Merlin*, 4 Nov. 1853), he states that he had

his wife and daughter to join him—he had even gone to Hobart to meet the boat on which he thought they had come, but had been sorely disappointed. His son now had a good position at Blaina, and to him he wrote commissioning him to send out 40 workmen (33 colliers, 2 blacksmiths, 2 sawyers, 2 carpenters, and an engineer) and forwarding tickets for their free passage to Van Diemen's Land. He also had 2,600 acres of agricultural land to dispose of, and would willingly help any farmers who were prepared to pay their own passage on the same ship as his workmen (a cost of £7. 10s.). Two years later (1855) he discovered 'tasmanite', a variety of yellow cannel coal from which paraffin could be extracted, and in the autumn of the same year he struck upon the valuable Mersey coal bed, some twenty-five miles from Launceston—a two-foot seam covering about 2,000 acres and only 35 feet below the surface. This was incomparably the best coal in the antipodes, and Williams was soon exporting it to Hobart and Melbourne, whereas hitherto most of the coal of Tasmania had been imported from Australia. His family never seems to have joined him. His wife all these years had kept the Boar's Head Inn at Caerphilly, and possibly felt too old to undertake the long journey to Tasmania, while he himself seems to have dreaded the sea voyage and never revisited his old home. His son, on the other hand, had now become a harpist of repute, under the bardic name of *Pencerdd y De*. Full of years and prosperity Zephaniah Williams died at Launceston on 8 May 1874, thirty-five years after the 'mad enterprise' (as he called it) which had brought him to Van Diemen's Land.[1] In strange contrast was the death only four months previously, and in the

obtained his conditional pardon. The announcement of the pardon for the three men was not made until 6 March 1854 (*Merlin*, 10 March 1854), but Frost also says that Williams obtained his pardon a year before he did.

[1] *South Wales News*, loc. cit.; *Cornwall Chronicle*, 7 April 1855, 11 April, 16 May, 8 Aug., 15 Aug., 22 Aug., 29 Sept., 9 Jan. 1856, 3 Sept., 3 Dec.

same town, of his old associate, William Jones. He had taken up innkeeping for a time, but with no more success than in his other ventures, and so great was his poverty when he died, after a long and painful illness, on 26 December 1873, that the Oddfellows bore the expense of his burial, for in the old days in Pontypool he had once been a brother of their order.[1]

When Frost had served his sentence of two years' hard labour, he was removed to Hobart, and indentured as a clerk and warehouseman in a large grocery store 'under one of the worst masters in the town'. He had to wait three years for his ticket of leave, and then for eight years afterwards he earned a very meagre livelihood as a schoolmaster at various places. He played no part in the public life of the colony, nor did the other transported Chartists —some sixty-two men in all.[2] With advancing age grew his interest in religion, and as his literary ambitions still remained, he contemplated writing on the evidences of Christianity. He announced a lecture refuting Hume's position on miracles, but only thirty attended it, and although he received high commendation no one expressed any desire to help a convict. Meanwhile his daughter, Catherine, had joined him. His wife had frequently expressed a desire to do so, but he did not wish to subject her to the indignity of a penal colony, and all the time he hoped to be able to return home. At last, in July 1854, the welcome news reached him of the conditional pardon granted four months previously. Aberdeen's coalition government were greatly in need of the Irish vote, and so conditionally pardoned Smith O'Brien; Duncome immediately raised the case of the Chartists in the House, and as the punishment of the lesser criminals could not now

[1] *Western Mail*, 17 March 1877.
[2] H. L. Harris, 'Influence of Chartism on Australia', *Journal and Proceedings of the Royal Australian Historical Society*, xi (1926), pp. 351–78.

The Aftermath

very well be continued, the Home Secretary, Lord Palmerston, announced their pardon, adding unctuously that 'Her Majesty was always glad when she could properly find an opportunity of tempering justice with mercy'. A number of Newport citizens then prevailed upon the Mayor (James Brown) to petition Palmerston for an interview, so that they could present to him a memorial praying that Frost should be allowed to return home, but he refused to see them.[1]

Frost did not want to end his days in Tasmania, and so, although he was now seventy years of age, he and Catherine started in December on the long journey to the United States. They called at Callao, and reached California in May 1855, eventually making their way to New York. Here a number of British residents held a meeting to congratulate him and to petition the queen for a free pardon, but Frost greatly injured his own cause by publishing a twenty-paged *Letter to the People of the United States* in which he sought to prove the interesting thesis 'that the aristocracy of the British Isles was the curse of the world'. In point of fact, the pamphlet was a vigorously written description of convict life, with its cruelty, vice, and horrors, but it was felt even by his supporters in Newport that his fierce denunciations made it impossible to hope for further relief.[2] Yet in the following May the successful conclusion of the Crimean War led to a grant of pardons to political prisoners, and among them was Frost. He wasted no time in getting home, for he arrived at Liverpool on 12 July. He proceeded immediately to London to pay his

[1] James Fenton, *History of Tasmania* (London, 1854), p. 154; *Merthyr Guardian*, 3 Jan. 1846, 26 Sept. 1846, 8 May 1852, 11 March 1854; *The Times*, 25 June 1844, 6 Aug. 1847; *Merlin*, 4 May 1850, 5 Oct. 1850, 11 March 1854, 14 April 1854, 21 April 1854, 15 Aug. 1855 (Frost's letter from New York, dated 15 Aug. 1855). *Star of Gwent*, 11 March 1854. Newport Library MS., Memorial of Inhabitants of Borough of Newport, signed James Brown.
[2] *Star of Gwent*, 15 Dec. 1855.

respects to Duncombe and others who had championed him, and attended a debate in the House of Commons, but in a few days he had joined his family at Stapleton.[1]

It was seventeen years since he had left them, but he was still strong and active, although his hair was pure white. Time had wrought changes in his family. His old mother had died just four years previously at the age of ninety-two. His wife also was ailing, and lived less than a year after his return. In all these years nothing seems to have been heard of his son John, and his eldest daughter Elizabeth also seems to have died. Catherine, who had accompanied her father round the world, soon returned to Tasmania.[2] Sarah had become a widow through the death of her husband, Dr. Harry Fry, the previous year.[3] But her matrimonial ventures were not at an end, for on 9 December 1857 she was married in Palermo Cathedral to the Marquis Giuseppe Pasqualino of that city. Her husband was descended from an old Venetian noble family, a branch of which had settled in South Italy about 1500. His father had been president of the Grand Council of the last king of the Two Sicilies, whose kingdom was soon to disappear beneath the hammer strokes of Garibaldi. Sarah was the Marquis's second wife, his first being also an Englishwoman, Mary Charlton, authoress of *Letters from Sicily*. Thus the Chartist's daughter had become a Marchioness and held a title older by centuries than that of the Russells, Dukes of Bedford. She does not seem to have lived long after her marriage, but she left her second husband a daughter named Emilia, who became the wife of the Cavaliere Giuseppe Spadafora di Oliastrello.[4] Frost's

---

[1] *Star of Gwent*, 19 July 1856; *Merthyr Guardian*, 17 May 1856.
[2] John Frost's will.   [3] *Merthyr Guardian*, 28 April 1855.
[4] Marriage notice, *Merthyr Guardian*, 5 Dec. 1857; information kindly supplied by the Marchese Firmato Fracassi, First Secretary of the Italian Embassy. The head of the Pasqualino family to-day is Generale di Divisione Grande Ufficiale Pasqualino Salvatore.

daughter Ellen had married William Davies of Blackwood. He had stayed away a whole year after absconding for the second time, but then had returned home. Octavius Morgan (Sir Charles's son) had written on behalf of the magistrates to the Home Office asking if they should apprehend him, for he had not only escaped being put on trial, but the Attorney-General had refused to distrain for his recognizance, and so, said the magistrate, he had completely slipped through the hands of justice. The Home Secretary, however, replied that it was not advisable to proceed on the former charges,[1] and Davies escaped scot free. After his marriage he seems to have emigrated to Australia.[2] Frost's remaining daughter, Anne, lived with her father after his wife's death, and was, he said, 'the solace of his declining years'.

Within a month Frost had visited the scene of his early activities. Here also there were changes. Sir Charles had been dead for ten years, and Thomas Prothero, Esquire, of Malpas Court, had just recently died. Sir Thomas Phillips had naturally ceased to be a country attorney. He had been called to the Bar, and his fame together with his undoubted ability secured him a highly successful career as a Chancery barrister and queen's counsel. Moreover he had rendered his fellow countrymen an important service. Three young barristers had been commissioned to inquire into education in Wales, and had produced a terrible indictment of the Welsh nation on the grounds of perjury and sexual immorality, attributing this state of affairs to nonconformity and the persistence of the Welsh language. This 'treason of the Blue Books' aroused an intensity of feeling in Wales which has never subsided. Nonconfromist leaders sought to provide a refutation by

[1] H.O. 40/57, letter dated, 20 Nov. 1840.
[2] *Western Mail*, 30 July 1877. (It is possible that Ellen is here confused with Catherine.)

pointing out that the government figures for bastardy (and bastardy was the commissioners' test for immorality) were actually higher in relation to the population in seven out of ten large rural areas in England than they were in Wales, whereas in Wales itself the figures were highest in Radnorshire and South Pembrokeshire, which were both Anglican and English in speech. But it was all of no avail. The *Morning Chronicle* declared that the Welsh were 'fast settling down into the most savage barbarism', while the *Examiner* thought that 'their habits were those of animals and would not bear description'. To all this Sir Thomas produced a reasoned reply in his book *Wales, its Language, Social Condition, Moral Character and Religious Opinions*, and to the judgement of this Anglican Sir Galahad (*sans peur* as well as *sans reproche*) even London periodicals had to pay some attention.

A committee had been set up at Newport to welcome Frost, and the theatre was taken for this purpose, but Samuel Homfray intervened and prevented the lessee, his tenant, from fulfilling his contract. The committee then thought it wise not to have a public procession. But the day of Frost's arrival (11 August) became known, and a thousand or more (the canaille of the town, according to the *Merthyr Guardian*) welcomed him as he stepped off the Bristol packet. They had provided a carriage, decked with flowers, and when Frost was seated the horses were removed and the carriage drawn in triumph through the town. Outside the Westgate Hotel the crowd halted for a minute or two and cheered. Then, from the window of a temperance hotel in Llanarth Street, Frost addressed them. He still held the same opinions, he said, as he had done seventeen years before, for there could be no change in a man whose convictions were based on principle. He was determined to work for a radical reform of Parliament (there could not be a worse set of men than those who

now ruled the country, he said), as well as for redress of
the evils of the convict system, and also for the removal of
abuses in Newport, for he still maintained that the lands
of the charity school, on which most of Commercial Street
had now been built, had wrongly been appropriated by
the Tredegar family. His ideas and interests, therefore,
had scarcely changed in forty years. But he caused much
offence to those who had expected him to end his days in
peace, and the *Manchester Guardian*, in particular, accused
him of ingratitude to the government which had pardoned
him.[1]

A still greater ovation awaited Frost in London. Ernest
Jones had seized upon his return to revive an interest in
Chartism, and elaborate arrangements were made for 15
September, when the Chartists were to meet at various
points with bands and banners, and march to Finsbury
Square. Frost was to be met by a carriage and four at
London Bridge, and brought to the square at twelve
o'clock. So large was the demonstration that *The Times*
devoted two full columns to it, and estimated that there
were 20,000 present. In spite of its extremely hostile
account, it again (as did the newspapers in 1839) admitted
with surprise that Frost's 'deportment was modest, and
his appearance prepossessing rather than otherwise'. Soon
after twelve o'clock the procession started from Finsbury
Square. Prominent among the contingents was one from
the exiles in Soho, with their banner 'Es lebe die allge-
meine soziale demokratische Republik', and one wonders
if Karl Marx was one of the crowd. They passed through
Cheapside, St. Paul's Churchyard, Ludgate Hill, into
Fleet Street and the Strand (stopping to burn a copy of
the *Daily Telegraph* when they came to its office) and then
through Trafalgar Square, Regent Street, Portland Place,

[1] *The Times*, 13 Aug. 1856; *Merlin*, 16 Aug., 23 Aug., 30 Aug.; *Merthyr
Guardian*, 16 Aug.; *Star of Gwent*, 16 Aug., 23 Aug.; *Two Lectures*, p. 4.

and Regent's Park to Primrose Hill. There Ernest Jones read an address to Frost, and he briefly responded, calling upon his listeners to be cool and determined, prudent but fearless, giving up no principle, being satisfied with nothing less than their due, so that they might yet live to see their country deserve the name of Merry England. The meeting ended by singing to the tune of the national anthem:

> God, hear the people pray,
> If there 's no other way
> Give us one glorious day
> Of Cromwell's time.[1]

Frost evidently intended to take an active part in public life. He waited on the mayor of Newport to ask that he should be reinstated in his rights and privileges as a freeman, only to be told that he would be entitled to them if he lived at Newport.[2] He announced his intention of becoming a lecturer, charging for admission in the manner of Vincent, Kossuth, and others, and from time to time notices of these lectures appeared in the press—in London, Manchester (where his friend W. P. Roberts took the chair), Nottingham, Burnley, and other places. In one of these, at least, he dealt with the riot of 1839, and declared that Hodge and Harford must have been government agents, for he had never spoken to them in his life, and that the story about the Welsh mail which they gave in evidence was nothing but a foul and flagitious falsehood. But his main topic was the horrors of transportation, and at one point in his lecture he would sententiously ask all women to withdraw, so that he could speak on the subject of sodomy. He declared that the authorities closed their eyes to this vice, in order not to give the colony a bad name, and he was a firm enough believer in the Scriptures to hold that this would certainly involve the British Empire

---

[1] *The Times*, 16 Sept. 1856; *Merlin*, 20 Sept. 1856.
[2] *Star of Gwent*, 30 May 1857, 30 Aug. 1857.

in the fate of the cities of the plain. This also was the subject of his *Letter to the People of Great Britain*, an amplification of his *Letter to the People of the United States*, which he forwarded to members of Parliament.[1] But soon no more is heard of his lectures, and possibly he found the people apathetic to the convicts' woes.

The years passed by at Stapleton, ten, fifteen, twenty years after his return. He had become interested in spiritualism, to which he had been introduced by a fellow Welshman in the United States, and on this he carried on a very amicable controversy in the *Star of Gwent*. Among his spiritual communicants was his son, Henry Hunt, the companion of his Chartist demonstrations, and the joy of his early manhood. On one occasion he evoked the spirit of Feargus O'Connor. There are many questions which one would have been glad if he had asked him, as, for example, where were the men of Merthyr on the night of 3 November 1839? But Frost's interests were both more trivial and more profound: Was there a God? Were the planets inhabited? Had Feargus visited Saturn? Was he present at Frost's lectures? to all of which the replies were in the affirmative.[2] He several times expressed his intention to write his autobiography, even listing the topics with which he would deal. This, unfortunately, he never did, although his early days were much in his mind, and he loved to dwell in his letters on his childhood in Newport and the pleasant evenings when he had wandered along the river to Caerleon. He attended to his financial affairs, and shortly before he died he sold the Royal Oak for £1,500. He maintained an interest in public matters, both in the Franco-German War and the municipal politics of Newport, and he recalled the time when Alderman Townsend

---

[1] Ibid., 23 Aug. 1856, 30 Aug. 1856; *Merthyr Guardian*, 6 Sept. 1856; *The Times*, 22 Jan. 1857.

[2] *Star of Gwent*, 1 Dec. 1860, 8 Dec., 22 Dec., 29 Dec., 5 Jan. 1861, 12 Jan., 26 Jan., 9 Feb.

(as he had now been for many years) and he had fought together at many a council meeting against as corrupt a crew as ever walked the deck of a pirate ship. But in his eighty-ninth year he had a bad fall from which he never completely recovered, and he made his will, leaving his property to his three daughters, Catherine, Ellen, and Anne. His handwriting had suddenly become that of an old man. Yet he still held to his idea of writing his life, but his sight began to fail him, and it was never done.[1] He died on 27 July 1877 in his ninety-third year. Few people had been aware that he was still alive; like the Chartism for which he had fought and suffered he had become an anachronism.

[1] Letters in *Star of Gwent*, loc. cit.; in W. E. Adams, *Memoirs of a Social Atom* (London, 1903), and MS. letters in Newport Library. Will dated 12 April 1874, proved by Anne Frost, 9 Jan. 1878, endorsed 'under £1,500'.

APPENDIX

CHARTISM IN WALES 1839–48

In Wales, even more than in England, the Chartist movement after 1839 was an anticlimax. Whatever may have been the purpose of the Chartists in marching on Newport, the unfortunate outcome of the affair had alienated and frightened liberal-minded people who might otherwise have sympathized with them, and, as well, had played into the hands of their opponents. These were determined to make a clean sweep of Chartism while they had the opportunity, and prosecutions for participating in the riot recurred at each succeeding Assizes. As late as June 1841, the landlord of the King Crispin Arms at Brynmawr was condemned to seven years' transportation by Mr. Justice Maule, though this sentence seems to have been annulled at the intervention of the Home Secretary—still another example, said the *Merthyr Guardian* of the duplicity of the 'brutal and bloody Whigs'.[1] By the end of 1840, there were 63 Chartists in Monmouth County Gaol, as well as 4 in the House of Correction at Usk, 12 in Brecon Gaol, 1 in Swansea, and 50 in Montgomery.[2] Deprived of its leaders, therefore, the movement could not but decline.

The influence of the churches was also brought to bear against Chartism. Anglicans strove to associate the riot with Nonconformity. The *Merthyr Guardian* declared plainly that there were many Baptists and Independents among the rioters, and the Nonconformists, it said, 'would now see, if they never thought of it before, that they have a character to be gained or lost'. It maintained that the Socinians were Chartists 'almost to a man', that they were 'corrupt and disloyal with hardly any exceptions'.[3] The Anglican monthly *Yr Haul* held its contemporary *Y Diwygiwr* responsible for the riot, because it had incited the people to agitate. If the three leaders were to be hanged and quartered, it declared, surely this should also be the fate of the editor of the *Diwygiwr*.[4] Still more striking is

---

[1] *Merthyr Guardian*, 26 June 1841.
[2] *Chartist Circular*, 23 Jan. 1841.
[3] *Merthyr Guardian*, 14 Dec. 1839.
[4] *Yr Haul*, 1840, p. 122.

Appendix

the report presented to the magistrates by the Reverend
Edward Gosling, chaplain of Monmouth gaol.

'It has been my custom since my appointment to the
chaplaincy of your prison at Monmouth', reported the chaplain, 'to obtain from each individual as soon as practicable
after his entering the prison, as well a portraiture of his
manner of life as an avowal of the particular church or sect
to which he might happen to belong. This I have usually
done solely with a view to the better discharge of my duties
as their minister. In the case of the Monmouth Chartists this
was not the only motive; the wish to discover in what con-
gregations sedition throve best was another. I am aware of
the objections that might be raised against an inference
drawn in such a manner as this, yet I allow that at the time
this formed one of my motives, and the following is the result
of my inquiry: of various sects there were 41; of the anglican
and Romish churches 8. I have since been told that some
who gave their name as belonging to the Established Church
were, for some motive or other, deceiving me. For instance,
John Owen has his name down as a churchman, whereas I
find that he is a dissenter, and warmly vindicates their tenets.
Indeed I think it would be difficult to find more than one or
two whose religious instruction was not derived from the
minister of the Meeting House as well as from the clergyman
of the Parish Church. Others there were who had been
members of the Established Church, and apparently strongly
attached to it, as they formed part of the choir, who afterwards left it, their lapse into dissent and their progress in
Chartism keeping pace one with the other.'[1]

Equally severe was the attack on the Nonconformists by the
incumbent of Dowlais, Evan Jenkins, in his sermon *Chartism
Unmasked*. This he preached two weeks after the riot and published early in the following year, and its popularity is shown
by the fact that within twelve months it had run into nineteen
editions. Chartism was diametrically opposed to the word of
God, said the preacher, for its two fundamental principles were
impious. The first of these was equality. Men were equal
only in the sense of being equally sinful by nature, for Scrip-

[1] Usk MS., Prison Report, Michaelmas Sessions, 1840.

ture proved conclusively that the Almighty had deliberately organized society in gradations. The devil, indeed, was the first Chartist, for he had wished to be on an equality with God. Secondly, poverty was not the result of unjust laws, as the 'infidel' Frost had claimed, but was part of the everlasting purpose of God. There were texts enough to prove this. Moreover, let not the labouring man think that his lot was worse than that of others; he slept sweetly and soundly and had no cares, while the rich men, the iron-masters and honest shopkeepers spent their nights in mental anguish. Turning to the points of the Charter, he dismissed them without difficulty. Annual elections would lead to constant turmoil; universal suffrage would mean universal confusion and the setting of one workman against another; vote by ballot would only be a cloak for rogues and knaves to cover their dishonesty, while the idea of the payment of members 'was too absurd for an idiot to be the author of it'. Chartism, therefore, was evil; it had its origin in the revolt of the angels; it had been manifest in the French Revolution and the Reform agitation in England, and God had now clearly shown His displeasure with it in the defence of Newport. The Chartists must be punished to render them incapable of future mischief, and the evil eradicated by the spread of true religion.

The Reverend Evan Jenkins soundly criticized the Nonconformists, 'degenerate followers' of the pious dissenters of old. Yet he had great praise for the Calvinistic Methodists and the Wesleyans. The former were able to claim that no member of their body was in any way connected with the riot, and the iron-master, Sir John Guest, showed his 'extreme satisfaction' at this by contributing £59 towards building their chapel in Dowlais.[1] Their association met at Blackwood a few days after the riot, and excommunicated two members who had joined a Chartist lodge.[2] At the Llanidloes meeting of the Association next year 'joy was expressed that not a single member of the connexion had joined the rioters', and their periodical, *Y Drysorfa*, pronounced Chartist principles to be contrary to the Christian religion.[3] The *Eurgrawn Wesleyaidd* adopted the same

---

[1] *Merlin*, 29 Feb. 1840; *Yr Haul*, 1840, p. 128.
[2] *Merlin*, 21 Dec. 1839.
[3] *Y Drysorfa*, 1840, pp. 45, 376.

standpoint, adding that the material condition of the workers had improved to such an extent that they had no cause to be discontented.[1] The attitude of the other denominations was not so clear. The Baptist *Seren Gomer* was inclined to sympathize with the exiled leaders, and declared their condemnation illegal. Yet it published in full the prize essay submitted to the eisteddfod of the London Cymreigyddion Society on 'The Evil Effects of Chartism in Wales'. This essay stressed the infidelity of Zephaniah Williams, who had apparently distributed the writings of Carlyle among the workers (possibly a confusion between Thomas Carlyle and Richard Carlile). It put forward a claim, which has frequently been repeated, that the troubles had begun among the English immigrants into Monmouthshire, and that the riot had been fomented by English missionaries.[2] This, also, was the argument of the Newport Welsh Baptist minister, Thomas Morris. He avowed himself a staunch supporter of the Whig reformers, and advocated the ballot, but universal suffrage he condemned on the novel grounds that it would give power to the Papists, who would pour over from Ireland, and the payment of members he maintained would open the House of Commons to all sorts of praters, tinkers, cobblers, and chimney sweeps. He was as convinced as the curate of Dowlais that God had revealed his wrath against the Sabbath breakers in the torrential rain of 3 November.[3] It was among the Independents that there was most difference of opinion. The Reverend Richard Jones of Sirhowy had suffered personally at the hands of the Chartists, for he had spent the night of the riot uncomfortably hiding among the reeds on the bank of the Sirhowy river. He may therefore be excused for solemnly excommunicating those of his members who were known to be Chartists,[4] yet when the Reverend Evan Williams of Cefn (near Merthyr) sought to do the same, he found that it was he who had to leave.[5]

In Newport, in particular, the blood letting of 4 November

---

[1] *Eurgrawn Wesleyaidd*, Feb. 1840.
[2] *Seren Gomer*, March 1841. Cf. Henry Richard, op. cit., pp. 81–2; *Udgorn Cymru*, March 1841.
[3] T. Morris, *Cynghor da mewn amserau drwg* (Cardiff, 1840).
[4] *Merlin*, 16 Nov. 1839; *Merthyr Guardian*, 16 Nov. 1839.
[5] *Yr Haul*, 1840, p. 41.

had destroyed the Chartist movement, and a new reminder of the consequences of sedition was provided by the second trial of Vincent and Edwards at the Monmouth Assizes in March 1840. They were charged with having conspired, together with John Frost, to subvert constituted authority and alter by force the constitution of the country, and with having used seditious language. The basis of the charge was the meeting held at Pontnewynydd on 1 January 1839, with Edwards in the chair, when Frost had referred to the grooms of the bedchamber, and Vincent had spoken of the time when the whole social system would collapse, bringing down with it that pretty little bauble, the Crown. The jury took only ten minutes to find the prisoners guilty, although they recommended them to mercy on account of the long imprisonment they had undergone. Nevertheless Vincent was sentenced to a further twelve months imprisonment, and Edwards to fourteen months, while both had to find sureties of good behaviour for five years, amounting in all to £700 each. They were thus effectively silenced, and their sentence gives an indication of the punishment which Frost would have received on one of the two charges against him before the Newport affair had occurred. Yet the authorities still feared that an attempt might be made to rescue them, and so they were immediately removed from Monmouth to the Milbank Penitentiary. Here they were subjected to all the rigours of the prison, although they had been condemned to simple detention only. Sergeant Talfourd, who had prosecuted them at Monmouth, honourably presented a petition to the House of Commons and intervened on their behalf. The reason given by the government was that it was dangerous to leave them in Monmouth, and it would be wrong to throw the cost of their imprisonment on any other shire, while at Milbank no distinction could be made between different classes of prisoners. In the debate which followed, Vincent's remark was compared with the seditious expressions used in 1819 by Cam Hobhouse, now a cabinet minister, and in the end it was decided to remove the prisoners to Rutlandshire. Their sentences were eventually reduced, so that they were released on 31 January 1841.[1]

Yet some interest in Chartism still persisted in Newport. On

[1] *Merlin*, 29 Feb., 4 April, 11 April, 6 June 1840; *Merthyr Guardian*, 4 April 1840; *Udgorn Cymru*, July 1840.

Appendix

Palm Sunday (1840) it was noticed that the graves of the killed were covered with flowers and laurels,[1] and in October handbills were distributed announcing a meeting at which two Bath Chartists would speak. The magistrates immediately forbade the meeting and swore in special constables, but nevertheless it was held, although the two speakers were arrested the next day.[2] When the anniversary of the riot approached, the magistrates feared a demonstration, and again swore in special constables,[3] and in the winter the Roman Catholic Bishop and Vicar-Apostolic in Wales (who resided in Newport) sent an alarming report to the Home Office. He had obtained information that the Chartists intended to hold great simultaneous meetings early in the New Year under the pretence of petitioning for Frost, and that if they were not successful there would be a general burning of houses and destruction of property.[4] The Bishop's information was incorrect. Black, a Chartist missionary, did announce at Merthyr on 25 December that simultaneous meetings would be held on New Year's Day,[5] but the precautions of the magistrates made these impossible, and although Black appeared in Newport,[6] the day passed without any demonstration. Yet a Chartist lodge now began to meet weekly in the town,[7] and interest revived with the prospect of a general election. In preparation for this, Black reappeared in Newport in June, when an important meeting was held. But it then became obvious that there was a division of opinion even in the attenuated ranks of the Chartists. Dickenson, the butcher, condemned the Reform Bill and the clap-trap promises of the Whigs, but he believed that the Tories would have been ten times worse, and he supported the anti-corn-law agitation. On the other hand, Black violently attacked the Whigs who had given the Chartists an example in their speeches and had then turned their bayonets upon them. He urged co-operation with the Tories. Townsend, also, declared that the Whigs 'had called the working class into existence',

[1] *Silurian*, 25 April 1840. [2] *Merlin*, 31 Oct. 1840.
[3] *Merthyr Guardian*, 7 Nov. 1840.
[4] H.O. 40/57, Bishop Brown to Home Office, 13 Dec. 1840.
[5] Ibid., Lord Bute to Home Office, 28 Dec. 1840.
[6] *Silurian*, 16 Jan. 1841.
[7] At the Llanarth Inn, Llanarth Street, *Merlin*, 16 Jan. 1841.

and then, like Frankenstein, had been terrified at their own work. The blood shed at the end of that street called for vengeance on the deceitful murderers. Edwards, who had recently returned from prison (where his constitution, he said, had been ruined by fifteen months of pigs' food) reappeared in public at this meeting. He, also, rejoiced that a Tory had been elected mayor of the borough, and claimed that opposition to the cornlaw agitation was already leading the Whigs to use violent language.[1] In addition to this difference of opinion, the meeting had a curious sequel. A parcel had arrived by the mail coach at Pontypool which had given rise to suspicion, and was found, according to several newspapers, to contain two muskets, two bayonets, a fowling piece, two pistols, five bullet moulds, a quantity of Chartist literature, and a book entitled *Instructions to the people, how to make combustible materials*. It was addressed to a person named Moore, but was called for by Black, who was promptly arrested. Yet the only charge brought against him, when his case came to be tried, was one of being a rogue and a vagabond, for which he was given a month's hard labour.[2] This was a fantastically light sentence if the newspaper story was true, and one is led to suspect that the object of the magistrates was to keep Black in gaol over the election.

The election for the Monmouth boroughs took place in July. Elsewhere an alliance between the Tories and the Chartists had led to a defeat of the Whigs, to their intense chagrin and surprise,[3] but in the Monmouth boroughs the Tories decided not to contest. Blewitt therefore turned up on nomination day accompanied by his friends, fully expecting to be 'chaired' without any opposition. But the Chartists, who had recently established a new lodge at Abergavenny[4] and possibly elsewhere, decided to put forward a candidate of their own, and chose Dr. William Price. This unaccountable person had returned to Newbridge after eight months abroad, a fact greatly deplored by the Lord Lieutenant,[5] but he did not appear at Monmouth for his nomination. At the last minute, therefore,

---

[1] *Monmouthshire Advertiser*, 12 June 1841.
[2] *Cambrian, Merthyr Guardian*, and *Silurian*, 19 June 1841.
[3] e.g. at Nottingham, *Merlin*, 1 May 1841.
[4] *Northern Star*, 26 June 1841; *Merlin*, 7 May, 21 May 1842.
[5] H.O. 40/57, Bute to Home Office, 10 July 1840.

Appendix

Edwards was substituted for him, and was proposed and seconded by two Monmouth Chartists. In his address Edwards dwelt upon the unequal distribution of wealth, on the origin of large estates and the evils of the new Poor Law, and on the customary show of hands Edwards was elected by a very large majority. Blewitt then demanded a poll, and Edwards thereupon announced his intention not to stand; it had been his object only to seize an opportunity to bring Chartist principles to the notice of the public, he said. But his proposer in a violent speech insisted upon a poll, and hinted at a compromise between Edwards and Blewitt. He was opposed by Dickenson, who supported Edwards, and deplored the turning of the Town Hall into a beer garden, whereupon Townsend jumped on to the table and accused both Dickenson and Edwards, his former fellow prisoners, of being bribed, even professing to know how much they had accepted. As the proposers still insisted, the mayor, after much consulting of the statutes, decided that it was in their power to demand a poll, even if their nominee had withdrawn, yet when the poll was taken a few days later it was announced that Blewitt had received 330 votes and Edwards 0, a result probably unique in parliamentary history. But some nights before this, Edwards's effigy had been carried through the streets of Newport, his windows and those of Dickenson smashed, and the troops called upon at midnight to restore order, Townsend being subsequently bound over to keep the peace.[1] From this fiasco, Chartism in Newport never completely recovered. Yet in December the Chartists captured a meeting called to congratulate the queen on the birth of her son, and substituted for the loyal address another drawing her attention to the condition of her people, and calling for the return of Frost, Williams, and Jones. Edwards ridiculed the idea of congratulation when no one could know whether the child would be a blessing or a curse, and he recalled the births of George III and George IV. He hoped that with Victoria monarchical government would come to an end, though he professed not to be concerned with the form of government provided the people were well fed, well clothed, well housed, well educated,

---

[1] *Monmouthshire Advertiser*, 3 July 1841; *Merthyr Guardian*, 3 July 1841.

and happy. As the Chartists were in a great majority, no resolution could be passed until the mayor (Frost's old enemy, Lewis Edwards) promised to call a meeting to petition for a pardon for Frost, Williams, and Jones.[1] After this Chartism lasped in Newport for years; there was a faint flicker of a revival in 1848, when Frost's cousin and namesake together with a few others issued a broadside and held a meeting to support the Charter, but with that it disappeared.[2]

After the failure of the Newport riot, the centre of Chartism in Wales had moved to Merthyr Tydfil. The situation there was difficult to explain. On the one hand the enraged colliers of Nantyglo were reputed to be threatening a nocturnal visit to Merthyr, after the fashion of the 'Scotch Cattle', in revenge for the neglect or failure of the Merthyr Chartists to join them.[3] On the other hand, the authorities were apprehensive lest the latter should attempt to rescue Frost. For some weeks Merthyr was reported to be in a disturbed state, and troops were continually held in readiness. When a Chartist meeting was announced for Christmas Day, the magistrates immediately forbade it; they even informed an innkeeper that they would deprive him of his licence if he allowed a Chartist dinner to be held at his house. They themselves remained in attendance at the Castle Hotel throughout the day, and a detachment of infantry was kept under arms at Dowlais. In these circumstances the meeting which was held in the open air was attended only by 600 men, and proved a failure[4]. Yet the leader of the Merthyr Chartists, Morgan Williams, bitterly repudiated the accusation brought against them by the *Merthyr Guardian* that they countenanced sedition and treason. Their society, he said, was no more illegal than the Glamorgan Conservative Association; the only difference between the two associations was that the one was composed of workers living honestly by their labour, while the other was composed of idlers, pensioners,

[1] *Merlin*, 20 Nov., 4 Dec., 18 Dec. 1841; *Merthyr Guardian*, 27 Nov., 18 Dec. 1841.

[2] Newport Library, Broadside, 29 March 1848.

[3] *Shrewsbury News*, 7 Dec. 1839, quoted by Miss Myfanwy Williams.

[4] H.O. 40/45, Col. Considine to Home Office, 14 Nov., 20 Dec.; H.O. 40/46, Bute to Home Office, 18 Dec.; H.O. 40/57, Bute to Home Office, 28 Dec.; Newport Museum MS., Samuel Homfray to W. T. H. Phelps, 24 Dec.; *Merlin*, 28 Dec.; *Morning Chronicle*, 28 Dec.; *Charter*, 29 Dec.

Appendix

sinecurists, pluralist parsons, lying newspaper editors, county squires, bull-frog farmers, and other fools of the same stamp.[1] It should be noticed further that Morgan Williams was a personal friend of Frost's. He was the recipient of one of the few letters written by Frost on board the *Mandarin*, a letter in which Frost hoped 'that the spirit which once animated the men of the hills was not extinct'.[2] Yet Williams remained also a faithful admirer of Feargus O'Connor,[3] another proof (if one were necessary) that neither O'Connor nor the Merthyr Chartists betrayed Frost.

Early in the new year Morgan Williams and his co-religionist, David John, the son of a well-known Unitarian minister of the same name, decided to publish a Chartist periodical. They acquired type, and both printed and published the paper themselves. Its first number appeared in March 1840, under the name of *Udgorn Cymru* ('The Trumpet of Wales') and was priced 3*d*. It greatly resembled the early Chartist periodicals in its attack on the poor law, on pensioners, and on the expense of royalty (which it estimated at £1,201,200 a year), but it repudiated violence, declaring both that the Newport affair was contrary to Chartist principles and that no riot had been intended.[4] It also resembled the Welsh Nonconformist periodicals of the day, of which there existed a surprising number, and much space was given to such matters as church rates, tithes, disestablishment, and temperance. In the early issues there was considerable material in English, and it was probably the demand for this which led Williams and John in July to publish an English periodical of the same nature, entitled *The Advocate and Merthyr Free Press*. They also issued pamphlets, among them a reprint of the *Dialogue* on government by the great orientalist, Sir William Jones. It was the publication of this pamphlet which had led to the trial of the author's brother-in-law, Dr. William Davies Shipley, Dean of St. Asaph, in 1784, a trial which Lord Campbell (who, as Attorney-General, prosecuted Frost) declared in his *Lives of the Chancellors* to be

[1] *Northern Star*, 14 Dec., replying to *Merthyr Guardian*, 6 Dec.
[2] Letter dated 4 May; MS. copy in Lord Tredegar's Library.
[3] *Udgorn Cymru*, March, April 1840.
[4] Ibid., Sept., Nov. 1840. See Charles Wilkins, *The History of Merthyr Tydfil* (Merthyr, 1908), 425; *Charter*, 5 Jan. 1840.

'ever memorable in our juridical annals', for it was Erskine's defence of Dean Shipley which established the principle that the jury should decide whether printed matter was libellous or not, and which led to the enactment of Fox's Libel Act of 1791. The Chartist pamphlets were sold about the country by hawkers, one of whom was arrested in October for doing so by the magistrates of Newbridge (Pontypridd). He was released on bail, one of his sureties being Dr. William Price. The latter still retained his interest in Chartism, and had helped to form a branch of the new National Charter Association in the previous month. The Marquis of Bute reported that he held Chartist meetings on Sundays, generally at his own house. But the number who attended never exceeded twenty—they were known as 'Dr. Price's Scholars'—and they were probably as much interested in the doctor's new druidical religion as in Chartism. The Home Office informed the magistrates that they had exceeded their authority in arresting the hawker, and with this Dr. Price's association with the Merthyr Chartists ceased.[1]

Both the *Udgorn* and the *Advocate* were unstamped, and therefore could give no news, though, as in the *Western Vindicator*, an attempt was made to obviate this by means of letters from David John. The Marquis of Bute forwarded copies of all issues of both papers to the Home Office, together with full translations of the *Udgorn*, and in October 1840 the editors were threatened with prosecution for contravening the Stamp Acts. They submitted the matter to Duncombe, who raised it in the House of Commons, but apparently with no success, for with its fifth issue in November 1840 the *Advocate* ceased to appear—thus being the second Chartist paper in Wales to be suppressed. The editors then sought to have the *Udgorn* stamped, yet this was not done until April 1842, when the revival of Chartism was at its height, but with the collapse of the second Petition in that year the *Udgorn* disappeared.[2]

---

[1] H.O. 40/57, Bute to Home Office, 6 Oct., 22 Oct. 1840; Llantrisant magistrates to Bute, 20 Oct.; Magistrates to Home Office, 30 Dec. 1840; *Merthyr Guardian*, 2 Jan. 1841; *Lovett Collection*, ii. 196.

[2] H.O. 40/57. Numbers 1, 2, 3, and 5 of the *Advocate* among the Home Office papers seem to be the only ones extant. The *Udgorn* became a fortnightly in April 1842; the last issue seen by the writer is that of 30 July 1842.

Appendix

After the debacle of November 1839 numerous suggestions were put forward for the reorganization of the movement. Among these was the suggestion that a new Convention should meet at Manchester, and as early as February 1840 the Marquis of Bute reported that a meeting of 3,000 Chartists at Merthyr had appointed a delegate. Their choice fell upon David John, and when the Convention met on 20 July, he represented Merthyr Tydfil, Pontypool, Newport, Newbridge, and Aberdare.[1] Out of this meeting grew the National Charter Association. Its object was to petition again for the Charter, and although it advocated none but peaceable means, it was decidedly an extremist body, supporting O'Connor and opposing the various forms of moral force Chartism, such as Christian Chartism and the Complete Suffrage Movement of Sturge, as well as the Anti-Corn-Law League. Lovett bitterly condemned it, and Place gave it as his opinion that it was an illegal body, each member rendering himself liable to transportation for seven years. It is therefore important to note that Merthyr played an active part in the N.C.A., and that Morgan Williams was elected to its executive of five members both in 1841 and 1842.[2] Nevertheless it made little headway for a time, although meanwhile the Merthyr Chartists had succeeded in holding a number of meetings (all carefully reported by the Lord Lieutenant) and in capturing others intended to present loyal addresses to the Crown or support the Anti-Corn-Law agitation.[3] When the 1841 election occurred, Morgan Williams opposed Sir John J. Guest, and on a show of hands was successful. He used the opportunity which his nomination gave him to attack the Corn-Law League. The employers of labour wished to reduce the price at which corn was admitted, he claimed, merely so that they could lower wages; cheap bread meant cheap labour, and he warned the workers not to be led astray. He announced his intention not to go to the poll, and fortunately for him, his supporters did not insist, so that the election did not have the disastrous consequences which it had in Monmouth.[4]

---

[1] H.O. 40/57, Bute to Home Office, 10 Feb.; *Northern Star*, 1 Aug. 1840.
[2] *Northern Star*, 7 June 1841, 25 June 1842.
[3] H.O. 40/57, Bute to Home Office, 18 April, 10 July, 27 Aug., 1 Sept., 1 Oct. 1840; *Merthyr Guardian*, 4 April, 26 Dec. 1840.
[4] *Merthyr Guardian*, 3 July 1841.

Chartism in Wales 1839–48

The winter of 1841–2 was one of intense depression throughout the country, and especially on the South Wales coal-field. The newspapers reported that hundreds of workmen were reduced virtually to starvation.[1] In these circumstances Chartism received a new impetus, and the N.C.A. called a Convention to London to supervise the presentation of another monster Petition to Parliament. Morgan Williams was present as a delegate. His departure provided the opportunity for a great demonstration. A large crowd accompanied him to the station (for the railway had reached Merthyr just twelve months previously) with two men carrying a Petition signed by 36,000 workmen from Merthyr, Tredegar, Aberdare, and Pontypridd. The Convention met on 12 April, once more at Dr. Johnson's Tavern in Bolt Court, and to it Morgan Williams presented an interesting report on Chartism in South Wales. He had no signatures from Pembrokeshire or Cardiganshire; those in 1839 from this area, he said, had been due to the exertions of Hugh Williams, who had since left the country. The conditions of the agricultural labourers there were deplorable, for their wages were only 7d. to 1s. a day, with no food provided. There was no lodge in Carmarthenshire, even in the growing town of Llanelly. He had recently lectured in Monmouthshire, and had found little enthusiasm there owing to the failure of the Newport riot. In Glamorganshire the cause was more flourishing, especially at Merthyr, where all were supporters of O'Connor and none were Sturgeites.[2] The new Petition was presented to the House of Commons on 2 May. It contained 3,317,702 signatures in contrast with the 1,280,000 of 1839, and in a sense, therefore, it marked the highest peak of the Chartist movement. But it met with the same fate as its predecessor, and was rejected by 287 votes to 49. Once more, the most remarkable of the speeches in the House was that of Macaulay, who held 'that universal suffrage would be fatal to all purposes for which government exists . . . and was utterly incompatible with the very existence of civilization'.

The Convention lasted only three weeks, owing to lack of funds. (The contribution of Merthyr to its expenses was only £19. 14s.) Yet it marked the complete disintegration of the

[1] *Silurian*, 8 Jan. 1842, 19 March 1842.
[2] *Udgorn Cymru*, 23 April 1842.

Appendix

Chartist movement, for it showed a division of opinion not only between O'Connor and the followers of Lovett and of Sturge, but between O'Connor and O'Brien. Nevertheless when Morgan Williams returned to Merthyr he was met by a large crowd of over 5,000 persons to whom he gave an account of his journey. His statement that they were all supporters of O'Connor was greeted with cheers, and he declared that the ministry would probably grant through fear what it denied in justice. Yet he implored his audience to maintain peace and order, for the times were critical.[1] For a month or two he and David John actively conducted meetings in the Glamorganshire valleys,[2] but the times were too severe for a purely political programme. The works were almost at a standstill, and wages were drastically reduced. Early in July a meeting addressed in Welsh by the Reverend David John (senior), and a grocer named William Gould, now an active Chartist, and in English by Morgan Williams and others, passed resolutions concerning the general distress. Williams once more appealed to the crowd not to infringe the law, and the meeting ended with cheers for O'Connor and the Charter, but whether or not Williams's moderation was now repugnant to the people in their distress, and their poverty too great for them to buy the *Udgorn* any more, both the editor and his periodical disappear from the movement.[3] There were, however, frequent meetings of workmen in the Merthyr district, but although these generally ended with cheers for the Charter, they were concerned exclusively with wages, which were now only 9s. to 10s. a week for miners. In August the Cyfarthfa workmen waited on Crawshay, the iron-master, but he declared himself unable to raise wages because of the low price of iron. They then decided to come out on strike for the wages of 1839, but their poverty was intense, and after a few weeks they were beaten and had to return to work. Nineteen leaders in the Cyfarthfa works, and all who 'favoured Chartism' in the Dowlais works, were then discharged. In this way, said the *Merthyr Guardian*, it was

[1] *Merthyr Guardian*, 14 May 1842.
[2] *Udgorn Cymru*, 30 July 1842.
[3] *Merthyr Guardian*, 2 July 1842. Williams reached the age of 73, and was one of the founders of the Merthyr Library. He died 27 Aug. 1886. Wilkins, op. cit., p. 425.

hoped to give Chartism a death blow, and apparently the device was successful. As in 1839, this newspaper was violently opposed to the workers, and constantly demanded that the military should be called upon. The disturbances of the times it attributed to lying incendiaries, Chartists, Anti-Corn-Law leaguers, and socialists, and it severely reprimanded the workers for resorting in their distress 'to the paltry remedy of politics, instead of turning their thoughts to religion'.[1]

It may possibly be the failure of orthodox Chartism which led in December to the sole appearance in Merthyr of the Complete Suffrage Movement of Joseph Sturge. This was an attempt to bridge the gap between the middle and working classes, but Sturge also hoped to heal the breach between O'Connor's followers and his opponents, and for this purpose he summoned a conference to Birmingham to meet on 27 December 1842. A meeting to elect a delegate took place at Merthyr on 22 December. The chief speaker was a Baptist minister, the Reverend Thomas Davies, who propounded the ideas of Sturge on the interdependence of the middle and working classes. He deplored violence, but deplored also the peremptory refusal of the workers' rights. The argument used in reply to the workers: 'Give up your rights and we will act for you with more wisdom and greater safety than you can act for yourselves' could be equally well applied to the other classes, he said. Two delegates were selected, one workman and one tradesman, but the detestation of O'Connor by his opponents was too strong to allow of any compromise, and the conference proved abortive.[2] Six months later (15 July 1844) the Merthyr Chartists met again to petition for Frost, Williams, and Jones. They were addressed by Gould, by David John, Senior, and by his son Matthew, and the opinion which had now become prevalent, that the violence at Newport had been the act of hired traitors, was strongly expressed.[3] But with this Chartism seemed to disappear for a time, for O'Connor's land schemes, with which the movement was occupied in the following years, found no echo in Wales.

[1] *Merthyr Guardian*, 20 Aug., 27 Aug., 3 Sept., 10 Sept., 8 Oct., 15 Oct., 5 Nov. 1842.
[2] Ibid., 31 Dec. 1842, 7 Jan. 1843.
[3] *Merlin*, 20 July 1844.

Appendix

Morgan Williams's statement that Chartism was non-existent in rural Wales raises an interesting problem. In Montgomeryshire all was quiet, although the education commissioners of 1846 reported that the working men still had their 'secret clubs', and spent their Sundays discussing the works of Paine, Carlyle, Volney, and Robert Owen, and other 'pernicious tracts and periodicals'.[1] But in West Wales there occurred the amazing incidents known as the Rebecca Riots, when bands of farmers and labourers, with blackened faces and in women's clothes, destroyed the gates on the turnpike roads. The riots had started in the summer of 1839, in the neighbourhood of Narberth, soon after the attempt to destroy the workhouse there, and soon after the visit of a Chartist missionary to the town. But after four gates had been destroyed, there was a complete lull for over three years. Then the riots broke out again, with increased violence and over a larger area, and culminated in an attack on the workhouse at Carmarthen on 19 June 1843. The rioters won the unexpected support of a special correspondent of *The Times* who described the situation in a series of remarkable letters. He reported that there was 'nothing like political disaffection, opposition to the government, or any Chartist crotchets' instigating the disturbances,[2] and his opinion has generally been accepted. Yet his contrast of Rebeccaism with Chartism arose from a complete misunderstanding of the latter, which was not exclusively a political movement, as its opponents claimed, but was essentially a social movement expressed in political terms. In Wales, in particular, Chartism was the outcome of discontent with the Poor Law Amendment Act. But Rebeccaism, also, was due to the same causes, for the gates were only something tangible on which the people could wreak their vengeance. Besides, the most spectacular incident in the riots was not the destruction of any gate, but the concerted attack on the Carmarthen workhouse. And further, one of the prime movers in the Rebecca movement was the solicitor Hugh Williams (who had certainly returned to Carmarthenshire in 1843, if he had been away in 1842). He it was who put the case of the farmers before the country and who defended the captured rioters. Indeed many

[1] *Report on the State of Education in Wales* (1847), iii. 153.
[2] *The Times*, 30 June, 18 Aug. 1843.

of the proclamations of Rebecca, illiterate though they pretended to be, showed a surprising acquaintance with legal terminology, and it has been claimed that Hugh Williams was 'Rebecca', himself.[1] There was, therefore, an intimate connexion between Chartism and Rebeccaism. The riots ended in sentences of transportation for ten men, and of imprisonment for several others, but also in the Turnpike Act of 1844, which removed one of the grievances of the farmers.

The year of revolutions, 1848, began in Wales with the gloomy prospect of trade depression. On 8 January wages in the Merthyr iron-works were reduced by 4*s.* in the pound, and in Pontypool by 5*s.*[2] This enormous reduction was made necessary, so the iron-masters claimed, by the drop in the demand for iron rails, and the workers, chastened by their experiences in 1842 and 1843, accepted the situation without a strike. But the outbreak of revolution in France gave them encouragement, and for the third time a monster Petition was determined upon, and a Convention to supervise its presentation. A meeting was held in the Market Square at Merthyr on 20 March to choose a delegate. Matthew John and Gould were the chief speakers. Both attempted to win the sympathy of the middle class, whose interests, they claimed, were identical with those of the workers, and both attacked the administration of the poor law. Even the *Merthyr Guardian* admitted that the meeting was orderly and conducted with much good humour. The choice of a delegate fell upon a cooper named David Thomas, and he proceeded to London to the Convention which opened on 4 April.[3] It is not necessary here to relate in detail the fiasco which ensued. The authorities feared the consequences of a demonstration, and preparations on an extraordinarily elaborate scale were made by the octogenerian Duke of Wellington. When 10 April, the day appointed for the presentation of the Petition, arrived, these preparations proved too effective for the Chartists, and the demonstration was a failure. Moreover, the Petition, presented by O'Connor himself (for he had become a member in the previous year by defeating Cam Hobhouse at Nottingham), was found to contain not 5,706,000, as O'Connor

[1] It is said that Hugh Williams was struck off the Roll of Attorneys for his part in the riots.   [2] *Merthyr Guardian*, 15 Jan. 1848.
[3] Ibid., 25 March.

had estimated but only 1,975,496—still a very large figure. The Whigs and Tories in their relief made great play of the false signatures of the queen and of the Duke of Wellington, and of the insertion of such names as Snooks, Pugnose, and Flatnose. But the temper of the people once more hardened at this ridicule, and the densely crowded meeting at the Market House, Merthyr, on 18 April was sterner in tone than the one held there a month previously. Edmund Jones, the delegate from Liverpool to the Convention, called upon the people to consider whether, if moral agitation would not produce results, they must adopt other means and risk an ignominious death. He even reminded them of Owain Glyn Dŵr, and asked if the Welsh of the nineteenth century were going to prove themselves degenerative cowards? Gould argued that no Chartist could have put nicknames in the Petition; it was only too obviously a trick on the part of their opponents to bring them to ridicule. The Chartists desired nothing but peaceful discussion, but every time they were met with an array of armed force. There were no disturbances at the meeting but the *Merthyr Guardian* now, again, became almost hysterical in its abuse: the Chartist leaders were ragamuffins, spouters of treason, earning their living in this way because of their aversion to honest work.[1] Three weeks later an opposition meeting was held to express loyalty to the throne. It was chiefly remarkable because of the speech in support of the address delivered by Thomas Stephens, a member of the Reverend David John's congregation and the greatest scholar in Wales in his day. He produced an economic interpretation of the history of political change. Political power, he said, had once been in the hands of the landed aristocracy; then commerce had developed and a new claimant for power—the middle class—had appeared; now there was a third claimant—the working class. But unlike Marx (whose *Manifesto* he can scarcely have seen) Stephens argued that in reality there was no difference between the middle and working classes; their interests were interdependent, and the two classes merged into one another. This meeting, again, the Chartists tried to capture. Gould attempted to speak on the distress of the workers, but the audience was

[1] *Merthyr Guardian*, 22 April. Jones proceeded to a meeting at Swansea, ibid., 29 April.

hostile, and when Matthew John moved an amendment in favour of the Charter, it was defeated amid great confusion.[1] In June there was a last attempt to hold a Chartist meeting, but the authorities intervened, and their superior force prevailed.[2] The Chartist movement in Wales had come to an end.

It has been customary to speak of the failure of Chartism, and to seek reasons for this failure. These have generally been found in the absence of solidarity within the working class and in the internal weaknesses of the movement itself. In Wales, in particular, there was a marked division between the heritage of the old Union Clubs and the violence of the 'Scotch Cattle', which had coalesced for a time in Chartism. There was in consequence no agreement on questions of policy or of method, and no leader arose capable of unifying the various elements. The movement's supreme misfortune was the leadership of Feargus O'Connor. Its relations with the middle class were a further source of weakness. As long as the Chartists hoped for success through Parliamentary action, they were dependent upon the good will of middle class radicals, for they had no representatives of their own in Parliament. Yet as Place so frequently pointed out, they seemed bent upon alienating those whom they should have tried to conciliate. In addition the success of the contemporary middle class agitation against the Corn Laws—that 'red herring trailed across the path of democracy' as the early Socialists called it—was in no small degree responsible for the failure of Chartism, through distracting public attention from it. No doubt, also, the return of prosperity in the fifties, and the increase in the general well-being of the working class through social legislation, may have removed much of the discontent behind the Chartist movement, although this can scarcely have decreased the workers' demands for the franchise.

Yet it is doubtful if one can consider as a failure a movement whose objects have in the course of time been attained almost without exception, and whose principles have come to appear so reasonable that they are now accepted without question as part of the political life of the nation. If judgement has to be passed in terms of success or failure, it was surely those who failed who

[1] Ibid., 13 May. [2] Ibid., 17 June

considered these reasonable principles 'too absurd for an idiot to be the author of them'. Moreover, if praise or blame is to be allocated, those who met reasonable demands with a blank refusal and a parade of armed force should be held responsible for the rioting which occurred, and the suffering which was its consequence. Resistance to authority in the interest of justice has, since Locke, always been a cardinal principle in British political theory. The failure of Chartism was therefore more apparent than real, even in the narrow sense of the attainment of the six points of the Charter. But Chartism was much wider than a movement directed towards six constitutional changes. It was the motive power behind the great social legislation of the period; it also marked the first emergence of the working class as a political force, and the experience which it provided taught the workers how to direct their energies in future. The political education of the working class was perhaps more apparent in England than in Wales, for in Wales the main stream of the nation's life was towards middle-class liberalism, drawing its strength from rural Nonconformity. This movement had its first marked success in the election of 1868, when Wales returned a majority of Liberal members for the first time in its history. With the passing of the Ballot Act—still considered too dangerous a measure to be placed permanently on the Statute Book, and therefore renewed from year to year —and with the Reform Act of 1885, Wales attained political consciousness, for in the election which followed the latter Wales returned thirty Liberal members and only four Conservative members to Parliament. Squire rule was thus at an end. It was only then that working-class radicalism broke away from its middle-class associations, and won its first victory with the return of Keir Hardie as member for Merthyr in 1900. In preparing the way for this development, Chartism had played an overwhelmingly important part.

BIBLIOGRAPHY

For bibliographies of Chartism see: H. U. Faulkener, *Chartism and the Churches*, New York, 1916, and Mark Hovell, *The Chartist Movement*, Manchester, 1918. For a list of broadsides, prints, &c., relating to Chartism in Monmouthshire see John Warner and W. A. Gunn, *John Frost and the Chartist Movement in Monmouthshire, Catalogue of Chartist Literature, Prints and Relics*, Newport, 1939.

MANUSCRIPTS

BRITISH MUSEUM:

Place MSS.
  (i) *Working Men's Association*, Additional MSS., 27281.
  (ii) *General Convention*, Additional MSS., 34245 A and B.

PUBLIC RECORD OFFICE:

King's Bench:
  (i) Easter Term, 1821, No. 1628, Margaret Foster against William Frost, John Frost, and Thomas Frost.
  (ii) Hilary Term, 1822, No. 289, Thomas Prothero against John Frost.

Home Office Papers:
  (i) H.O. 11, Transportation, 1840.
  (ii) H.O. 40, Disturbances; No. 40, Wiltshire, Wales, 1838; No. 45, Monmouthshire, 1839; No. 46, Montgomeryshire, 1839; No. 51, Yorkshire, Wales, 1839; No. 57, Scottish and Welsh Miscellaneous, 1840.

NEWPORT MUSEUM:

Papers formerly in the possession of W. T. H. Phelps, solicitor to the magistrates conducting the preliminary examination of the Chartist prisoners.
  (i) Miscellaneous: Solicitor-General's brief; notes for the use of the Attorney-General and various papers.
  (ii) Examinations and depositions of witnesses.
  (iii) Correspondence, mostly addressed to W. T. H. Phelps.

Bibliography

NEWPORT LIBRARY:
  (i) Miscellaneous letters and papers.
  (ii) Overseers of the Poor, Minute Book, 1773–1812.
  (iii) Newport Improvement Commissioners, Minute Book, 1826–45.
  (iv) Borough Council Minutes, 1836–43.
  (v) Rules for the Borough Court of Record, 1838.

BIRMINGHAM PUBLIC LIBRARY:
Lovett Collection, *Proceedings of the Working Men's Association*, 2 vols., Newspaper cuttings and MS. correspondence.

USK:
Quarter Sessions Records of the County of Monmouth.

LORD TREDEGAR'S LIBRARY:
Copies of three MS. letters from Frost and Zephaniah Williams.

NATIONAL LIBRARY OF WALES:
Llangibby MSS. Correspondence.

CARDIFF PUBLIC LIBRARY:
Solicitor's accounts. Montgomeryshire Chartist prosecutions.

PRINTED BOOKS AND PAMPHLETS

A. PRIMARY

ANON. *Address and Rules of the W.M.A. for benefiting politically and morally the useful classes*, Newport, (1838).
—— *Report of the Proceedings of the great Anti-Chartist meeting held at Coalbrookvale, 29 April 1839*, Monmouth, (1839).
—— *Ymddiddan rhwng Mr. Bowen, deiliad ffyddlon i'r Frenhines, a William Thomas, Siartist, ar ol y terfysg yn y Casnewydd*, Llandovery, 1839.
—— *The Two Colliers, a Dialogue*, Monmouth, 1840.
—— *Riots in South Wales. An Address to the working classes of Wales, by one of the people*, Swansea, (1840).
—— *Particulars of the trial of Mr. John Frost for High Treason with an account of his life and other interesting facts*, London, (1840).

Bibliography

ANON. *Full report of the Trial of John Frost for High Treason, with a sketch of his life. By a Barrister*, London, 1840.

—— *The Life of John Frost, Esq.*, London, 1840.

—— *History of the Chartists and the bloodless wars of Montgomeryshire*, Welshpool, 1840.

(BROUGH, BARNABAS.) *A Night with the Chartists, Frost, Williams, and Jones. A Narrative of Adventures in Monmouthshire*, London, (1847).

DAVIES, JOHN. *Y Ffordd Dda, neu bregeth a draddodwyd yn Aberdâr*, Merthyr, 1839.

(DOWLING, EDWARD.) *The Rise and Fall of Chartism in Monmouthshire*, Newport, 1840.

EDWARDS, WILLIAM. *An Address to the Working Men and Women of Newport and of the Monmouthshire Hills*, Newport, (1839).

ETHERIDGE, SAMUEL. *Letter 2nd: to the Burgesses of Newport*, Cardiff, 1820.

—— *The Charter of the Borough of Newport*, Cardiff, 1821.

—— *The Newport Review*, No. 1, 19 Aug. 1822—No. 12, 20 Nov. 1822, Newport, 1822.

—— Preface to reprint of Nathan Rogers, *Memoirs of Monmouthshire*, Newport, 1826.

—— *The Oppressors' Chronicles*, Newport, (1831). (Anon., probably by Etheridge.)

FROST, JOHN. *A Letter to Thomas Prothero*, Cardiff, 1821. (Two editions.)

——*A Letter to the Mayor and Aldermen of Newport*, and *A Letter to the Independent Burgesses of Newport*, Newport, (1821).

—— *A Sermon for the Lawyers*, Cardiff, 1821.

—— *A Letter to Sir Charles Morgan*, Cardiff, 1821.

—— *Part the first: the Trial between Thomas Prothero and John Frost*, Newport, 1822.

—— *Part the second: the Trial between Thomas Prothero and John Frost*, Newport, 1822.

—— *To the Benefit Societies of Monmouthshire*, Newport, (1822).

—— *A Letter to Sir Charles Morgan and other Commissioners of the Highways*, Newport, 1822.

—— *A Second Letter to Sir Charles Morgan*, also *A Letter to the Farmers in the County of Monmouth*, Newport, 1822.

—— *A Letter to J. H. Moggridge, Esq.*, also *A Letter to Parson Thomas of Caerleon*, Newport, 1822.

345

Bibliography

Frost, John. *A Letter to the Farmers of Monmouthshire*, Newport, 1822.

—— *A Letter to the Radicals of Monmouthshire, written in Monmouth gaol*, Newport, 1822.

—— *A Lawyer in a Panic: or the Client's Revenge*, Newport, 1822.

—— *A Christmas Box for Sir Charles Morgan*, also *A Letter to the married and single women of Monmouthshire*, Newport, 1831.

—— *The Welchman. No. 1, Cheap Government, Cheap Law, Cheap Religion*, Newport, 1832.

—— *A Letter to the Reformers of Monmouthshire*, Newport, 1832.

—— *A Letter to the inhabitants of Newport*, also *A Letter to the ratepayers of St. Woollos*, Newport, 1832.

—— *A Letter to Sir Charles Morgan . . . showing how the Tredegar Family obtained possession of the school-lands at Newport*, Newport, 1833.

—— *Letter the second to Sir Charles Morgan*, Newport, 1833.

—— *A Letter to the Whig Magistrates of the County of Monmouth*, also *A Letter to the Radicals of the Borough of Newport*, Newport, (1837).

—— *A Letter to the Working Men's Association of Newport and Pillgwenlly*, Newport, (1839).

—— *A Letter to the People of the United States showing the effects of aristocratic rule*, New York, 1855.

—— *The Horrors of Convict Life, two lectures*, London, (1856).

—— *A Letter to the People of Great Britain and Ireland on Transportation, second edition* (London, 1857).

Francis, James. *A Sermon to the Working Classes, preached at St. Paul's Church, Newport, 21 April 1839*, Newport, (1839).

Gurney, Joseph and Thomas. *The Trial of John Frost for High Treason*, London, 1840.

Jenkins, Evan. *Chartism Unmasked*, Merthyr, 1840.

John, David, and Williams, Morgan. *The Question: What is a Chartist? answered*, Merthyr, 1840. (Bilingual.)

—— *Cyfieithiad o lythyr diweddaf Mr. Feargus O'Connor at weithwyr Prydain Fawr*, Merthyr, 1840.

Kenrick, G. S. *The Population of Pontypool, situated in the so-called disturbed districts, its moral, social and intellectual character*, Pontypool, (1840).

Morris, Thomas. *Cynghor da mewn amserau drwg, sef pregeth a draddodwyd yn y Tabernacl, Pontypwl*, Cardiff, 1840.

Bibliography

Parliamentary Debates, Hansard, 3rd Series, vol. l, 1839; vol. lii, 1840; vol. lxiii, 1842.

PHILLIPS, THOMAS. *Wales. The Language, Social Condition, Moral Character and Religious Opinions of the People*, London, 1849.

(PROTHERO, THOMAS.) *Trial of Prothero against Frost in the Court of King's Bench*, Newport, 1822.

State Trials Committee: The Queen against Vincent and Others, *Reports of State Trials*, iii. 1831–40.

—— The Queen against Frost, *ibid.* iv. 1839–43.

TAYLOR, J. R. *A Sermon on the late Chartist insurrection, preached at St. Woollos Church, 10 Nov. 1839*, Newport, 1839.

TOWNSEND, W. C. Report of the Trial of John Frost, *Modern State Trials*, vol. i, London, 1850.

ULLATHORNE, W. *The Horrors of Transportation briefly described*, Birmingham, 1841.

WALKER, C. H. *Monmouthshire Summer Assizes, 1832. Walker at the suit of Phillips upon a charge of defamation*, London, 1832.

WATKINS, JOHN. *John Frost, a Play*, London, 1841.

WILLIAMS, HUGH. *National Songs dedicated to the Queen and her countrywomen*, London, 1839.

WILLIAMS, ZEPHANIAH. *A Letter to Benjamin Williams, a dissenting minister*, Newport, 1831.

B. SECONDARY

ANON. Review of Rise and Fall of Chartism in Monmouthshire, *Dublin Review*, 1840.

ADAMS, W. E. *Memoirs of a Social Atom*, 2 vols., London, 1903.

BROUGHTON, LORD (J. C. Hobhouse). *Recollections of a Long Life*, vol. v, London, 1911.

DODD, A. H. *The Industrial Revolution in North Wales*, Cardiff, 1933.

EDWARDS, NESS. *John Frost and the Chartist Movement*, Abertillery, (1924).

—— *The Industrial Revolution in South Wales*, London, 1924.

EVANS, THOMAS. *Background of Modern Welsh Politics*, Cardiff, 1936.

FENTON, JAMES. *History of Tasmania*, London, 1884.

FORSYTH, W. D. *Governor Arthur's Convict System*, London, 1935.

GREVILLE, CHARLES. *The Greville Memoirs* (ed. Strachey and Fulford), vol. iv, London, 1938.

347

Bibliography

HAMER, EDWARD. *A Brief Account of the Chartist Outbreak at Llanidloes*, Llanidloes, 1867.

HANWORTH, LORD. *Lord Chief Baron Pollock*, London, 1929.

HARDCASTLE, MRS. *Life of Lord Campbell*, vol. ii, London, 1881.

JENKINS, R. T. *Hanes Cymru yn y Bedwaredd Ganrif ar Bymtheg*, Cardiff, 1933.

JOHNS, W. N. *The Chartist Riots at Newport*, Newport, 1889 (2nd edition).

MOLESWORTH, SIR WILLIAM. *Speech on Transportation*, London, 1840.

MORGAN, JOHN. *Four Biographical Sketches*, London, 1892.

POWELL, DAVID and EVAN. *History of Tredegar*, Cardiff, 1885.

REES, T., and THOMAS, T. *Hanes Eglwysi Annibynol Cymru*, 4 vols., Liverpool, 1871–5.

ROBERTS, W. G. 'Y Siartiaid yng Nghymru', *Cymru*, 1909.

SAMUEL, J. E. 'The Montgomeryshire Chartist Riots', *Cymru Fu*, 1889.

SPENCER, J. D. 'The Chartist Movement in Wales', *Wales*, 1895.

URQUHART, DAVID. 'The Chartist Correspondence', *Free Press Serials*, no. xiii, 1855.

—— 'The Chartist Movement', *Diplomatic Review*, 1872–3.

WARNER, JOHN. 'The Marshes Estate and other Properties of the Newport Burgesses', *Monmouthshire Review*, 1933.

—— *Local Government in Newport, 1835–1935*, Newport, 1935.

(WARREN, SAMUEL.) Review of Townsend, Modern State Trials, *Blackwood's Magazine*, 1850.

WEST, JOHN. *History of Tasmania*, Hobart, 1852.

PERIODICALS

BRITISH MUSEUM, PLACE COLLECTION:

Set 56, *Reform*, 1836–47, 29 vols.

Set 66, *The Charter*, Jan. 1839–March 1840, 1 vol.

BIRMINGHAM PUBLIC LIBRARY, LOVETT COLLECTION:

Proceedings of the Working Men's Association, 2 vols., as above.

CHARTIST.

Advocate and Merthyr Free Press.
Charter.
Chartist Circular.

Bibliography

Northern Star.
Udgorn Cymru.
Western Vindicator.

NATIONAL:
Annual Register.
The Times.

LOCAL:
Bristol Mercury (Bristol).
Cardiff Times and South Wales Weekly News (May–June 1888;
    23 Jan. 1893; reminiscences and obituary notice of Dr.
    William Price).
Cambrian (Swansea).
Merthyr Guardian (Merthyr and Cardiff).
Monmouthshire Advertiser (Newport).
Monmouthshire Beacon (Monmouth).
Monmouthshire Merlin (Monmouth and Newport).
Silurian (Brecon).
South Wales Daily News (1877, Letters of Zephaniah Williams).
Star of Gwent (Newport).

WELSH DENOMINATIONAL:
Diwygiwr (Independent).
Drysorfa (Calvinistic Methodist).
Eurgrawn Wesleyaidd (Wesleyan Methodist).
Haul (Anglican).
Seren Gomer (Baptist).

TASMANIAN:
Cornwall Chronicle.
Launceston Gazette.

349

INDEX

Index

Firman, Israel, 243–4, 253, 300.
French Revolution of 1789, 13–14, 52, 72, 128, 289, 325; of 1830, 63; of 1848, 339.
Follett, Sir William, 88, 91, 109, 286.
Foster, Margaret, 17, 34, 35, 37.
Foster, William, 11, 15, 16, 33, 35, 267.
Fothergill, Richard, 21, 26.
Frost, Henry Hunt, 16, 53, 167, 179, 209, 224–5, 245–6, 297, 305, 321.
Frost, John (of London), 13–14.
Frost, John, birth, 9; parentage, 10; education, 11; in London, 12–14; return to Newport, 14; marriage, 15; religion, 16; children, 16; radicalism, 14, 19; intervenes in struggle of Monmouth borough against Beaufort, 27; supports Newport freemen, 29; election of 1820, 33; aids William Frost, 34–5; private letter to Prothero, 35; indicted at Usk, 36; made responsible for uncle's debt, 37; libels Prothero, 38–9; prosecuted, 40–4; criminal prosecution of, 45; in Monmouth gaol, 46; bankruptcy, 46, 92; in Cold Bath Fields prison, 48; reception at Newport, 49; social and political ideas, 49–54; appeals against rates, 58; supports agricultural labourers, 60; demands Parliamentary reform, 62–4; becomes printer, 62; prevents assault on Marquis of Worcester, 67, 126, 280; defends curate of St. Woollos, 68; forms Patriotic Society, 68; attacks Wellington, 69; starts periodical, 70; welcomes Reform Bill, 74; opposes harbour bill, 77; elected councillor, 79; becomes magistrate, 81; improvement commissioner, 82; poor law guardian, 82–6; mayor, 86; proclaims Queen Victoria, 89–90; inquires into fines paid to borough magistrates, 91; revives Court of Record, 92; seeks re-election as mayor, 92; joins Chartist movement, 94, 107; elected delegate to Convention, 109, 122; letter to Lord John Russell, 124–6; in Convention, 128; dinner of Marylebone association, 129; at Crown and Anchor meeting, 132; defends physical force Chartists, 132; dinner in honour of, 133; removed from magistracy, 136; speaks at Stroud, 140–1; sent to South Wales, 161; arrest expected, 162; charged with using seditious language, 163; proposes simultaneous meetings, 164; at Glasgow, 168; proposes securing hostages, 169; indicted for libel, 169; favours sacred month, 171; speaks at Dukestown, 180; agitates for Vincent's release, 181–2; gives casting vote for dissolution of the Convention, 184; explains failure of the Convention, 185; organizes groups of ten, 188; attends Coalbrookvale meeting, 188–91; attends secret meeting, 191; movements, 197–8; relations with Price, 203; at Blackwood secret meeting, 207–9; meets delegate from North, 209–11; leads march on Newport, 213–16, 222–5, 227; in hiding, 232; arrest, 233; indicted for treason, 244–5; True Bill found against, 264; provision for defence of, 266; trial, 269–84; sentenced, 285; motives in attack on Newport, 289; sentence commuted, 294; removed to hulk, 295; illness, 300; voyage to Tasmania, 301–2; at Port Arthur, 303; sentenced to hard labour, 307; conditional pardon, 314; in America, 315; full pardon, 315; return, 316; reception at Newport, 318; reception in London, 319; at Stapleton, 321; death, 322.
Frost, Mary, 15, 17, 209, 301.
Frost, Sarah (mother of John Frost), 10, 14, 47, 267, 296.
Frost, Sarah (daughter of John Frost), 16, 141, 316.
Fry, Harry, 141, 145, 316.

Geach, William Foster, 15, 17, 86–8, 93–4, 246, 251, 259–60, 267, 275, 290, 296, 300, 303–5.
Gray, Lieutenant, 226, 229, 237, 279.

Index

Greville, *Memoirs* of, 238, 291.
Guest, Sir John Josiah, 213, 325, 334.

Hall, Benjamin, 22, 33, 65, 66, 72, 73, 75, 76, 77, 81, 89, 244, 262.
Hampden clubs, 30, 106.
Haul, Yr, 99, 323.
Heckmondwick, 199, 202, 210.
Hetherington, Henry, 100, 104, 143–5, 156, 202.
Hobhouse, John Cam, 102, 290, 291, 293, 294, 327, 339.
Hodge, James, 214, 222–3, 251, 253, 255, 277, 279, 282, 299, 320.
Homfray, Samuel, 21, 26, 118, 180, 240, 262, 318.

Industrial distress, 49–50, 95, 110–14, 335–6.
Irish and Chartism, 111, 225, 240.
Iron industry, 5, 20–2, 49, 336.

John, David, Jnr., 332, 333, 334.
Jenkins, William, 102, 120, 121.
Jones, Charles, 105, 106, 143, 144, 158, 159, 200, 210, 214.
Jones, Ernest, 319–20.
Jones, John Gale, 13.
Jones, William, 'the watchmaker', 148, 160, 166, 170, 180, 181, 189, 191, 196, 204–8, 212, 232, 245, 264, 269, 285, 295, 309, 310, 313–14.

Kelly, Sir Fitzroy, 266, 267, 271, 274, 275–7, 280–1, 286, 297, 298.

Leigh, Capel Hanbury (Lord Lieutenant), 81, 145, 146, 165, 167, 187, 225, 244, 261, 287.
Llanelly, Breconshire, 57, 207.
Llanelly, Carmarthenshire, 96, 97, 102–3, 335.
Llanidloes, 63, 83, 103–6, 144, 145, 156–8, 174, 325.
Lovett, William, 101, 134, 140, 141, 162, 198–203, 334.

Macaulay, Lord, 293, 298–9, 335.
Mail, non-arrival of, 210, 223, 252, 255, 277, 278, 287, 320.
Malpas, 220, 221, 317.

Man with glazed hat, 214, 252.
Man with lantern, 222, 225, 252, 253.
Marx, Karl, 248, 319, 340.
Melbourne, Lord, 62, 290, 293.
Merlin, 57, 61, 94, 117, 153, 160, 179–80, 194, 195, 204, 226, 228, 236, 237.
Merthyr Guardian, 94, 119, 174, 189, 194, 237, 244, 318, 323, 331, 336, 339.
Merthyr riots of 1831, 95, 115–16.
Merthyr Tydfil, 63, 72, 84, 101, 111, 112, 114, 119, 155, 156, 157, 158, 167, 170, 198, 205, 231, 252, 256, 260, 288, 296, 331–40.
Moggridge, John Hodder, 30–1, 32, 33, 34, 44, 45, 46.
Monmouth, 3, 27, 56, 165, 190, 193, 209, 241, 245, 268, 269, 279, 287, 292, 329.
Monmouth boroughs, political representation of, 8, 32, 59, 66–7, 73, 76, 90, 329.
Monmouthshire, political representation of, 8, 31, 32, 59, 66, 73, 76.
Morgan, Sir Charles, 6, 24, 25, 26, 29, 31, 34, 35, 36, 39, 40, 47, 52, 57, 59, 60, 63, 65, 73, 74, 79, 172, 223, 236, 241.
Morgan, Sir Charles Gould, 6, 21, 26.
Morgan, family of, 5, 8, 52, 65, 73, 74, 285.
Morgan, John, 5, 6, 33, 62.
Morgan, Octavius, 76, 262, 317.
Municipal Corporations Act, 29, 58, 78.

Nantyglo (*see* Coalbrookvale), 20, 21, 150, 170, 212, 216, 231.
National Charter Association, 334, 335.
National Petition, 102, 119, 121, 129, 156, 163, 173, 334, 335, 339.
Newbridge (Pontypridd), 23, 149, 187, 257, 333, 335.
Newport, appearance, 2; bridge, 2, 23, 223, 252, 278; government of, 3; growth, 5, 22–3, 55–6; canal, 22; tramroad, 22; coal trade, 22–3; turnpike, 23, 46; population, 23, 55; struggle between freemen and corporation, 28;